T0360517

It is rare to come across an individual who is so passionate in the field of Marketing. Having known Pak Hermawan for more than 40 years, it is not a surprise at all that the firm he founded is synonymous with his love for Marketing. This book succinctly captures both the personality of the founder and the dynamism of the firm. If you wish to learn more about what drives marketing and what drives a person to love marketing, you would miss so much if you pass up on reading this book.

**Professor Kuntoro Mangkusubroto**
Chairman of the School of Business Management, ITB, Indonesia

The world of marketing evolves and expands its horizons with visionary leaders in the sphere of marketing. Pak Hermawan is one such visionary leader who had the foresight a couple of decades ago to establish the Asia Marketing Federation (AMF), which would become the focal point in Asia for the development and permeation of future marketing. His intuition that Asia would turn out to be a formidable economic powerhouse in the world stage led him to conceive several marketing theories and invent many supporting drivers such as MarkPlus to elevate the stature of marketing and management. Being the architect of awards ceremonies such as the Asia Marketing Excellence, 3.0, and Youth, Netizens & Women awards, his attempt to enhance the value proposition of the Asian brands and brand icons was successful indeed. This book elaborates on the learning of this legendary marketing guru and his kingdom, an impetus to the development of marketing together with the expansion of readers' conviction on the philosophy of Marketing.

I wish him all the best for his future endeavours.

**Rohan Somawansa**
President, Asia Marketing Federation

This book is an elegant story about Pak Hermawan, the company, MarkPlus Inc., he founded, and his passion in the marketing world. I have known Pak Hermawan since he was still in Surabaya in the late 1970's. We have developed a very close relationship after he moved to Jakarta until today. He is the soul of MarkPlus that makes it a renowned marketing firm. He is also the driver and architect of the marketing movement in the region. His passionate works in the dynamic changing of the marketing concept has also influenced the companies in adopting the new marketing strategies in business. If you wish to learn his insights into marketing and business, this book is an inspiring read.

**Y. W. Junardy**
Chairman, Asia Marketing Federation Foundation;
President, Indonesia Global Compact Network


*MarkPlus Inc.* by marketing guru Philip Kotler and Hooi Den Huan is a book that opens up new horizons in marketing. This book commemorates the 30th anniversary of the founding of MarkPlus by Pak Hermawan Kartajaya.

"Entrepreneurship without marketing is directionless. Marketing without entrepreneurship has no innovation." I am very interested in Humane Entrepreneurship, and Entrepreneurial Marketing is a new area of focus that deserves significant attention.

There is a famous business principle called High-Tech, High-Touch. The more advanced technology is introduced, the more humanity and warmth are required as a reaction to balance it out. K-pop boyband BTS uses a lot of cutting-edge non-face-to-face technology but creates a fandom through humanity. This is the result of integrating Humane Entrepreneurship and marketing. AI (appreciative inquiry) becomes more important as artificial intelligence, or AI (Artificial Intelligence) is emphasised. We are grateful that this book also contains the meaning of Humane Entrepreneurship based on the High-Tech, High-Touch principle.

**Ki-chan Kim**
Honorary Chairman, Asia Council for Small Business
Professor of Humane Entrepreneurship, Catholic University of Korea
President, Korea Indonesia Management Association (KIMA)

# WINNING
## THE FUTURE
**MARKETING AND ENTREPRENEURSHIP
IN HARMONY**

MARKPLUS.INC
THE LEADING MARKETING CONSULTING IN INDONESIA

Founder
# Hermawan Kartajaya

# WINNING
## THE FUTURE

## MARKETING AND ENTREPRENEURSHIP
## IN HARMONY

## Philip Kotler
Kellogg School of Management, Northwestern University,
USA

## Hooi Den Huan
Nanyang Business School, Nanyang Technological University,
Singapore

 **World Scientific**

EW JERSEY · LONDON · SINGAPORE · BEIJING · SHANGHAI · HONG KONG · TAIPEI · CHENNAI · TOKYO

*Published by*

World Scientific Publishing Co. Pte. Ltd.
5 Toh Tuck Link, Singapore 596224
*USA office:* 27 Warren Street, Suite 401-402, Hackensack, NJ 07601
*UK office:* 57 Shelton Street, Covent Garden, London WC2H 9HE

**Library of Congress Cataloging-in-Publication Data**
Names: Kotler, Philip, author. | Hooi, Den Huan, author.
Title: MarkPlus, Inc. : winning the future, marketing and entrepreneurship in harmony /
    Philip Kotler, Kellogg School of Management, Northwestern University, USA,
    Hooi Den Huan, Nanyang Business School, Nanyang Technological University, Singapore.
Description: New Jersey : World Scientific, [2021] | Includes bibliographical references and index.
Identifiers: LCCN 2020040392 | ISBN 9789811221712 (hardcover) |
    ISBN 9789811222177 (paperback) | ISBN 9789811221729 (ebook) |
    ISBN 9789811221736 (ebook other)
Subjects: LCSH: Kartajaya, Hermawan, 1947–  | MarkPlus, Inc. | Marketing--Indonesia. |
    Marketing research companies--Indonesia. | Marketing consultants--Indonesia.
Classification: LCC HF5415.12.I6 K68 2021 | DDC 381.06/5598--dc23
LC record available at https://lccn.loc.gov/2020040392

**British Library Cataloguing-in-Publication Data**
A catalogue record for this book is available from the British Library.

For any available supplementary material, please visit
https://www.worldscientific.com/worldscibooks/10.1142/11862#t=suppl

Desk Editor: Ong Shi Min Nicole

Printed in Singapore

# ABOUT THE AUTHORS

 Dr Philip Kotler is the S.C. Johnson Distinguished Professor of International Marketing at the Kellogg School of Management, Northwestern University. He has been honoured as one of the world's leading marketing thinkers. He earned his MA degree in economics (1953) from the University of Chicago and his PhD degree in economics (1956) from the Massachusetts Institute of Technology (MIT), and has received honorary degrees from 22 foreign universities. He is the author of 90 books and over 150 articles. He has been a consultant to IBM, General Electric, Sony, AT&T, Bank of America, Merck, Motorola, Ford, and others. *The Financial Times* included him in its list of the top 10 business thinkers. They cited his *Marketing Management* as one of the 50 best business books of all times.

Hooi Den Huan is an associate professor of Marketing at the Nanyang Business School, and former Director of the Nanyang Technopreneurship Center, Nanyang Technological University, Singapore. He is an advisor of the Asia Marketing Federation Foundation and the Asian Council for Small Business. Den schooled at St. Michael's Institution in Ipoh, received his bachelor's degree from the University of Bradford, and his PhD from the University of Manchester. He was a visiting scholar at the Sloan School of Management, MIT and is a chartered marketer (CIM UK) and a chartered accountant (ICAEW).

# ACKNOWLEDGEMENTS

The authors are grateful for the invaluable help given by all staff of MarkPlus including Michael Hermawan, Stephanie Hermawan, Jacky Mussry, Taufik, Iwan Setiawan, Hendra Warsita, Vivie Jericho, Anggia Aryandita, Andi Magie Fitrahnurlia and Rifeldo Meiza, and for the book endorsements from Pak Kuntoro Mangkusubroto, Pak YW Junardy, Rohan Somawansa and Kim Ki-Chan.

We also wish to acknowledge with deep appreciation the very strong support for Pak Hermawan and MarkPlus from member organisations of the Asia Marketing Federation and the Asia Council for Small Business:

**Members of the Asia Marketing Federation (AMF)**

China Council for the Promotion of International Trade (CCPIT) Commercial Sub-Council
Hong Kong Institute of Marketing
Indonesian Marketing Association
Institute of Marketing Malaysia
Japan Marketing Association
Macau Marketing Institute

Marketing Association of Cambodia
Marketing Association of Thailand
Marketing Institute of Singapore
Marketing Society of Bangladesh
Marketing Society of Korea
Mongolian Marketing Association
Myanmar Marketing Society
Philippine Marketing Association
Sri Lanka Institute of Marketing
Taiwan Institute of Marketing Science
Vietnam Marketing Association

**Members of the Asia Council for Small Business (ACSB)**

ACSB Bangladesh
ACSB China
ACSB Sri Lanka
ICSB Indonesia
ICSB Laos
ICSB Macau
ICSB Myanmar
ICSB Taiwan
ICSB Thailand
ICSB Vietnam
ICSMEE Malaysia
ICSMEHK
Japan ICSB
Korea ICSB
SEAANZ

# PREFACE

The year 2020 marks the 30th anniversary since the founding of MarkPlus by Pak Hermawan Kartajaya. It is no mean feat, to grow a microenterprise to become one of the most respectable marketing consultancy firms in the region. By the turn of the 21st century, not many first-time entrepreneurs would start up a business in the professional advisory field, given its inherent intangible nature and the critical need to build up the commensurate credibility at least in terms of skills, reputation, and trust. This is all the more so in the field of marketing consultancy services, where many believe that they already have the marketing know-how and what matters more is the know-who. This poses an almost insurmountable challenge to any tiny setup and many of Hermawan's friends cast doubt on the sustainability of such a venture and sincerely persuaded him to stay on with his successful corporate career with a large local company. Notwithstanding an established career and his more than 40 years of age, Hermawan pursued his mission in life to promote marketing for a better world.

Having worked with Hermawan for more than 20 years and as his coauthors for quite a few publications, we have witnessed how passionate Hermawan is with Marketing and as we have the same love for marketing, we are happy to coauthor this book, as a tribute to a person and a firm that fully deserves the recognition. While we may have various publications to our names, and especially Professor Philip Kotler, this is the first time ever that both authors have decided to publish a book about a firm and its founder and examining its formula and its future perspective. The Founder, Firm, Formula, and Future framework, which is covered in the respective four parts, lay the foundation and structure for this book. Part 1 is about the founder of MarkPlus, Hermawan Kartajaya — what drove him to start MarkPlus. Part 2 is about the firm's 30 years of journey through the decades — what it first started as and what it is today. Part 3 is the firm's formula as a thought and practice leader through its various concepts and frameworks and Part 4 looks at the future of the firm.

We believe that Hermawan Kartajaya and MarkPlus have contributed significantly to the body of knowledge of marketing theory and practice, not just in Indonesia but the region and the world and will continue to do so. Our faith is further strengthened by the strong support and respect that both have earned from the various marketing and entrepreneurship communities including the Asia Marketing Federation and the Asia Council for Small Business.

**Philip Kotler** and **Hooi Den Huan**

# CONTENTS

# Part I

## FOUNDER: Hermawan Kartajaya, The Man Behind MarkPlus

Have you ever wondered about the life of a start-up founder? What is the story behind the establishment of a business? Many founders have their passion as the main reason for starting a business. Other founders observe what people need and then start a business to serve them. There are many different reasons why a business is established.

Hermawan Kartajaya founded a company called MarkPlus in 1990, a company focusing on marketing, a subject which he has a deep passion for. This year marks MarkPlus's 30th anniversary. Hermawan faced many challenges along the way to build the firm to become what it is today. He made a life-changing decision in starting the firm and could very well have jeopardised his life and even his children's in the course of establishing this business. No one can say that establishing a business and becoming an entrepreneur can be easy.

The founder of MarkPlus, Hermawan Kartajaya, or HK, has a very strong will and unwavering focus on what he sets out to do. He gave his all in managing and building the firm. He has a strong entrepreneurial mindset, which became one of the critical factors in his success in building MarkPlus.

Today, HK is well known, not only in Indonesia but also globally. Many intellectuals know this name as someone who has created many breakthrough concepts in Marketing. He is also very well known among many practitioners who also see him as someone successful in building a business literally from scratch. Many know his name because of several reasons, including his ways of thinking or doing things.

This section aims to provide a thorough story about the founder of MarkPlus. It will cover his early days, the process in establishing MarkPlus, and the journey he took in becoming the father of Indonesian Marketing.

CHAPTER 1

# HERMAWAN KARTAJAYA: AN ENTREPRENEUR

May 1, 1990, was a historic day for a man named Hermawan Kartajaya. A man whose name is now widely known and well respected nationally and globally as the Father of Indonesian marketing. This was the day that he started a company called MarkPlus, and this also marked his first day as an entrepreneur. Prior to that, he was holding a prestigious position as a distribution director of one of the biggest cigarette company in Indonesia, PT HM Sampoerna.

## YOUNG HERMAWAN KARTAJAYA

Hermawan is a brilliant person who started to independently earn his own money as young as 17 years old. He then became a teacher for 20 years and after that, was appointed as a general marketing manager in PT Panggung, an electronics company in Surabaya. Next, Hermawan joined one of the largest cigarette companies in Indonesia as a distributor director, which he subsequently left to be the founder of MarkPlus, a marketing consultancy practice that has been in the industry for 30 years. Looking at his track record, you might think Hermawan had it easy. But this is not so.

He was born into a lower to middle-class family. His father was a civil servant and also worked as a treasurer in a school in Surabaya. From him, Hermawan learned to be active in organisations and was bright enough to be "the top of his class," due also to his father's way of teaching and support. With his good results, he was accepted into one of the best technology schools in the country, the Institute of Technology

Surabaya (ITS) as an engineering student. This is arguably one of the best Institutes of Higher Learning in Indonesia and his father was so proud of him, to the point that he bragged to his friends about his son's acceptance into ITS. Unfortunately, he wasn't able to graduate as the family was poor at that time.

Even though he had to drop out from the ITS for financial reasons, it didn't stop his desire to complete his university studies. Several years later, he continued his studies, no longer as an engineering student and no longer at the ITS. He switched to a management course at the University of Surabaya because he had taken a strong interest in the management and marketing fields.

## TAKING RISKS IS NECESSARY

Before starting MarkPlus, Hermawan was in a prestigious and highly desired position with his own office, a highly prized job benefit, which is located in an Industrial Estate Complex in Surabaya, the second largest city in Indonesia. He was leading 1,600 people and covering a huge geographical span throughout Indonesia, which was divided into 54 market areas. At the age of 42, he decided to let go of all the prestige and material comforts that came along with this senior executive position with one of Indonesia's largest companies. He made a quantum leap into a totally new territory, or someone might have considered it as a "gamble" by switching from his senior corporate executive career to become an entrepreneur. It takes immense courage to do so and if anyone is in his shoes, would the person have such a drive or be brave enough to take such a leap?

On that memorable day, Hermawan started his new job, as indicated by his new card that stated "MarkPlus Professional Service." The name MarkPlus was adopted because Hermawan envisioned this company to provide "Marketing plus other services."

> *"At that time I was ready and prepared to do any 'professional services,' hence the name is **MarkPlus Professional Services.**"*
>
> **Hermawan Kartajaya**

Similar to some other successful entrepreneurs' stories that you might have heard of, everything started in his own home — a home located in a neighbourhood, which might not have been too suitable as an office. But Hermawan believed he had to start somewhere, and as an entrepreneur who had just begun, a home located in a good neighbourhood was sufficient to be his office. What other choices did he have at that time? In one's own home, one can save on rental costs.

On his first morning as an entrepreneur, he felt something was "missing." Usually, in the morning, he would wake up early, then take a shower and prepare to change into his office "uniform." This used to be his regular morning routine, every day for years. But on that day, he slept in and woke up late. The moment he woke up, he was confused about what activities he should do on his first day as an entrepreneur.

The decision that Hermawan made in becoming an entrepreneur was not risk-free and there was no guarantee of success. But, he still took the risk. At that time, he only had Indonesian Rupiah (IDR) 50,000,000 (approximately US$3,300) as his savings after his resignation from his previous position. Then, he spent almost half of it for the down payment for his new car (because his last company owned the vehicle he had been using). The remaining of the savings was used as his reserve and for his business's starting fund. For some, his decision could be considered reckless, but for the others, his decision could be categorised as brave.

## GRAB EVERY OPPORTUNITY

In the beginning, there were no clients who wanted to use Hermawan's professional services. But, he kept trying, in various ways, to find customers for the firm's professional services. He then decided to focus on becoming a writer for one of the newspapers in Surabaya at that time. A few years back, Hermawan was asked to be one of the writers for this newspaper by the director himself. Hence, once he no longer had a "routine" job and had more time, he solely focused on writing articles that will be published every Wednesday.

He remembered clearly and related to his colleagues about the very first article he wrote for the newspaper, as it was a monumental moment for him. It was about a concert held by Pepsi Cola in Jakarta, which had invited a famous singer, Tina Turner. He talked about how Tina Turner, with the power of her strong voice, could strengthen Pepsi's positioning as a brand that would differ from the classic Coca-Cola at that time. Another interesting article he wrote was about how Lady Di, also known as Princess Diana, faced a difficult situation in the British royal family. However, she was considered as a "People's Princess."

There was also another article Hermawan talked about; it was about the dedication of Mother Teresa, known as someone who always helped those who were sick, neglected, and even shunned. She took care of every single person who needed help, without even knowing their backgrounds. No wonder she attracted the spotlight from the global community. He discussed these three different cases with the same approach and analysis to elaborate on them.

At that time, Hermawan realised the power and effectiveness of newspapers, as a media, in society. Then, he used this media to market and developed himself in the community. He positioned himself as a "Professional Marketing Analyst," and the differentiation was clear because, in that period, there were relatively few professionals in the marketing field.

## BIG FISH IN A SMALL POND

In the early days after Hermawan founded MarkPlus Professional Service, he was anxious. The thing he worried about the most was not being able to pay for his needs, especially the car he had just bought. At that time, he still had 24 months on the credit instalment payment. Not only that, unlike in the past when he had been a director of a big cigarette company, in MarkPlus Professional Services, he did not have a paid position. He did not want to put "director" or "managing director" on the business card. The reason was that he did not have any other person working with or for him, at that time. It would not be very pleasant to have a designation, for a one-man company, according to him.

Hermawan faced a lot of questions about his decision. "Why did you let go of your position?" It was a big thing and more so at that time, for a person doing well as a distribution director of a big company, to resign and set up his own one-man business. He was even asked whether the reason behind his decision to leave his distribution director position was because of corruption, as corruption was not uncommon.

One of the activities he did during his early MarkPlus days was to join a weekly Rotary Club Surabaya meeting. The first time he came to the meeting after his resignation, people noticed that something had changed because he did not wear his usual "uniform." His friends in the club doubted his decision to become an entrepreneur, especially as a marketing professional. Marketing was not a common thing back in the 1990s, and people did not pay too much attention to it. At that time, businesses in Indonesia were dominated quite significantly by monopolies and oligopolies.

Hermawan told us one of his friends in the Rotary Club even remarked, "Who understands marketing and needs it? Tax consultants and accounting consultants are so much better! And the market is big. Everyone needs an accountant, and everyone pays tax."

Even though he was questioned and doubted by many, he stayed firm to his belief and decision. He remembered what his previous boss had told him.

> *"It is better to be a Big Fish in a Small Pond, rather than to be a Big Fish in a Big Pond."*
> **Putera Sampurna (Hermawan's previous boss)**

Hermawan knew the accounting and tax consulting market was huge. But, many players have jumped in the "same pond." Hence, he decided he would be the pioneer in the marketing consultancy market, with MarkPlus. However, one of his friends predicted MarkPlus would only last for three months. It turns out, his friend's prediction was totally off the mark! This year, MarkPlus is celebrating its 30th anniversary. Not three months, but 30 years. How remarkable!

## NETWORK, NETWORK, NETWORK

In MarkPlus Professional Services's first year, Hermawan used his time to widen his network. He joined as many relevant nonprofit organisations as possible. His fondness for joining such organisations began when he was a student. The first organisation was the Rotary Club in Surabaya because the members of this organisation were highly regarded and well connected. Then, he took the initiative to start a new Rotary Club in the Metropolitan area of Surabaya where he became the Chartered President.

Other than the Rotary Club, Hermawan was also involved in establishing AMA Indonesia, also known as the Association for Managers in Indonesia. He was the president of AMA Surabaya and succeeded in making this organisation grow. It had 400 members with a routine monthly meeting.

His networking efforts did not stop there. He then joined another prestigious organisation, Bhakti Persatuan Foundation, that counts famous people as some of its members, volunteering as the foundation's secretary. Membership of this club was dominated by bosses or CEOs. This organisation provided opportunities for Hermawan to get to know those bosses and develop connections with them. However, trying to establish a strong relationship with the "real bosses" was not an easy task, for a person with no position and who had just barely started his business. He sometimes felt inferior and uneasy, but his strong determination helped him to overcome these inhibitions.

His involvement in these three different organisations had significant impacts. In the Rotary Club, he had the chance to experience world-class networking. In AMA Indonesia, he got to polish his creativity in managing an organisation. And lastly, in the last organisation he joined, he gained a valuable skill, which is to understand better the way of thinking of "real bosses." The experiences of such networking were immensely beneficial to Hermawan in his efforts to build MarkPlus.

## SUCCESS BREEDS CONFIDENCE, NOT THE OTHER WAY AROUND

As an entrepreneur, Hermawan started to gain his confidence around one year after he founded MarkPlus Professional Services. This is mainly because during this time, he was able to increasingly secure jobs. He received several invitations to be a speaker from some of his friends. Every single opportunity to speak, whether it was paid or not, provided him with a "laboratory." He was always very well prepared — not only about the material but also the suitability of the content for the participants. Gradually, he was invited to speak not only by his friends, he started to get requests to speak for the public.

Hermawan never does things half-heartedly, no matter what the job is. As a speaker in public, he performed very conscientiously. He always considers the audience as his customers, who need to be satisfied with his service. He considers other speakers at the same seminars or events to be as competitors and according to a basic tenet of marketing, he has to try to be better compared to competitors in satisfying and fulfilling the customers' needs.

These exposures as a speaker led to more opportunities to gain more clients for MarkPlus Professional Services. At around this time, he decided to recruit MarkPlus's first employee. As more jobs came in, this provided more assurance for the company's revenue. This was the tipping point where he gained his confidence as an entrepreneur and confidence in running this business.

> *"It is not confidence that makes you successful, but success that makes you confident!"*
> **Al Ries and Jack Trout**

Hermawan believes that it would be useless to have high self-confidence but not be successful. He prefers to have a small success first that will eventually lead him to gain more confidence. Furthermore, one success will usually bring more confidence and leads to another greater success.

## PRACTICE WHAT YOU BELIEVE IN

Managing a business is not easy, and this is what he experienced. The consulting industry is an "abstract" field and poses a lot of challenges to market this type of service to potential customers. The key success for him is that he practices what he believes in, and this applies to MarkPlus as well.

> *"I am not only preaching but also practicing."*
> **Hermawan Kartajaya**

This can be seen from his approaches to developing MarkPlus throughout the years. He created a strategic forum for MarkPlus in order to differentiate it from other similar businesses. The forum was mainly focused on marketing and he was the moderator. For a long time, he has always tried to be "different" — to practice one of the key concepts in marketing.

## THE POWER OF THREE

One of the most valuable lessons learned by Hermawan while being an entrepreneur is "The Power of Three." He learned this from Dr. Ida Bagus Mantra, former Country CEO of IBM in Indonesia. At first, he was amazed by Ida Bagus Mantra's way of presenting and talking. Everything was systematic. The secret behind it was "The Power of Three."

Why three? Because two seems too little and is often perceived as not too detailed. And more than three items makes it harder for people to digest. If there are more than three, five would be better, just like Indonesia's Pancasila ideology. And if five is still not sufficient, go with ten, just like 'The Ten Commandments'. However, three is more practical and more concise.

An entrepreneur's way of thinking needs to be systematic. This will come in handy in managing and developing a business. The power of three can be a tool for entrepreneurs in organising their thoughts, ideas, solutions, or identifying challenges. He himself has been using this in running MarkPlus for the past 30 years.

The power of three can be used to be systematic. Two popular dimensions are often used to implement "the power of three". For example, the time dimension can be be broken down into three aspects: past, present and future. Another dimension which can also be broken down into three is the "space" dimension with internal, external and environmental sub-dimensions. Hence, one problem can be dissected into various aspects, and only the affected dimensions need to be changed.

After identifying the first three aspects for a given dimension, each element can also be further developed into three more aspects. This will result in a more systematic way of thinking which is easy for others to understand. Some of the examples of how he incorporated "the power of three" are the first logo of MarkPlus Professional Services. The logo consists of three cubes, totaling nine squares. The top line spells out 'MAR', the middle one 'KET', and the bottom one 'ING'. Not only that, the application of "the power of three" can also be seen from Hermawan's Nine Core Elements framework. The framework starts with Strategy (Segmentation, Targeting, and Positioning, or STP) to win the mind share. They are followed by Tactic (Differentiation, Marketing Mix, and Selling) to win the market share. Then, there is Value (Brand, Service, and Process) to win the heart share. Looking at this, everything follows the power of three.

"The power of three" is also in line with the 'Why (reasoning) — What (strategising) — How (executing)' framework used in Harvard Business School.

## WHY-WHAT-HOW

The story of how Hermawan Kartajaya became an entrepreneur and established MarkPlus can be broken down into three parts: why–what–how. He first founded MarkPlus Professional Services because of three 'whys'. The first one is because he saw signs that globalisation was inevitable, especially with the president at that time, Mr. Soeharto. Globalisation means competition, and competition requires marketing. Hence he decided to found MarkPlus.

As for the second "why," Hermawan noticed various multinational companies (MNCs) had demonstrated marketing practice during that time. The method of marketing in those companies led to more significant and sustainable profitability. The third one is because customers expect a good brand and services at that time. Not only price! Even though customers might seem price sensitive, they are willing to pay more, as long as it is better or more convenient for them.

The next part is on, "What will MarkPlus be all about?" Hermawan aims for MarkPlus to be a company that will provide professional services to various companies in Indonesia and to be competitive by using marketing as the primary strategy. As earlier mentioned, it was called MarkPlus because Hermawan was envisioning this company to be "Marketing plus others." It means that client requests outside the marketing field can still be served, but only as a supporting service and as long as MarkPlus has enough competence. This is MarkPlus's grand strategy.

What about the next step, "How"? According to him, it is all about tactics that must be in accordance with strategy. He pictured strategy as an F1 "race-track," which must be passed through by the racers. Each racer has its tactics. It depends on how many times they will change their tires, when they hold their position, and when they will overtake the opponents. But in the end, every racer needs to stay on track.

In his case, Hermawan started from talking, writing, establishing clubs, training, consulting, and then research. These are the things that match his competences and skills. Therefore, he started to be a speaker for companies or for the public. Later, he published many articles and several books. After that, he established a club that was started with his fans as the members. Furthermore, he provided consultants or advisors to companies in need of marketing strategy. Lastly, he and the MarkPlus staff decided to include research as well and this requires a methodology and people management in the field.

Hermawan believes in being an entrepreneur and doing something; you need to remember the why–what–how. Even though you are interested in doing something quickly (how), do not ever do something if you are not in line with the existing strategies (what). And more importantly, there must be a strong reasoning (why) behind everything you decide to do, or will do in the future. An entrepreneur needs to be able to determine their strategies (what) based on explicit reasoning (why). Then, in the end, everything you do will have a good result. And this was proven by his journey in being an entrepreneur.

### 3E: EXPLORE, ENGAGE, AND EXECUTE

In running a business, changes are unavoidable. In his 30 years running MarkPlus, Hermawan believes in using the 3Es (explore, engage, and execute) to deal with changes in the business environment. The first E is explore. It means to explore the market, whether it is a new market or an old one. Before making any decision, it is crucial to explore the available options out there.

The second E is engage. After exploring and deciding on a new market, a business needs to engage with the newly targeted market. An example is to utilise the resources available, to meet the needs of the newly targeted market. It can be in a form of developing new products that suit the new market, or even collaborate with the local businesses. This is the best way to engage a new market.

The third E is to execute. An example for this is selling a locally made product, or developing a regional value chain to include different competences from different areas. In conclusion, the 3Es are applied when changes in the business landscape occur. First, one needs to start exploring the various possibilities. Then, one needs to do an engagement by investing in a marketing mix and a new way of selling. Lastly, one needs to execute the plan by establishing the new process and or new service.

## CHALLENGES ARE INEVITABLE

The biggest challenge Hermawan encountered as an entrepreneur was in 1998. That year was the "Asian Crisis." At that time, like most people, he suffered from the crisis. His kids, Michael and Stephanie, were in the United States pursuing their studies. Mike was a student at the University of Texas at Austin (UT Austin), and Stephanie was in St. Stevens High School also in Austin. That time, the rupiah weakened significantly — the exchange rate from IDR to USD went from Rp. 2.500 to Rp. 15.000 — a six times decrease! Hermawan was anxious, felt uncertain, and did not know when the crisis would be over. He was not sure if he could afford to send money to his kids, especially when there were barely any clients at that time. One by one, the clients left because they were not even sure whether they could survive and what would happen in Indonesia. They no longer needed any of MarkPlus's services, because they did not see these as essential while they themselves struggled to survive. Hence, MarkPlus was left with not too many clients.

However, Hermawan stayed strong and did whatever was necessary in order to survive the crisis. He did not want to let his kids know his struggle and condition at that time. Fortunately, his firstborn, Mike, finished his studies with an excellent GPA of 3.97 and within only six semesters, which meant some cost savings. On the business side, Hermawan had to be creative and think of ways to survive. One of the things that he did at that time was to "barter" with his clients. He managed to build a good relationship with his clients during those difficult times and got help from them. One of the clients helped him by giving him the opportunity to join an executive education program in the United States. In return, He provided training to the client's employees. It was a win-win solution for Hermawan and his client. He got a chance to update his knowledge from a world-class level school, and his client's employees got training with the updated knowledge, without the need to send many of them to the United States. Moreover, as the training was conducted in the national Bahasa Indonesia language, it was more effective and better suited for the participants. He was also able to "barter" with one of his other clients to have a rent-free office in Jakarta, in return for free consultancy services for the client.

Another challenge for Hermawan came in the form of the riots that took place in Jakarta in May 1998. When he flew into Jakarta from Surabaya, at midnight on May 13 that year, the condition was chaotic with fires in several areas, but fortunately, he could reach his house safely. The next day, May 14, 1998, when he was in the office, there was an announcement on the radio that Jakarta was under riot conditions. Everyone in the office was sent home. The situation at that time was out of control. People were stopped and mugged. He and his kid witnessed with their own eyes the fire and riot in Jakarta from the office. Smoke and fire could be seen in various places. On the streets, many people looted from stores and there were massive demonstrations.

At that time, Hermawan tried to cheer up his son by telling him that everything would get better. Indonesia would get better. The day after the riot, images of the chaos, the fire and the uprising ran through his mind. But when he brought himself back to reality, he had a feeling that a new version of Indonesia would come. And MarkPlus, which at that time had been running for eight years, would go up to the "next level." He believes that crises can both be a threat and an opportunity. And it turned out to be true! After the crisis was over, a new chapter for Indonesia, and MarkPlus, began.

One of the ways to keep MarkPlus alive during the crisis was by having a MarkPlus Club — a gathering for members to share and exchange knowledge, discuss specific topics and led by Hermawan himself. During the crisis period, Hermawan still held the monthly meeting for the members in Jakarta and Surabaya. The meeting was always packed with members, even in May 1998! It was a surprise! The club was successful, because Hermawan always tried to deliver interesting topics that would attract members. One of Hermawan's strong points as an entrepreneur is that, even in difficult times, he always tries to find ways and opportunities to help keep the business running.

After the crisis period was over, Hermawan decided to give awards to companies that had creative ways to face the crisis and survive. The award was named "Crisis Award of the Month" because it was given out during the monthly MarkPlus Club gatherings. Having this award boosted the confidence of companies in facing difficult times and also inspired the members at the same time. This award strategy worked well, and the members of the club increased each month. At that time, the crisis was far from being over, but he managed to keep MarkPlus occupied and survived the challenging period.

The peak was in December 1998, when Hermawan held his very first marketing conference and succeeded in attracting an audience numbering 1,000. Even though there were still demonstrations in several areas, many people still came to the conference. This helped to build the image of MarkPlus as a Marketing firm that was always "in" and able to stay strong during the crisis and creatively survives.

## EAT, SLEEP, AND DREAM WITH YOUR BUSINESS

The idea and implementation of "eat-sleep-dream" with each business might differ from entrepreneur to entrepreneur. In Hermawan's case, this starts with understanding trends from multiple perspectives. In the 1990s, he was not only reading books and journals to discover the prevailing "intellectual" trend. He also used his sense and sensitivity to understand the "emotional" trend during that time, by observing none other than the president of Indonesia himself.

What does understanding the "emotional" trend mean? In the 1990s, it meant observing the president of Indonesia's directions, which can help in predicting various possible outcomes. At that time, when the president announced that globalisation would occur in Indonesia, it meant that Indonesia and its citizens had to be ready and be prepared to face greater competition in the near future.

Not stopping in understanding "intellectual" and "emotional" trends alone, Hermawan also observed the "spiritual" trend. The "spiritual" trend is obtained by sensing the changes in the people. He shared the idea of these three trends: intellectual, emotional, and spiritual with Philip Kotler, whose response was:

*"This is the highest level of science in social science, especially in Business and Marketing."*

**Philip Kotler**

For Hermawan, building and developing his MarkPlus business for 30 years wasn't just all about looking for opportunities. He loves his business deeply and marketing is ingrained in his blood. He never stops thinking about marketing, even when he showers. For him, the most productive and enjoyable time to think is during a long flight. There is no disturbance from anyone. He can think deeply for himself.

According to him, there are three things that an entrepreneur should have. The first is that, no matter what the industry is, an entrepreneur should focus on and appreciate his own business. There should be something more significant than money and profit as a goal. Money and profit should be considered as a bonus or appreciation for your efforts and hard work.

Second, reading journals and books is a must. Because this is the easiest way for an entrepreneur to find out other experts' thoughts and opinions. Then, an entrepreneur can follow and apply the knowledge that is suitable for their situation and business.

Third, it is not sufficient to only read journals and books; an entrepreneur should learn from success and failure stories as well. By reading real stories and experiences, an entrepreneur will gain a deeper understanding of how to run a business. They can then identify the characteristics and points on how success or failure occurs in a business.

By combining these three with a considerable amount of focus in running a business, an entrepreneur then can eat, sleep, and dream with their business.

## RIDING THE WAVE, WINNING THE MOMENTUM

The Asian Crisis that happened in Indonesia in 1998 was indeed extraordinary and unforgettable. Luckily, in 1999, Indonesia started to recover. Even though not all of MarkPlus's clients had recovered from the crisis during that year, Hermawan tried to raise their sense of nationalism. Why nationalism? Because the crisis left a big scar for many people, and people were not really sure what would happen next to Indonesia. Would Indonesia able to recover from the crisis? Would everything go back to normal, just like before the crisis? Many questions were lingering in people's minds, especially questions toward Indonesia's situation and future.

In order to raise the sense of nationalism of the people at that time, Hermawan decided to create a big event called "New Indonesia in New Millennium." He invited national companies to the event, to strengthen the concept of the event itself. This event was a big success. This can be seen from the number of people that came to the event: 2,500 people! And the event was also broadcasted live by one of the biggest television channels in Indonesia. Many were surprised about the scale of this event, even his friends. The crisis was not really over at that time, but what he did strengthened the position of MarkPlus in Indonesia as a world-class marketing institution. He could see opportunities when others couldn't, and seize them right away. Be bold!

*"Don't lose the momentum to ride the wave!"*
**Hermawan Kartajaya**

## KNOW YOUR LIMIT

The temptation to lose focus on business is always there. Especially when one begins to succeed in developing one's business. Hermawan knows his limit. He also knows his true calling! He doesn't need to be someone else, as long as he enjoys what he does. Ever since MarkPlus was established on May 1, 1990, the company has always focused solely on marketing, and nothing else. Looking at this, some people snickered and told him that he did not dare to enter "real" business, and only focused on the "consulting business." Those people did not realise that "consulting business" is an abstract business, which in many ways can be more difficult and challenging, compared to some other businesses, because one couldn't see the products physically!

Hermawan faced several obstacles in his journey building MarkPlus. He got questioned a lot by those around him and sneered at by those who did not believe in MarkPlus's credibility. Not only that, credible competitors also came from outside of Indonesia and they carried strong brand names, technology, and systems. Furthermore, many joined MarkPlus to learn initially, and when they left, they started their own companies and became MarkPlus's competitors.

Having gone through different kinds of challenges as an entrepreneur and business owner for 30 years, according to him, the keys to being a successful entrepreneur are to know your limits and to focus. Especially when competition is more intense and global, an entrepreneur needs to be more focused!

> *"In a quiet and calm lake, a small boat is sufficient. While in a vast ocean, a ship needs to be a mother ship. And, a mother ship needs to be more focused!"*
>
> **Hermawan Kartajaya**

## GROWTH IN A BUSINESS

In running a business and being an entrepreneur, Hermawan was inspired by a book called *Every Business Is a Growth Business!* The book explained two findings.

Firstly, a business that doesn't grow will die! Why? Because at the same time, competitors are growing and will then have a better bargaining position. Not only that, but the customer also doesn't like stagnant companies that doesn't have any development and innovation. Customers will most likely prefer a more creative competitor. There will also be internal pressures. Employees will feel that they have no future in the company. The good ones will leave, and the "deadwood" will stay. This will result in a company that is not sustainable. So, if a company wants to be sustainable, there is a strong imperative for it to grow.

Secondly, the growth of a company must be accompanied by an increase in quality as well. According to Hermawan, it is essential not to chase the top line or market share only. The bottom line or profit is important to make sure the growth of a company is healthy. Therefore, there must be profitable growth, and growth is sustained by the power and drive to continue to grow.

Hermawan believes in the word "grow." MarkPlus needs to grow, and so does its employees (MarkPlusers). Without this, MarkPlus would not have been able to stay for 30 years in the industry. Both he and the MarkPlus staff believe that growth with quality can only be achieved when everyone also believes in "excellence." If a company is able to grow with excellence, then the company can deliver remarkable growth!

## INSPIRATION, CULTURE, AND INSTITUTION

According to Hermawan, there are three components to a dynamic enterprise. These are inspiration, culture, and institution. A company must have inspiration when it is first founded. Without inspiration, a company will quickly go down because it has no reason and goals to be achieved. Therefore, in this inspiration, he includes mission and vision.

Many are familiar with the terms 'mission' and 'vision'. But people's understanding of their meanings may differ. Some are still confused between these two. Mission can be defined as "what businesses are we in." Without a mission, a company doesn't have any reason for its being, when it is first founded.

On the other hand, a vision is a big picture of a goal to be achieved within a specified period. Without vision, a company doesn't have any dreams. The company doesn't have any ambition or goal to be accomplished in the future.

Thirty years into the business, MarkPlus has modified and altered its mission and vision several times. The changes in the mission and vision are to be aligned with the changes in the business landscape. For him, the same mission and vision may be useful for three to five years. If it's longer than that, the mission and vision might not be relevant any longer. Because the landscape keeps changing, and no one can predict it. Three to five years is quite an ideal period based on his experiences as an entrepreneur.

The second aspect of a dynamic enterprise is culture. Aside from mission and vision, there is one other thing that can differentiate one company from others, and that is the corporate culture. In MarkPlus itself, Hermawan builds the corporate culture by applying four passions. The first one is passion for knowledge, then passion for business, followed by passion for service, and last is passion for people. These four passions are embedded in MarkPlus and have become the culture of the company.

The third aspect of a dynamic enterprise is institution. According to him, institution consists of the organisational structure and its system. Culture, as a second component, will not be useful without the presence of the institution. As an illustration, culture is the software, and institution is the hardware. A good business will need good management as well, and this includes the measurement tool for measuring performance; Key Performance Indicator (KPI). For him, this is an important aspect for any business to have, and a crucial point for an entrepreneur to be aware of. This is because there must be a comprehensive measurement, to make sure one knows how well the company is doing and hence gauge its sustainability.

# CHAPTER 2

# HERMAWAN KARTAJAYA— THE FOUNDER OF MARKPLUS

What distinguishes one company from other companies? Its mission and vision will be important, but these may only be fully understood and appreciated by its employees. Other than that, there is another thing that is important and visible to others. These are its values, which can be conveyed not just through its statements but also by the concrete results that are delivered.

A company's culture is its shared values and the common behaviour of its employees. Shared values are the values that are ingrained in the employees, whereas common behaviour is the behaviour of the employees and can be easily seen by others.

Being an entrepreneur, a leader, and particularly as the founder of MarkPlus, Hermawan Kartajaya initiated his own 4Ps. It's not the 4Ps of the marketing mix that all marketers know, which are product, price, place, and promotion. His 4Ps stands for **"Four Passions,"** that act as a guide for all *MarkPlusers* (the name for MarkPlus's employees) in their day-to-day work.

What is passion? Simply put, passion can be interpreted as a powerful feeling in someone for something. Passion is often the root driver of things before someone does something. The stronger the passion is, the stronger the drive to the extent that a person is willing to do something even with great sacrifice. Passion is often built up gradually, usually through a complicated and winding stage of development. So, someone may not necessarily find their passion at the start, but instead in the middle of the project they are focused on. To become truly proficient, they also need to perfect or fine-tune themselves, which may take years and enormous effort.

Figure 2.1. The Four Passions of MarkPlusers

Throughout his life, Hermawan realised the importance of having passions in four aspects. This is proven true, from years of experience and practice. From his perspective, the four passions are *passion for knowledge, passion for business, passion for service,* and *passion for people* (Figure 2.1).

## Passion for Knowledge

Hermawan chose Passion for Knowledge as the first passion to be embedded in MarkPlusers. For him, knowledge is the life of MarkPlus. Without strong knowledge and its continuous development, a company will be irrelevant and left out. How can a company become a trendsetter or leader, when its knowledge is outdated?

For an individual, the passion for knowledge needs to be owned by the person, so that there is a strong willingness to learn a new skill or knowledge. Hermawan believes that knowledge comes first before anything else, because it is the foundation or what he called "a soul" of one's identity. Knowledge is the first pillar that needs to be mastered by oneself, because one can only develop this optimally or help others if one has sufficient capabilities.

> *"Possessing passion for knowledge in oneself*
> *means having the desire to always develop continuously."*
> **Hermawan Kartajaya**

An ever-changing landscape requires one to develop continuously. And having passion for knowledge will be the key to be dynamic and adapt to the constantly changing situation. This kind of thinking is exactly what has driven him since his early days.

- **Visionary in Marketing**

  In the 1990s, at a time where many industries were being monopolised by few businesses, Hermawan had already envisioned the importance of marketing for all businesses, before anyone else. At that time, he believed the situation would shift from a monopoly or oligopoly business format and hence effective marketing would be crucial for all companies. His prediction came true during the 1998 crisis. Not surprisingly, in this hard-hitting crisis, companies faced difficult times. Some companies went bankrupt and some experienced tough challenges. Some even lost their monopoly/oligopoly businesses. In order to overcome the crisis, businesses realised the importance of and the need to have effective marketing. Hermawan had foreseen this possibility and was well prepared in advance to help promote effective marketing.

- **Knowledge Sharing**

  Hermawan's passion is not just to obtain and update knowledge for himself; he is also known to be keen and generous in knowledge sharing. In the last 30 years, he had been earnestly sharing his knowledge through several different platforms and this is an indication of his strong passion in knowledge.

  He first started by conducting marketing training programs to some companies and then continued by establishing a marketing club, a place where he provides exclusive knowledge updates in marketing for the members every month. His knowledge sharing is not only limited to companies or members, but is also conducted on a bigger, national scale. He had his own television program in the early 2000s where he explained what marketing is, discussed real case studies, and shared his views and updates on marketing. To help the audience accept and understand marketing, his presentations were supported by various illustrations.

After the name of Hermawan Kartajaya became widely known, both nationally and internationally, he received many invitations to speak or lecture in several different countries. A memorable experience for him was teaching in the MBA program of St. Gallen Business School, a top business school in Europe according to the German business weekly magazine, *Wirtschaftswoche*. He was invited to give lectures about marketing for a week, twice a year. The students there came from various countries and different backgrounds. He was also given the opportunity to give lectures at the University of Michigan, United States of America, and the University of Western Australia.

Even now, he still shares his knowledge from time to time. He has his own session in an education program held by MarkPlus and he also delivered lectures to the students of a master program in marketing, that is, offered by SBM-ITB, a top Indonesian Institute of Higher Learning, in partnership with MarkPlus. He often got invited to speak in both national and international events.

At the end of every year, he also shares his views on marketing and development for upcoming years in MarkPlus's biggest annual event, the "MarkPlus Conference." His passion in knowledge is very much aligned with his main purpose in life, which is teaching and sharing of marketing knowledge.

*"I am a teacher but I am also a thinker! I do not like being called as a motivator, because I am a composer who can sing!"*

**Hermawan Kartajaya**

The biggest influence in terms of teaching for Hermawan is his late father. His father always feels so proud to see his son having so many opportunities to teach not only in Indonesia, but also in other countries!

- **Simplify the Complex Things**

Hermawan's passion in knowledge is effectively shared by his ability to simplify complex topics and his development of new frameworks or concepts. He learned from journals, books, magazines, conferences, schools, and businesses; he would then generate, simplify and syn-thesise the content, together with his additional inputs and refine-ments, into his own model. His models and concepts contribute to his fame today.

*"We don't only read and teach other people's concepts,*
*but we also write and practice our own model!"*
**Hermawan Kartajaya**

Looking back, in the early days when MarkPlus was established in the 1990s, it started with the "Marketing Plus 2000" concept. Hermawan was a pioneer to shift the paradigm of seeing marketing not merely as part of the body of an organisation, but also its soul. Through the Marketing Plus 2000 concept, he succeeded in changing the views of marketing as being complicated, into something simple. Like one of the titles written in a book, *Grow with Character* (2010), 'Keep It Simple Stupid!', he explained that through logical reasoning, a simple umbrella, and redefined model can be created, without the need for complex concepts.

Ever since then, he kept writing and publishing books which demonstrates the brilliance of his mind, from *Repositioning Asia* (2000), *Rethinking Marketing* (2002), *Marketing 3.0* (2010), *Think ASEAN* (2007), *Think New ASEAN* (2014), *Marketing 4.0* (2016), *Marketing for Competitiveness* (2017), *Asian Competitors* (2019) and many others that will be discussed further in the next chapter.

The passion for knowledge runs not only in his blood but also in that of all MarkPlusers. No firm, MarkPlus included, can rely just on one person, even if he were the founder. Indeed MarkPlus, which is currently dominated by young people, is a strong resource base for him. He was able to develop the MarkPlus concepts because of the intensive discussions and exchange of ideas with MarkPlusers, including the young people who are able to come out with fresh ideas and are also both innovative and creative.

Hermawan's role is now more leaning toward listening, even though, in many ways, he still plays a direct role. This collaboration of wisdom and experience from the established with the energy and curiosity for knowledge of the younger generation has become a powerful source of strength for MarkPlus. MarkPlus is characterised by the youth. Currently, 81% of its staff belong to either Generation Y or Generation Z. The younger generation is a strength for MarkPlus and as a "teacher" — which has been one of Hermawan's passions for a long time — they always engage with each other through dialogues and discussions. Hence, he dubbed MarkPlus as *a school of life* or *a university of life*.

> *"Keen to continuously learn, develop, and share knowledge with others.*
>
> *Enthusiastic to learn new stuff, keep updated with the latest data, information, and concepts and yet able to apply the knowledge to practice."*
>
> **Passion for Knowledge of MarkPlus**

## Passion for Business

Hermawan's passion for business needs no questioning. Throughout his 30 years' journey, his experience and creativity in building and managing MarkPlus had shaped him into the kind of entrepreneur he is today. Every experience along the way, good or bad, was his platform to learn more about business. Various crises and obstacles arise along the way and the way he deals with and overcomes these provide invaluable business experience. According to him, there is a close relationship between the first and the second passion, passion for knowledge and passion for business, respectively.

> *"MarkPlus is a Business Knowledge but also a Knowledge Business."*
>
> **Hermawan Kartajaya**

During his time in MarkPlus, he developed several marketing concepts that are applicable for businesses to use. At the same time, MarkPlus also specialises in the knowledge sphere, particularly the field of marketing. As MarkPlus is a company, business calculation is important not just for it to grow, but in crisis times, even to survive.

The Passion for Business is important so that people can become independent even in facing a crisis. In MarkPlus, Hermawan always encourages everyone to have an entrepreneurial spirit. This was shown even in the first decade of MarkPlus where, since the very beginning, he had given full trust and freedom to MarkPlusers to do their job. For example, he would only instruct them on the main objective without meddling in the process. MarkPlusers are given full authority to take care of the job and they can be as creative as possible, as long as it's within the boundaries of the main objective. By giving trust and freedom to them, he is also cultivating and supporting their entrepreneurial spirit at the same time. That's how Hermawan built the entrepreneurial spirit in the company and helped employees develop the passion for business.

*"Keen to seek business opportunities, sell, and be concerned about the target achievements. Always be aware and evaluate potential opportunities. Actualise the potential opportunities by proactively engaging, either directly or indirectly, in selling activities and have a target-and-cost-conscious attitude."*

**Passion for Business of MarkPlus**

MarkPlusers do not only pay attention to the ability of businesses to increase profits and returns but also to business sustainability. They not only strive to be better compared to their competitors but also to be able to make a meaningful difference to the surrounding environment. Their mindsets no longer focus only on solving problems and avoiding obstacles but also on seeking collaborations with various parties.

Business growth is carried out in a healthy manner while at the same time having a positive impact on the surrounding environment. The spirit that is encouraged is not just to focus on being superior and leading in various fields but on how to grow and develop together.

### Passion for Service

Throughout his life, Hermawan came to realise that the more he teaches, the more he gives service to others. He deeply held this passion even when he had been an executive at PT Panggung and also HM Sampoerna, prior to starting up MarkPlus at the age of 42 years old.

The passion for service grew even more, when he started his own business, MarkPlus. Basically, MarkPlus is a service knowledge business in all its business units.

In 1993, Hermawan separated Service from Product. For him, Service has a very big meaning. It encompasses not only after-sales service, which often is treated as a package with the product, but before-sales service as well. The reason is service must be the paradigm of all marketing-oriented businesses. No matter the industry, from hotels, restaurants, or transportation, these are in the service industry. This also applies to non-service industries such as consumer goods, cement, and even infrastructure. The same goes for B2B and B2C businesses.

The service culture that Hermawan Kartajaya has built in MarkPlus is "Service with Care." He wants everyone in MarkPlus to be willing and brave enough to provide service with care. Not like serving a king, but providing caring service like a friend we care about.

> *"Giving service doesn't mean giving everything to the customer, but it means to have sincere relationship with the customer, just like with friends."*
>
> **Hermawan Kartajaya**

As a leader and a role model for his employees, he needs to apply this passion in his daily life. If the leader is consistent in applying this passion for service in his day-to-day activities, the employees will feel embarrassed if they don't follow. Hence, he is always trying to show a concrete example of passion for service in the office. He does not hesitate to welcome and escort guests that come to the office. Even from the simplest thing, he is willing to pour water, tea, or coffee for the guests. Therefore, all the employees in MarkPlus never hesitate to do the same things for any visitor, because their boss also does the same! He even invited a trainer who specialises in giving hospitality training to new hotel staff to train MarkPlusers about this. The passion for service has become part of the culture of MarkPlus.

*"Keen to serve customers both externally as client and internally as friend. Genuinely care about customers, be sensitive to sense customers' needs, be courageous to apologise, and give immediate service recovery in case of failures in satisfying customers."*

**Passion for Service of MarkPlus**

Fellow humans can work together and collaborate very flexibly, even with people we have never met before. Not only that, we can also work with each other even in big numbers to achieve a particular goal. Such cooperation continues to enrich the progress of our civilisation because humans are social creatures and are more effective in doing things by working together.

So, what matters most is not what we do for ourselves, but what we do for others. Our existence becomes increasingly meaningful if we can benefit the surrounding environment. With passion for knowledge, we can identify what to do and how to execute it. Not only that, with passion for business, we are also capable of making a more significant contribution, whereas passion for service encourages us to help others more.

## Passion for People

The fourth passion is passion for people. Hermawan wants MarkPlusers not to look down on other people. Not only that, he also wants MarkPlusers to put aside differences between nations, tribes, races, and religions, and to build good relationships with others. There's a strong relation between the third and fourth passion, between service and people.

*"MarkPlus is a People-oriented Service and a Service-based People Organisation!"*

**Hermawan Kartajaya**

He wants everyone to be horizontal citizens of the world. He himself has been practicing this kind of passion for people since his early days.

He talks to anyone, networks with anyone, and opens himself to anyone, regardless of race, nationality, or religion. This can be seen from his network, from the past until today.

In the early days of MarkPlus, Hermawan learned a lot from his networks including networks from his previous jobs. During the crisis period, in order for MarkPlus to survive, he received help even from clients at that time. In the process of becoming the Father of Indonesian Marketing, he did not hesitate to learn from experts, inside as well as outside the country. No matter what the challenges were, he was able to connect and have networks with a lot of people. These are just small examples of his passion for people.

One thing Hermawan always does before he meets someone is he will get to know the person beforehand. No matter who the person is: Whether the person is a CEO, government agent, artist, or even an ordinary person. He will try his best to know their personality, their interests, and their values. Hence, when they meet in person, the likelihood of having an interesting and memorable conversation is higher. And this will lead to a bigger impact toward their relationships and connections afterwards.

> *"Keen to socialise with others to build relationships.*
> *Be confident to interact with other people, easily initiate conversation, establish good connections and also eager to be part of social activities to meet new people."*
> **Passion for People of MarkPlus**

Human relations are indeed very complicated, ranging from identifying problems, looking for alternative solutions to actions. Not to mention if there are issues in communication or differences, such as generational differences, that can cause differences in perspective on the problem.

For various reasons, arguably, perfecting passion for people is very difficult to do. Because in passion for people, the focus is no longer on oneself, but how one's presence can have a positive influence on others. Even though it is very complicated, particularly when dealing with relationships between people, if appropriately managed, passion for people can give birth to a beautiful relationship. The positive synergy between people or even the community can produce wonderful results. And this is what Hermawan has in mind as a goal for MarkPlus. When MarkPlusers possess the passion for people that can result in an excellent and synergic working environment, it will then lead to better results and better productivity as well.

In its 30th year, 1% of MarkPlus's employees are baby boomers, 18% are from Generation X, 72% from Generation Y, and 9% from Generation Z. As we know, each generation has its own style, working preferences, and virtues. The baby boomer's style and Generation Z's style are very different. One is likely a thinker, and the other is likely a doer. However, in spite of these generational differences, the current MarkPlusers make it work. The main reason is that they can understand and quickly adapt to each other, and these sprouted from their passion of people in the first place. Even though Hermawan Kartajaya is a baby boomer, he still discusses and is open to suggestions from the younger generations. Similarly, his actions are reflected by MarkPlusers as well.

# CHAPTER 3

# HK—THE FATHER OF INDONESIAN MARKETING

## WHERE IT ALL BEGAN

It all started in 1993 when Hermawan had the ambition to develop a new marketing concept that could be applied in the new millennium, starting from 2000. There are three important underlying principles which he believes are important to develop a new concept, which he later named it, "Marketing Plus 2000".

The first is simplicity. Hermawan strongly believes that a concept needs to be simple. The main reason is that the more straightforward a concept is, the easier it is for people to understand. A concept needs to be as simple as possible so that people who don't have any business background or even those who did not go to college, will be able to understand and accept it. They should not only accept the concept, but should also like the idea.

> *"Simplicity is Power!*
> *What's the use of a sophisticated model if it's difficult to understand?"*
> **Hermawan Kartajaya**

Hermawan realised that a concept or model which looks sophisticated but is challenging to understand would be useless. As a form of social science, marketing should be useful for many people through its simple application and execution.

The second underlying principle is that the concept needs to be an "umbrella" concept. It means that the idea must be able to cover all other existing concepts at that time. This is essential because, at that time, people had many misunderstandings about marketing. Marketing is often thought to be the same thing as selling, promotion, public relations, advertising, discounts and promotions, and so on. As there had been many studies and researches on various aspects of marketing, it is essential to develop a new marketing concept that can be used as an "umbrella" concept for marketing.

Studies, research, and textbooks that explained marketing at that time usually consist of several marketing concepts. One of the weaknesses of such an approach is that practitioners, with limited time, would face difficulties in reading all or a lot of them. Hence, Hermawan wanted to develop a concept that would offer a "big picture" about marketing.

The third underlying principle in developing a new concept is that it should attempt to redefine existing concepts, to make them more relevant and current. Hermawan felt that the existing definition of marketing was lacking and was not satisfied with what was explained to the people. He thought that redefining marketing was necessary for it to be well accepted by the others. There were many new ideas about marketing but these seem divided in several different aspects.

Looking at the situation, before Hermawan started to develop a new concept, he read and explored the different definitions out there in the market and tried to understand the meaning of marketing itself, from the very beginning. Moreover, the newly developed concept, as a new definition, had to be relevant to the modern era.

As his influence grew, so did his determination to finish developing a new marketing concept. He believed that to be acknowledged as a marketing teacher and for any new concept to be well accepted, two things were required. First is to write a textbook that would be widely used throughout the world. This is not an easy task. Writing marketing textbooks is already highly competitive in particular among marketing professors. And after all, textbooks are usually written by academics.

The second one is to write a trade book, instead of a textbook. This one is also not easy, but it would be possible and helpful if a writer can find a "non-mainstream" path. The main reason for this is textbook writers have already compiled many, if not all, marketing concepts.

Hermawan saw an opportunity to jump into the trade book path. His first teacher, who could help him on this path, was no other than Al Ries, a well-known marketing professional and author with multiple best-selling books. One of his most recognised books was *The Battle for Your Mind*, co-written with Jack Trout. Both of them are known to be the first to use and define the term "Positioning".

Hermawan did not stop there and also learned from other writers. Another writer he learnt from was Kenichi Ohmae, a Japanese business strategist who published the book *The Mind of the Strategist*. This book explained a company's strategy in a clear but yet simple manner. In addition to Ohmae, Hermawan also learnt from Leonard Berry, Zeithaml, and Parasuraman who came out with their fantastic concept: Service Quality Excellence. These three authors succeeded in redefining "service."

Each writer came from a different background. Al Ries and Jack Trout were former practitioners in the advertising industry. On the contrary, Kenichi Ohmae was a former consultant, and Berry, Zeitaml, and Parasuraman are professors. All these writers seem to have something in common in their writings — their concepts are simple, are an umbrella concept, and are a redefinition.

In the process of developing his marketing concept, Hermawan was heavily influenced by Kenichi Ohmae who in his most famous book, *The Mind of the Strategist*, wrote about the Three Cs. Ohmae writes that the company's strategy must be based on three choices. First is a company-based strategy. A company needs to identify its strengths and weaknesses before anything else. Then, the company needs to develop an approach based on strengths, not weaknesses. Don't force a company to "enter" into an area that is not suitable and doesn't have the competence. The second strategy is customer based. It means a company can synthesise its approach based on the needs and wants of the customers. This might seem too simple for some, but this is essential. It would not be suitable for a company to offer products or services that are not required and wanted by the customers. Many companies in the past, trying hard to be "unique" and "different" from others, came out with products that customers did not need, which led to failure. The reason is that customers may not need products or services that are too "unique" or too "different." The third one is the competitor-based strategy. It means that a company can decide their next plan based on the competitor's strategies. If the competitor does something, a company will then have a choice to follow or to surpass, or even to be completely different to attract potential customers' attention. Another thing a company can do is ignore the competitors. People say the latter is the most risky, because it often fails.

*"Think of a strategy as a triangle with three sides: company, customer, and competition."*

**Kenichi Ohmae**

Hermawan was impressed by Ohmae's writings, and he always thought about this day and night. One day, he discovered his AHA! moment. He got the idea to have the fourth C, Change, that needs to be considered in the process of making strategies.

His way of thinking was simple. If people only made strategies based on the first three Cs, the strategy might not be sustainable, because it would not take into account the changes that will occur. As changes may not just be from customers and competitors, it is better if changes are first considered.

After having this AHA! moment, Hermawan then combined these four Cs into his first model: CHANGE–COMPETITOR–CUSTOMER–COMPANY.

After he developed the 4C model, he continued to perfect his concept. If the 4C is considered an illustration for an outside competitive setting, there is a need for an inside competitive strategy. This was the forerunner to the legendary Nine Core Elements of the Market-ing Model. At that time, Hermawan was thinking about how to combine all the major marketing elements into one model. These include more established elements such as marketing mix and selling and relatively newer ones such as segmentation and targeting.

He also wanted to combine them to align with the positioning concept, which was a hot topic at that time. In terms of positioning, he was heavily influenced by Al Ries who stated that positioning is the core strategy.

## POSITION HIMSELF WITH AL RIES

It can be said that developing the Marketing Plus 2000 concept gave Hermawan the opportunity to meet with Al Ries. He became enthusiastic about developing a marketing concept, after reading the legendary book by Al Ries and Jack Trout called *Positioning: The Battle for Your Mind*. The first encounter with Al Ries was possible because of Hermawan's friends. His friend invited Al Ries for a workshop in Jakarta. Knowing this, Hermawan offered to deliver a keynote speech for the event. His friend agreed to his idea, but he was only given five minutes for his speech.

Due to the limited time, he needed to make the speech as compact as possible but still deliver what he wanted to say. While constructing his speech, he assumed he had three types of customers. The audience of five hundred people, his friend who was the organiser of the event, and Al Ries himself, the person he wanted to ask to be an endorser. For that reason, he reviewed positioning, marketing warfare, bottom-up marketing, and other concepts, so that he was very well versed with the ideas and the connection with the books written by Al Ries.

Hermawan needed to go the extra length for this keynote speech because of many reasons. For the audience, this speech should be an executive summary of the event. For the good of the organiser, it was essential to deliver the content of the keynote speech in a manner that the audience would find it easy to understand. He also wanted to impress Al Ries with the quality of his speech.

He spent one week working on developing an effective and efficient keynote speech which could be delivered in five minutes. He could not afford to fail, because he knew that this kind of opportunity would not knock twice. This keynote speech was Hermawan's moment of truth to make or break it.

On the day of the event, he arrived at the venue an hour before the event even started. He was hoping to get a chance to speak with Al Ries and share the story of MarkPlus with him.

After successfully delivering the speech, Al Ries shook his hand and complimented him. At first, Hermawan thought that he was merely being courteous, until he received a fax from India, the venue of Al Ries's next event.

> *"Thanks a lot for a great opening speech. You are truly amazing."*
>
> **Fax from Al Ries to Hermawan**

He did not expect to get a fax from Al Ries. He then replied to the fax saying that he would visit him in New York the following month. To which Al Ries replied, "I will welcome you in Manhattan. Please do come."

The next month, Hermawan flew to New York. He had scheduled a meeting with Al Ries at 10 am at the hotel's lobby. But Al Ries had not arrived, even at 10.45 am. He began to grow nervous as he wondered why Al Ries had not shown up at the designated meeting time.

When he called Al Ries's office, Al Ries himself happened to answer the phone and apologised profusely for forgetting about the meeting. With discussions finally underway Hermawan explained the Marketing Plus 2000 model and asked for Al Ries's endorsement. Other than that, he also asked to be Al Ries's representative in Indonesia. At the end of the meeting, Al Ries agreed to Hermawan's ideas. The meeting progressed smoothly and was very fruitful.

Hermawan flew back home with a big smile on his face. The reason was that he was allowed to use Al Ries' logo. He also had Al Ries' endorsement on his newly developed concept. That was the beginning of the relationship between Hermawan and Al Ries.

There was one input from Al Ries when he was shown the illustration for Marketing Plus 2000 concept.

*"It is a very good model, a world class model.*
*But it is better if you can make it simpler."*

**Al Ries**

Al Ries liked the overall concept, and Hermawan confirmed that "positioning" was very important and should be under the "strategy" dimension, not a tactic. According to Al Ries, the Marketing Plus 2000 concept would be easier to understand if it was made into some kind of a marketing law. At that time, Al Ries had just launched a new book with Jack Trout called *22 Immutable Laws of Marketing: Violate Them at Your Own Risk.*

Hermawan then decided to follow his advice. He modified his Marketing Plus 2000 concept into The 18 Guiding Principles of Marketing Company, changing some concepts into several imperative sentences. As it turned out, Al Ries' advice was indeed useful!

The relationship between the two did not end there. Al Ries had helped Hermawan in one of his projects in Indonesia, for a car company in Indonesia and its strategies. During the project, Al Ries gave him some pointers and ideas. Even though they worked in their own offices, one in Jakarta and the other in New York or Atlanta, they succeeded in helping the car company to develop a very suitable strategy.

## MEETING WITH WARREN KEEGAN

Hermawan met Warren Keegan for the first time because of his Marketing Plus 2000 concept. It all started when Hermawan came up with Marketing Plus 2000. Advertising this concept was not easy, in particular with his background as an Indonesian with no doctorate or professor background. Particularly at that time, MarkPlus was still a very small business. Despite all these hardships, Hermawan did not lose hope.

*"If you are small, you must be creative!*
*Don't only complain, but please be creative!"*
**Hermawan Kartajaya**

These are the words that he always lives by. That's the motto he still holds, teaches, and executes. Regarding Marketing Plus 2000, he used his creative mind to promote it. He did many things to raise awareness and acceptance of this concept, starting from being consistent in using the idea for several occasions. He also collaborated with different parties, and he subsequently decided to write a small book about Marketing Plus 2000 in English.

Hermawan always carried the book with him, no matter where he went and he always had a couple of extra copies on hand to give away. During that time, he joined an Executive Education Program at the Wharton School of the University of Pennsylvania where he met Professor Warren Keegan, who is renowned for his work and textbook in global marketing. From there, Hermawan managed to build and maintain a strong relationship with him.

He invited Warren Keegan and his wife to visit Bali and welcome them there. This also gave him an opportunity to seek Keegan's feedback on Marketing Plus 2000. At the end of the discussions, Keegan decided to include this concept in the book he was writing in the form of an appendix for the first chapter. This marked the start of a professional relationship, and Keegan was invited to come to Indonesia again to be a speaker in one of the events by MarkPlus. In return, Keegan invited Hermawan to the United States to be a speaker at the American Marketing Association Education Winter Conference where he spoke about market segmentation in a time of crisis.

*"Hermawan Kartajaya is to Asian Marketing what Philip Kotler is to Global Marketing."*

**Warren Keegan**

Having his concept included in Warren Keegan's book was his first step into the international domain, making his name known not just nationally but globally too. According to Philip Kotler, who used Keegan's book for one of his teaching materials, this was the first time he came across the name of Hermawan Kartajaya.

## FIRST ENCOUNTER WITH PHILIP KOTLER

1998 would be a year that Hermawan would never forget. It was not only the year of the Asian Financial Crisis but more importantly for him was also the year he first met the Father of Marketing, Philip Kotler.

It all started when he was elected as the president of the Asia Pacific Marketing Federation (APMF). When he was first given the role in Tokyo in June 1988, Hermawan explained his concept Marketing Plus 2000 concept. As the president of the Russia Marketing Association heard it and found it interesting, he invited Hermawan to be a speaker at the World Marketing Conference in Moscow and also because Hermawan was the president of APMF and from Indonesia. They wanted to hear the story of the Asian crisis from an Indonesian perspective, as Indonesia was one of the countries that had been most severely hit by the Asian financial crisis at that time.

It was amazing to be invited to be a speaker in a global event that attracts many famous and influential people across the globe. Hermawan was extremely excited about this event not only because of the conference itself but also because of the presence of Philip Kotler in the event as the main speaker.

## Meeting with Hermawan — from Philip Kotler's Perspective

I was the first speaker, and Hermawan was the second speaker. In fact, only the two of us, out of 10 speakers, were asked to meet the press before lunch. As the questions given were more focused on the Asian crisis, Hermawan confidently responded that Asia would not only survive but will rise again. He was presenting his views not just as an Indonesian but also in his capacity as the then president of APMF.

During lunchtime at the event, Hermawan was left alone with me. Everyone at that time was busy preparing for the conference. I was interested in Hermawan's statements regarding the Asia crisis during the press conference, and I was also curious to know the basis for his optimism in Asia. This led to a deep conversation between us.

## Meeting with Philip Kotler — from Hermawan's perspective

Looking at this situation, Hermawan knew that it was the golden moment of truth for him. He needed to seize this opportunity to impress Philip Kotler. The window of opportunity was very rare. He carefully explained the Asian crisis from the perspective he knows best — a marketing perspective. To him, many Asian conglomerates didn't use marketing at that time and depended only on corruption or nepotism which is not sustainable. Hermawan also explained the nature of Asian people; they are hardworking, not easy to give up, good savers, and are also flexible in adapting to changes. For these reasons, Hermawan strongly believes, that the crisis would be a turnaround for Asians to realise the importance of marketing and to use it. It was a wake-up call for Asia. Moreover, several Asian countries such as Japan and Korea already had strong infrastructure at that time. Not to mention Singapore and Hong Kong, which were often referred to as the New Asian Tigers!

**Meeting with Hermawan — from Philip Kotler's Perspective (cont)**

Upon hearing the explanations, I appreciated Hermawan's knowledge. On top of that, I also remembered Hermawan's model that was included in Warren Keegan's textbook, as I had used it for my international marketing teaching at Kellogg. I can remember the model well as my students asked about this particular model.

Hermawan and I then discussed the model that he had developed. For almost two hours, I probed Hermawan and asked a lot of questions regarding the model. In the end, I was impressed by his way of thinking and agreed to co-author a book with him relating to the Asian Financial Crisis that was prevailing at that time. The 4C model was the one that triggered my interest in Hermawan's concept. I was amazed at how he can simplify complex theories about strategies and made it into a new easier model. Despite not being a native English speaker, having no Ph.D., and no professorship, Hermawan successfully convinced me about his model and to write a book together.

## INDONESIA MARKETING ASSOCIATION

Hermawan founded the Indonesia Marketing Association (IMA) on May 20, 1996. There were two reasons behind the establishment of this association. The first is at that time, Hermawan wanted to focus more on marketing and this is aligned with what MarkPlus is about. There was no such national organisation or association that focused on marketing at the time.

The second reason was the path for international involvement. At that time, there was the APMF, which is now called Asia Marketing Federation (AMF) and the World Marketing Federation (WMF), which was subsequently called the World Marketing Association (WMA). These two international bodies were focused on marketing and provided opportunities for international exposure.

The IMA focuses on marketing development activities as a profession in Indonesia. IMA carries out various activities, including events and programs relating to improving marketing knowledge and practices throughout Indonesia.

Hermawan himself was a two-term president — the first term starting from the time he founded IMA, from 1996 to 1998, and the second being the time he continued to carry on that role of president during the crisis in Indonesia from 1999 to 2001.

IMA has grown significantly from the time of its founding. It is now an association that is well known throughout Indonesia, and as of today, there are 54 chapters across the whole of Indonesia. Currently, Hermawan is the Honorary Founding Chairman of IMA.

## ASIA MARKETING FEDERATION

Hermawan's first significant involvement in the Asia Marketing Federation (AMF), formerly known as the Asia Pacific Marketing Federation or APMF, was being elected as its president during the 1998–2000 period. The official inauguration was held in Tokyo in June 1998 and he made use of the opportunity to explain his "Marketing Plus 2000" concept to event attendees. As this concept had already been included in the textbook by Warren Keegan, it was not too difficult to explain the concept to those who have already read it in Keegan's book. It was at this event that Hermawan got the opportunity to be invited as a speaker at the World Marketing Conference in Moscow in September 1998. As mentioned, this event in Moscow turned out to be one of his monumental moments in life, as this was where he got the opportunity to get to personally know the Father of Marketing, Professor Philip Kotler. Hermawan would not be what he is today, if not because of this opportunity to spend some time with, and the support from, Professor Kotler.

The crisis happened at a time when Hermawan was president of the APMF. He came out with various initiatives to help APMF survive and sustain itself. He took steps to lower the membership fee for all the marketing association members under APMF and to ensure that APMF stayed liquid; he also pledged not to use any of the APMF's money in running APMF. He wanted to prove that a president from one of the countries worst hit by the crisis, Indonesia, could deal with the severe crisis and save APMF from challenges posed by the crisis.

In 2000, when his presidency term was duly fulfilled, the APMF Presidency position was succeeded by Khun Supat Tansanthitikorn, from the Marketing Association of Thailand (MAT). Hermawan and his secretary-general could be proud that APMF was handed to the next president, with funds, unlike the time when he took over the presidency and this is inspite of the difficult Asian Financial Crisis time. During his time as president, he managed to run the organisation without spending any of AMPF's money. When he handed over the presidency, the organisation's accounts were practically untouched. It was possible because of his creativity in seeking funding sponsorships to organise various activities. IMA members who helped out could also be proud of this achievement.

The APMF Presidency handover ceremony in Bangkok at the Chulalongkorn University campus was attended by none other than Princess Sirindhorn, the beloved daughter of King Bhumibol. This was a special experience because the inauguration of Hermawan as the APMF president in Tokyo 1998 had been graced by the Princess of Japan. It was indeed very honourable for the handover ceremony to also be graced by a princess.

In APMF, there were five active marketing associations from ASEAN. They were the IMA, Marketing Institute of Singapore (MIS), Malaysian Institute of Marketing (IMM), MAT, and the Philippine Marketing Association (PMA). As President, Hermawan always fostered cohesiveness and unity among all of them. The IMA was appointed as the coordinator for these five national marketing associations from ASEAN.

In 2003, Hermawan organised the first ASEAN Marketing Conference which took place at the ASEAN Secretariat in Jakarta. Several prominent speakers were invited. From Indonesia, these included the minister of political, legal, and security affairs of Indonesia at that time and also Ibu Martha Tilaar with her well-known "Sari Ayu" business. From Malaysia, the speaker was Tony Fernandes, who at that time quite recently started his Air Asia business.

The APMF went through a rebranding exercise and, with the support of Philip Kotler as the Honorary Patron, the organisation's name was changed to the Asia Marketing Foundation (AMF). A major difference is that the current one comprises members from Asia instead of the Asia-Pacific.

## WORLD MARKETING ASSOCIATION (WMA)

Hermawan was not only the President of IMA and APMF but also of the WMA, a position he held from 2002 to 2003. With his impressive performance as the president of APMF, his colleagues in that body advocated for him to be the president of the WMA, which was another significant milestone for him. All these hard work and efforts helped contribute to Hermawan being unofficially recognised as the Father of Indonesian Marketing.

## 50 GURUS WHO HAVE SHAPED THE FUTURE OF MARKETING

Being recognized by and working with Professors Philip Kotler and Warren Keegan, helped to make Hermawan well known. This is particularly so, when he was given the opportunity by Philip Kotler to co-author multiple books together.

The contributions of Hermawan to enrich marketing thoughts and practices did not go unnoticed. The Chartered Institute of Marketing, United Kingdom (CIM-UK), one of the world's oldest and most established marketing organisations, recognized Hermawan as one of "50 Gurus Who Have Shaped The Future of Marketing" in 2003.

This is a prestigious list of some the world's most famous and influential people in the world of marketing.

### The 50 Gurus Who Shaped the Future of Marketing

- David Aaker
- Tim Ambler
- Simon Anholt
- Michael J. Baker
- Drayton Bird
- Stephen Brown
- Dave Chaffey
- Hugh Davidson
- Leslie De Chernatony
- Mark Earls
- Barry J. Gibbons
- Malcolm Gladwell
- Seth Godin
- Dr. Evert Gummesson
- Gary Hamel
- Sam Hill
- John Philip Jones
- **Hermawan Kartajaya**
- Bruce Kasanoff
- Philip J. Kitchen

- Naomi Klein
- Ardi Kolah
- Philip Kotler
- Theodore Levitt
- Martin Lindstrom
- Steve Luengo-Jones
- Malcolm McDonald
- Regis McKenna
- Frederick Newell
- Kenichi Ohmae
- Stanley Paliwoda
- Parasuraman
- Don Peppers
- Tom Peters
- Nigel Piercy

- John Quelch
- Cees Van Riel
- Al Ries
- Martha Rogers
- Don E. Shultz
- Peter Senge
- Patricia B. Seybold
- Jagdish N. Sheth
- Rajendra Sisodia
- Merlin Stone
- David Taylor
- Jack Trout
- Hugh Wilson
- Yoram Wind
- Sergio Zyman

Hermawan is the only person from ASEAN in the list. He specially flew to London to receive this honor and the CIM-UK committee praised him with the following comment:

*"You deserve more than this."*
**CIM-UK Committee**

Even though it was a short sentence of no more than five words, it was significant to him. They had taken notice of his marketing models and were very much aware of the three books that Hermawan had co-authored with Philip Kotler.

Ever since his name was listed by CIM-UK, invitations to speak in various other countries increased significantly. These came particularly from friends in the APMF, with invitations from Kuala Lumpur, Singapore, Bangkok, Manila, Ho Chi Minh City, and Brunei Darussalam, and some of these became quite regular invitations.

Being listed as one of the "50 Gurus Who Have Shaped the Future of Marketing" was a tremendous achievement and a milestone for Hermawan. He was the first Indonesian ever to be awarded with such a prestigious recognition and also the first Indonesian to enter the international league in marketing, with his concepts and work acknowledged by none other than the Father of marketing, Philip Kotler.

## PUBLISHED INTERNATIONAL BOOKS

### 1. Repositioning Asia: From Bubble to Sustainable Economy

This is the very first book that Hermawan Kartajaya co-authored with Philip Kotler. Given the title and the coverage of this topic, Hermawan, with support from his colleagues in MarkPlus, had to put in a lot of efforts and he wanted to figure out the things that would make this book successful.

The book was about the Asian crisis, which is very macro perspective. Asia looked like a "bubble" at that time akin to "something big but hollow inside" but positioned as heading toward sustainability. The authors would like to view this crisis problem from a marketing perspective and must therefore, include marketing terms.

Secondly, this book needed to present the Asian view so that readers, including Westerners, would understand and appreciate the different aspects of Asian values. Some may still have misconceptions about the Asian culture and way of life. Hence, it is essential that this book is presented from the standpoint of Asians which can help to bridge the understanding between Asia and other continents.

To make sure this book would be successful, Hermawan connected with Professor Linda Lim, an Asian expert, from the ASEAN Center at the University of Michigan in Ann Arbor. In MarkPlus's early days (in 1990), Hermawan had attended a Michigan Executive Education program in Jakarta, and Linda was one of the lecturers. Even though she was an expert in macro-economics, she also paid attention to and appreciated marketing. They grew to know each other well and their friendship deepened when his daughter, Stephanie, pursued her undergraduate studies in Economics at the same university in Michigan, Ann Arbor.

At that time, Linda, who is from Singapore, had been at the ASEAN Centre doing in-depth research on the Asian crisis. Having her views and inputs for the book would further raise its quality and credibility which could further differentiate it from other books in this field.

Hermawan was also able to get many study materials from Andersen Consulting, where his son, Michael, worked at that time. He got official permission from Andersen Consulting to do so. With inputs from these various sources, a 2 × 2 matrix, where the X-axis is financial soundness, and the Y-axis, is competitiveness, became the core of this book. Companies that are low in both aspects are called bubble companies. Companies that are highly competitive but low in terms of financial soundness are called aggressive companies. These companies were in a lot of debt, but were still in business and were capable of dealing with the crisis. Companies that are low in competitiveness but high in financial soundness are called conservative companies. Some state-owned plantation enterprises were examples for this quadrant. They did not face any critical bankruptcy situation, with their financial health, but they were not competitive at that time.

On the contrary, companies that are high in terms of both high competitiveness and financial soundness are called sustainable companies. These companies can be considered as very well run professional companies. With the crisis happening at that time, these companies also slowed down just like others, but they were still solid as ever.

The fifth aspect Hermawan did was asking his colleague, Taufik, to help enhance the macro contents so as to add more depth to it. These macro contents would also reflect the Asian crisis at that time. In the end, the macro content of this book could adequately cover the Asian crisis.

By doing those five things, Hermawan succeeded in convincing Kotler that a book on the Asian Crisis could be written from a marketing perspective. Subsequently, the book, *Repositioning Asia: From Bubble to Sustainable Economy,* was published and was made available in many bookstores around the world in 2000. Hermawan was extremely happy that he could witness his book, co-authored with the father of marketing himself, Philip Kotler, being displayed in bookstores around the world. This was also with the support of the publisher, John Wiley, and the book appeared on the best-seller shelves for weeks in bookstores in Singapore.

The book was officially launched with Philip Kotler in Bangkok in 2000, right after Hermawan handed over the position of President of

APMF to Khun Suphat from MAT. The book also brought MarkPlus to the world stage.

**2. *Rethinking Marketing: Sustainable Market-ing Enterprise in Asia***

The second book Hermawan co-authored with Philip Kotler and also with Hooi Den Huan, *Rethinking Marketing: Sustainable Market-ing Enterprise in Asia* was published by Prentice Hall in 2003. In this book, the third version of the Marketing Plus Model 2000 was included (the second version of this model was included in the earlier book *Repositioning Asia: From Bubble to Sustainable Economy*).

In this third version of the model, marketing is not the most crucial function in a company — more than that, it is the soul of the company. If the marketing spirit is in all the employees' attitudes and behaviour, there is no need to have a separate marketing division anymore. Why have one division fully dedicated as a marketing department if everyone in the company is already practicing marketing in their daily work?

Sustainable Market-ing Enterprise (SME) is an illustration of such a company — a company that embeds marketing in its people and their daily activities. With this, it always continuously undertakes 4C analysis which results in a company that is always alert to changes in the business landscape and responding to them. If a company is always alert, the company can adapt its strategy from time to time, depending on the changing situation and its needs, before change is forced on it by the business landscape or the environment.

If a change is required, a company that is alert will quickly change itself first. For those which are not alert, they risk taking actions that are too late. Hence, the 4C model remains as a fundamental analysis tool.

A company that adapts to changes in its environment is likely to be sustainable. After the 4C comes the next sub-model the 9 Core Elements that includes Positioning, Differentiation, and Branding (PDB). In this book, he added a new aspect called 3E (explore, engage, and execute). 3E was created to strengthen an understanding of the 9 Core Elements concept which is based on Strategy, Tactic, and Value. The first E (explore) is for a new strategy, the second E (engage) is for a new tactic, and the third E (execute) is for creating new value.

Because of the continuous changes and transformations, where necessary, Hermawan decided to change the Marketing on the title to

Market-ing. What were his reasons? The main reason is that he wanted marketing to be a dynamic verb (market-ing), rather than being a passive noun (marketing). After all, it is in line with his belief below:

*"The real marketing company doesn't need to have a marketing department."*

**Hermawan Kartajaya**

For this reason, the second element of SME is written as Market-ing, not Marketing.

The third element in this book is the enterprise, where all stakeholders must be satisfied. If a company cannot achieve this, then the company will not be sustainable. For this particular reason, a 3C aspect was added in the book. The 3C stands for Capital, Customer, and Competency market. It means that in order to be sustainable, an enterprise must pay attention to all the 3Cs.

Those who have the capital are shareholders. They can be the founder, partner, or investor. If these are not satisfied, then they can easily move their investment to another company.

The competency market refers to the human resources who work in a company. They also have needs to be satisfied. Hence, the essence of an enterprise is very different from just a company as they have many stakeholders' needs to satisfy.

The diagram that is used to describe an enterprise is a circle which shows the balance among the three main stakeholder groups. Although the description of a company is usually a pyramid or a triangle that is vertical and not comprehensive, in this book, the reciprocal transactions between the company and the three Cs are illustrated. The logical flow from the 4Cs to the 9 Core Elements (with 3E as the connector) to the comprehensive circle (with 3C as the link) is the core of the SME model.

### 3. Attracting Investors: A Marketing Approach to Finding Funds for Your Business

When Hermawan joined a week-long executive program in INSEAD in 2003, he found the lectures by Prof. David Young, the writer of *EVA Value-Based Management*, very interesting and wanted to dive deep into this topic. At the end of the program, he approached David Young to collaborate in writing a book, as he wanted to merge marketing and finance through Young's EVA (Economic Value Added) concept. To convince him of his credentials, he explained his past experiences in marketing and also in writing books including the books with Philip Kotler. After some discussions, David Young was willing to consider, if Philip Kotler agreed to join in. Hermawan had a hunch that this could be of interest to Kotler as it meant extending the boundaries for marketing.

In order for David Young to have a better understanding of MarkPlus, he invited him and they subsequently spent the whole day at the MarkPlus office discussing the book. After listening to an explanation of the SME model, David shared the belief that marketing and finance could be combined — where marketing could be employed to look for business opportunities and create real value, whereas finance can be tasked with finding efficient financial resources to achieve maximum economic value creation.

Subsequently, Hermawan explained three interesting things about the potential book to Kotler. First, this book project was very much a marketing book too, as it used the SME model as a base. In addition, this book would also show another perspective of marketing — that marketing can be used not just for external and internal customers, but also for investor customers, as a third group of customers.

Second, this is a significant opportunity to incorporate marketing and finance. Usually in companies, finance is valued higher than marketing. Most, if not all companies, have a chief financial officer (CFO). Whereas in some companies there may not be a chief marketing officer (CMO), or the highest position for the marketing professional in many companies is the marketing director, which is generally not considered a "C-suite" executive.

Third, the book would be unique as the three co-authors would hail from three different continents; Philip Kotler from America, David Young from Europe, and Hermawan represents Asia. Kotler agreed and the rest is history.

> *"This is a very unique project Hermawan, the first in the world."*
>
> **Philip Kotler**

This book came into fruition and was published by John Wiley with the title *Attracting Investors: A Marketing Approach to Finding Funds for Your Business*. It was launched in 2004.

### 4, Think ASEAN! Rethinking Marketing Towards ASEAN Community 2015

This is the fourth book that Hermawan co-authored with Philip Kotler. To convince Kotler to co-author a marketing book focusing on ASEAN (Association of Southeast Asian Nations), Hermawan presented some data and explained the importance of ASEAN, both as its own entity and as a mediator between India and China. Philip Kotler agreed and Hermawan also invited Hooi Den Huan from Nanyang Business School in Singapore, another ASEAN country, to write the book with them. This book was published by McGraw-Hill Asia with the title *Think ASEAN!*.

In this book, the authors introduced the glorecalisation concept which encompasses global values, regional strategy, and local tactics. This concept is helpful, for example, for multinational companies that wish to enter the ASEAN market. Their head offices may be located in other countries such in the United States, Europe, or Japan, but they must have their own sets of values that must be upheld throughout the world. When the companies decide to enter regional markets such as ASEAN, the marketing strategy, including the order processes, service, and often even new product development should be executed through the regional office. As for the ground marketing tactics, these should be implemented through the local office in each country as they would have a much better understanding of the local circumstances and situation.

This book also explained the attractiveness of the ASEAN market to the world. With a population of 570 million people at that time, ASEAN should be sufficiently large to provide the economies of scale for multinational businesses. ASEAN was growing, not just in numbers, but in standards of living too. ASEAN which comprises the 10 different countries in Southeast Asia is not homogenous and this book explained the social-cultural similarities and differences among the ASEAN countries. Such an understanding is important for any company that wishes to penetrate the ASEAN market.

*Think ASEAN! Rethinking Marketing Towards ASEAN Community 2015* was launched in 2005 in Jakarta by Ong Keng Yong, the secretary-general of ASEAN, together with the launching of the Philip Kotler Center for ASEAN Marketing. A book launch event was also held at the Indonesian embassy in Singapore and the book was translated into several different languages, including Japanese, Korean, and Mandarin.

The book's primary purpose was not just to provide a better understanding and encouragement for businesses to view ASEAN as a potential market but also to discuss about how to market to countries in this region. Hermawan, at the time, said that what would become the next trend was regionalisation, not just globalisation. If the company thinks globally, companies must also prepare themselves regionally.

The publication of this book provided a speaking opportunity for Hermawan, who was invited to speak at the only ASEAN research center in the United States, the Center for South East Asian Studies at the University of Michigan in Ann Arbor.

### 5. Marketing 3.0: From Products to Customers to the Human Spirit

This book by Philip Kotler, Hermawan Kartajaya, and Iwan Setiawan (currently the CEO of MarkPlus), and published by Wiley, took two years to complete and it was launched at Kellogg School of Management, Northwestern University. To Hermawan, this was the most memorable gift he could have received for MarkPlus's 20th birthday. More information about Marketing 3.0 concepts is available from this book.

### 6. Think New ASEAN!

In 2015, Philip Kotler, Hermawan Kartajaya, and Hooi Den Huan launched another book on ASEAN, called *Think New ASEAN!*, which was published by McGraw Hill.

Since the first book was published, the region had changed a great deal. This book explores deeply about ASEAN, which has grown to become a new regional power in the world. It looked at the ASEAN market and how companies can use marketing strategies and tactics to connect with well-informed and empowered customers in the ASEAN countries.

*"Forget the world, think new ASEAN."*

**Philip Kotler**

*Think New ASEAN!* also discussed how the forces of globalisation, over the past three decades, had changed the face of the world today. Globalisation had been a hot button topic that was frequently discussed by statesmen, policymakers, business leaders, students, activists, and so on. It is a process that continues to advance in various aspects and Kotler asserted that the winners of globalisation are not necessarily the rich countries. The winner is a country that can adopt an open market policy, for the flow of capital and technology and to manage cross-border trade competitively.

How about ASEAN? ASEAN cannot be separated from the Asian context. In the past, relations between Asian countries were driven by social, political, and economic ties. A Japanese economics expert, Kaname Akamatsu, described the strength of the Asian economy like the formation of "flying geese" that forms the letter "V." The term was popularised by Akamatsu in the 1930s and reappeared in 1961 through a book called *A Theory of Unbalanced Growth in the World Economy.* In this book, Japan was illustrated as the leading goose who flies at the front of the pack followed by various Asian countries.

Unfortunately, from 1997 to 1998, a financial crisis hit Asia, creating immense legal, political, and social chaos, which ended in a crisis of trust. ASEAN countries were hard hit by the crisis, and the Japanese banking system collapsed. The flying geese formation was finally dispersed.

After the crisis, the geopolitical landscape in Asia has changed. New economic powers emerged such as China and India, along with Korea and Japan, which continued to rise. Countries in the ASEAN organisations such as Indonesia also started to rise. ASEAN has become an active and substantial economic zone. After the crisis ended, a new force emerged, popularly known as ASEAN Plus Three (APT), referring to the ASEAN countries plus China, Japan, and South Korea.

At the regional level in Southeast Asia, several ASEAN countries with hidden market potential, such as Myanmar and Vietnam, also started to open up. At the same time, the ASEAN founding countries, such as Indonesia, Malaysia, the Philippines, Singapore, and Thailand, were promoting the integration of the ASEAN market through the ASEAN Economic Community (AEC). AEC had been in force for some time, but not actively implemented.

The *Think New ASEAN!* book, following the previous *Think ASEAN! Rethinking Marketing Towards ASEAN Community 2015* book, explained the updated information about ASEAN countries and the marketing implications. It provided various information including the changing lifestyle, needs, wants, and even the culture of customers in these countries. Such information would be helpful for businesses who are interested in entering the ASEAN market.

### 7. Marketing for Competitiveness: Asia to the World! In the Age of Digital Consumers

Apart from the *Rethinking Marketing: Sustainable Market-ing Enterprise in Asia, Think ASEAN! Rethinking Marketing Towards ASEAN Community* and the *Think New ASEAN!* books, Philip Kotler, Hermawan Kartajaya, and Hooi Den authored another book, *Marketing for Competitiveness: Asia to the World! In the Age of Digital Consumers*, which was published by World Scientific.

This book provides information about how the market condition and situation in Asia has changed quite significantly and how organisations compete in such a dynamic and rapidly developing market. The authors' primary purpose in writing this book was to elaborate on the dynamic business landscape of Asia, which is influenced by internal and external factors. The business landscape included the challenges and opportunities in the Asia market.

The Asian market had been evolving and transforming in various aspects in the past years. Some variables such as the fast-developing technologies, globalisation, and the spread of information caused the change to accelerate. This book also discusses the rapidly evolving digital technology and its influence in Asia.

Understanding the changes in Asia will allow marketers to understand the market better and to seize available opportunities. Also, it helps marketers to prepare to tackle possible challenges that might arise in the ever-changing landscape in Asia.

### 8. Marketing 4.0: Moving from Traditional to Digital

The concept of marketing continues to evolve, from product-driven marketing (Marketing 1.0) moving toward customer-centric marketing

(Marketing 2.0) to human-centric marketing (Marketing 3.0). The Marketing 4.0 concept combines offline and online interactions between companies and customers. More information about Marketing 4.0 is available from this book.

# Part II

## FIRM: The 30 Years' Journey and Beyond

Since starting up MarkPlus in 1990, Hermawan Kartajaya has consistently aimed to develop both his business and individuals in the fields that the company is best in — marketing and entrepreneurship. MarkPlus has since grown to become Southeast Asia's premier marketing consulting firm with a reputation for its consulting expertise in various business aspects.

MarkPlus offers comprehensive services ranging from consulting, marketing research, education, media, and community service under its business units — MarkPlus, Inc., MarkPlus Institute, MarkPlus Tourism, and Marketeers. **MarkPlus Inc.** focuses on consulting services and offers integrated solutions for various business problems. It also provides marketing and social research services that produce not only useful information but also relevant customer insights, to support a business decision-making process. **MarkPlus Institute** is the training and education business unit of MarkPlus. It offers world-class people development solutions through in-house and public training as well as other education programs in collaboration with prestigious institutions.

**Marketeers** is MarkPlus's media business unit, acting as a connecting platform for marketing enthusiasts in Indonesia and beyond. The award-winning magazine provides the latest dynamic content that helps to inspire businesses and marketing professionals. Annually, Marketeers holds over 300 events, from campus-based gatherings to events for professionals, state-owned enterprises, and small and medium enterprises (SMEs). **MarkPlus Tourism** is the newly established business unit in MarkPlus that offers relevant business solutions to support the development of sustainable tourism.

This part elaborates on the untold stories, including the ups and downs, behind the success of MarkPlus's business units over the 30 years of MarkPlus's existence. It also provides the highlights from each decade, information about MarkPlus's various services and other details of each business unit.

# CHAPTER 4

# THE THREE DECADES JOURNEY

## THE FIRST DECADE — STARTING FROM ONE-MAN SHOW

Seeing MarkPlus today, it is hard to believe that this was all started 30 years ago and in a completely different situation. Looking back, the first 10 years' journey might be the essential phase that was very crucial in shaping the well-known MarkPlus, Inc today. At the very beginning of its lifespan, the company was not able to employ any staff. The company did not have the resources to pay a salary, and nobody was willing to work for MarkPlus Professional Services since it was just a start-up.

Given that Hermawan Kartajaya was the firm's only employee, it is not incorrect to describe MarkPlus Professional Services as a one-man show. MarkPlus did not have a proper office at that time; the founder's house was utilised as the temporary office. The company's logo and business card were the first two things that the company invested in. This just goes to show how important identity is for any company, especially a new company. Moreover, he believes that the company's brand must reflect its reason for "being." This is why the first action he took when he started the company, was to establish a meaningful name and logo.

Figure 4.1 First Logo of MarkPlus Professional Service.

The name MarkPlus consists of two words, Marketing Plus! It can be seen in the first logo that the company adopted. It represented Hermawan's belief that business is marketing, plus others. So, all other business functions, such as finance, operations, and human resources, should make decisions based on marketing considerations. He believes that marketing has a higher level of importance compared to other business functions (Figure 4.1).

This faith provided him with the driving force to establish his own marketing consultancy firm. It was then 1990 and marketing was not considered as something popular, because business was highly dependent on connections and not so much on competitiveness. Many people were questioning his decision to resign from his position as director in one of Indonesia's national companies to start this venture. Furthermore, many were also questioning why a service-based company, and why focus on marketing? Finance and accounting were considered as more useful areas to venture into. However, Hermawan believed that if the market had potential, the level of competition would likely be tighter. He drew on lessons that he learned from Putera Sampoerna, and one such lesson is, "It is better to be a little different than to be a little better."

In a very highly competitive market, customers would not prefer a less well known brand even if it offers a slightly better product because nobody believes in it. Therefore, it has to be different than what most competitors offer. This is quite in line with Michael Porter's theory of differentiation strategy. He believed that it is better to be a big fish in a small pond than to be a small fish in the mighty ocean.

On top of these, establishing a marketing consulting firm was not only a matter of business opportunity. For Hermawan, marketing has always been part and parcel of him.

*"I have indeed fallen in love with marketing. It is ingrained in my blood, and not a day goes by that I do not think of it. Thinking about marketing for me has always been AHA and WOW moments."*

**Hermawan Kartajaya**

## THE FIRST PROJECT — DO ASK THEREFORE YOU WILL BE GIFTED!

The early days of MarkPlus Professional Services were definitely among the most challenging. Hermawan was quite well-known and popular at that time, since he actively wrote weekly articles for *Jawa Pos*, a popular Indonesian media newspaper, and people have always recognised him as a very impressive marketeer. Despite this, it was hard to convince anyone to start using MarkPlus Professional Services. His presence at the Rotary Club in Surabaya Rungkut also helped him to connect with many people from different backgrounds. It was there that he started offering to talk "for free," although it turned out to be not as easy as was expected.

Hermawan's writings were everyone's favourite since they were easy to understand, but that was not enough to gain the public's trust in MarkPlus. Everyone he met was concerned about the uncertainty of MarkPlus's future. Fortunately, he also had other occupations that helped keep him going. Not only was he active in the Indonesia Marketing Club, but he also taught part-time at the Faculty of Economics in Ubaya.

The one thing that he would not want to do was to stay at home all day. He needed to do something, and so he went literally everywhere, going from office to office to advertise MarkPlus Professional Services for free, but nothing substantial really worked out. In his previous career, he had many friends. Since his resignation, many seemed to turn their back and felt hesitant to meet up with him.

It was a month of exasperation and desperation, and he really thought of giving up, but something hit him really hard. It was the look in his children's eyes and their future. He knew he could not give up, and he would not want to give up. He needed to be able to stand up, for himself and his family, and so he made a hard decision to approach his previous employer, Putera Sampoerna. Hermawan admitted that he needed something to help launch his new career, and asked Putera Sampoerna if there was anything he could do. By asking and with luck, he was offered the opportunity to train his former colleagues, who were in all parts of Indonesia, for one whole year. That was his first significant achievement since the company was established.

The moment Hermawan grabbed the first opportunity to prove himself was when his struggle and the MarkPlus journey began. Over the next 12 months, he dedicated himself to train his former colleagues in the Distribution Division of Sampoerna. Within one year, he traveled all over Indonesia to revisit the projects he had done in the past.

He knew that every single former colleague that he would be training was very skillful. They had deep expertise. A key question that arose was *if they are so good, what more could I give them?* He found an answer — a potential void that he could fill, and that was to focus more on strategic development rather than tactical training. He respectfully encouraged them to look at things more deeply and from a bigger picture and not only focus on the surface of the problem. He emphasised that anyone, regardless of his position, should master these three underlying principles, the first being to acquire projects and establish the ideal outcomes. The second is to prepare oneself for a higher stage in his career, by deepening and broadening one's knowledge, and the third is to prepare one's own apprentices for the future. Having demonstrated these three principles and how they worked earned him a lot of respect from his trainees.

Hermawan also realised one significant change — that he had to be fully prepared to reposition himself from being an insider to being an outsider. Educating his trainees to think strategically was his ultimate goal. It was not something easy, but that was a challenge he set for himself to engage in.

As far as he could remember, he earned at least twice as much, when he was an employee. Through this project, he saw that this was the first step for MarkPlus to grow even more significantly and to do so, he knew that the firm could not continue to be just a one-man show

— he had to start looking for his own staff, his own office, and to broaden his network.

The lesson that he learned was that he had to approach his ex-boss at the right time and in the right place. That was what he called the exact psychological moment when every element around you seemed to work out. He was really grateful for that turning moment in his life.

*"To be successful, you must be able to reposition yourself in different situations. Be the water that always fits wherever it flows."*

**Hermawan Kartajaya**

### FROM LOCAL TO NATIONAL

MarkPlus's start was tough. Remember the days when Hermawan had to train his former colleagues? Yes, those days had passed, and after a one-year contract with Sampoerna, he decided to progress further. During that one year, he had been able to expand his network not only in Surabaya but also in Jakarta.

Nothing significant was coming off quickly, and expanding MarkPlus to Jakarta took a lot of efforts. In the third year since MarkPlus's establishment, Hermawan tried to raise the company's national image by regularly writing articles, mostly about exceptional marketing cases in Jakarta. He was building a solid perception of the services offered by MarkPlus Professional Services. He emphasised that the strength of his approach was to create a positive perception among his network and going all the way to turn it into reality.

The relations he managed to grow and the positive brand image he created in Surabaya brought him a lot of satisfaction and feelings of self-actualisation. Within three years of MarkPlus's founding, it had established a pioneer market and had become a practical leader, without any strong competitor, in the field of marketing consulting. It was important for him to move to Jakarta, which is not just the political but also commercial capital of Indonesia — where every business would need to be, to tap on the economic benefits offered by the city.

The MarkPlus Strategic Forum was the platform for MarkPlus Professional Services to spread its wings to Jakarta. Regularly conducted at the Mercantile Athletic Club every month, it became the billboard for MarkPlus to make its mark and to step ahead. The fundamental purpose of the forum was to showcase MarkPlus Professional Services in Jakarta.

Every day had been a struggle, and the firm's real breakthrough came when he finally secured his first consulting client, Bogasari. The first project was to reorganise the salary structure for its employees. Even though this was far from the nature of a marketing project, Hermawan did not want to miss the chance for MarkPlus to secure its very first notable project in Jakarta. To successfully manage this project was a huge challenge that was full of risks. However, failure for one's first notable project was not an option.

Dealing with human resources issues was more complicated than it seemed, as the project was closely intertwined with the organisation's internal structure. There were serious implications to consider, as the project could mean a significant change in the employees' job descriptions, performance expectations as well as their salary range. Employees who performed well would really be able to reap the commensurate benefits, while it could be detrimental to low or nonperforming employees.

To complete the project, Hermawan went back and forth between Jakarta and Surabaya multiple times. In restructuring the compensation scheme for Bogasari's employees, he adopted the principle of internal marketing. He believed that a close relationship between workers and management was akin to customers' relationships with a company — where both parties had to satisfy one another's needs in the long term. Any company had to have both loyal workers and loyal customers. Without such loyalty, they may leave, and it would be much more costly to attract a new worker or customer than to retain one. Indeed, human resources and marketing have a lot in common, and both areas cannot be separated.

A successful business relation with Bogasari would be a good indication that MarkPlus Professional Services could succeed at the national level, especially in Jakarta. A year of hardship and efforts with Bogasari's project had proven its worth. Satisfied with the result of MarkPlus Professional Services, Mr. Sudwikatmono, the head of Bogasari, acknowledged Hermawan for his work and gave him due credit.

Hermawan knew that he had seized the right opportunity to work with a giant company like Bogasari, where discipline and teamwork were some of its hallmarks. Employee satisfaction was critical in increasing the productivity of a company.

This was but the starter project for MarkPlus Professional Services, and it subsequently opened the doors to many other opportunities. It took some five years since its founding for MarkPlus to establish itself nationally, and for its services to be widely recognised.

## 1998 — A BLESSING IN DISGUISE

Within eight years of the founding of MarkPlus, a serious crisis hit Indonesia in 1998. There were lots of major riots and demonstrations everywhere. The riots were triggered by the economic crisis that caused mass unemployment and shortages in food supply. It also led to the resignation of President Soeharto. The crisis days were very difficult for everyone and for every company. In those challenging times, MarkPlus did not step back or nor became weaker. It was still able to serve its clients through research, consultation, and training and luckily, it had one very important and large client, Indofood.

While dealing with the crisis, Hermawan had been thinking of the post-crisis scenario and what should be done. He foresaw that there could be more serious consequences for Indonesia due to corruption. As some say, "Power corrupts, and absolute power corrupts absolutely." The crisis spared no one and MarkPlus was also significantly affected. The market was dying.

It was not just an economic crisis but also a crisis in confidence. Everybody was unsure about the future of Indonesia. At that time, lots of MarkPlus clients stopped using its consulting services, cutting off research and giving up staff training. The only way MarkPlus could survive was to keep the MarkPlus Forum alive. It never missed a single month, not even during the chaotic month of May 1998. On the contrary, the MarkPlus Forum even reached its peak and was able to attract 150 people to join the forum.

1998 proved to be a turnaround point for Indonesia to shape a brand-new country through a significant transformation that many were grateful for. Every month after the crisis, Hermawan was giving away awards for creative companies that were outstanding in facing the crisis. Sari Ayu was the first company awarded by MarkPlus Forum. It was because it succeeded in surviving during the crisis without mass retrenchment of its employees. Sari Ayu even launched a brand-new product, in reaction to the crisis. Following Sari Ayu, the next Crisis Award of the Month went to Telkomsel. Many MarkPlus Forum members were inspired both by such companies and by such recognition. Far from ending MarkPlus, the 1998 crisis was more of a boon than a bane for MarkPlus Professional Services!

Refusing to surrender to the crisis, Hermawan continued writing for various media in Jakarta. He propagated effective ways to survive the crisis and drew examples from role model companies such as those awarded by MarkPlus.

In December 1998, MarkPlus held "The First Indonesia Marketing Conference" in Manggala, which was attended by 1,000 participants. This was the result of MarkPlus's breakthrough efforts against the crisis. It showed that the company was creative enough not just to survive but to grow its reputation and image, and all based on its own efforts. It was all too evident that it had a strong foundation in positioning, differentiation, and in its brand.

## MARKPLUS FORUM, THE FIRM'S PROMOTION ARM

Long before the MarkPlus Forum was created, Hermawan established the Indonesia Marketing Association (IMA). The reason he established IMA was for it to focus on and to promote marketing. This would be aligned with MarkPlus's purpose too. It also had an international dimension, being a member of the Asia Pacific Marketing Federation (APMF) and the World Marketing Federation (WMF). From 1998 to 2000, Hermawan was the president of APMF. His experiences with these various organisations was helpful in further strengthening the MarkPlus Strategic Forum, which was already was well-known as the MarkPlus Forum in Surabaya, in 1992.

The MarkPlus Forum was an effective platform to publicise MarkPlus Professional Services. Managing a marketing club was something that nobody would have thought of, back in 1990. It was believed as something unbeneficial, but Hermawan found it as a way to differentiate his services — as person who walks the talk — by practicing what he preaches.

As time went by, some people were curious and kept asking him about the business he was running. Nobody would ever have any idea how complicated his business was, compared to the others. Why? The answer is that the advisory business is an abstract thing and not easy to 'tangibilise' and more so, given the specific environment it was operating in. Hermawan offered something that nobody wanted. He would, in the first place, have to create or raise potential customer awareness of the need for such services. When, finally, more potential customers saw the need and engaged MarkPlus, a few competitors started to emerge. Such competition further triggered him to invent brand-new differentiation strategies to maintain the company's competitive edge.

In its early days, starting MarkPlus and running its activities, such as the MarkPlus Forum, was not at all easy. The risks were always there. He had to start from the very beginning and did not have enough members. However, as time went by, most of the people who came for the forum found it worth their while. They loved not just the entertaining talk but also valued the tips and tricks of what and what not to do to stay relevant and competitive. Hermawan was always there to moderate the forum discussions, which was one more way for it to be different from other talks.

During the first year, the MarkPlus Forum was able to attract various speakers from Jakarta. At that time, every speaker who came was really someone and considered to be of a top national class. Within a relatively short one year period, the MarkPlus Forum had gained 60 prominent members.

With an aim to increase its memberships, Hermawan felt it would be helpful to learn and share from distinguished global programmes such as the Harvard Business School Executive Education Program. Given that MarkPlus Professional Services was relatively unknown, he was not successful in enrolling into such programmes initially. He subsequently managed to gain admission through the office of Bogasari. Subsequently, the alumni of this executive program were recruited as founding members of the MarkPlus Strategic Forum. As his confidence in the MarkPlus Forum grew, he finally bought a small house in Duta Merlin to be utilised as an office and started to further build MarkPlus with help from various people, including his associate, Vivie Jericho. The MarkPlus Strategic Forum grew both in numbers and in stature with high-level speakers.

Through time, MarkPlus Forum was able to grow even bigger and recruited more members. *SWA* (previously known as *SWASEMBADA*), a highly regarded publication, was one of the reasons behind the progressive growth of the MarkPlus Forum. While leading the forum, Hermawan regularly wrote articles for *SWA*.

Unlike his work for *Jawa Pos*, what he produced for *SWA* was slightly different especially in the way he wrote the stories. He was promoted as an executive editor which further boosted the image of the MarkPlus Forum.

The MarkPlus Forum, played a significant role as the PR arm of MarkPlus Professional Services. This was something unique about MarkPlus Professional Services that made it so special and different from other business advisory firms.

The forum was able to meet the needs and wants of its distinguished customers, especially as it focuses a lot on relevant and very exciting topics that are delivered by well-respected speakers.

The rapid growth of the MarkPlus Forum cannot be separated from the struggle of the very man behind it. Through thick and thin, Hermawan finally saw through the development of the MarkPlus Forum, which further strengthened the image of MarkPlus as arguably the first highly respected and largest marketing consulting firm in Indonesia.

This created a breakthrough for MarkPlus to make its presence well known nationally. The accomplishment that MarkPlus achieved was not enough. It was merely a stepping stone to strive for more goals in the future. At this point, he could see a bright light shining ahead for MarkPlus.

## THE SECOND DECADE — INSTITUTIONALISING MARKPLUS

MarkPlus had slowly grown into a giant firm in its first decade. While Hermawan was developing his trust in the team, he realised that the demand for MarkPlus's services would begin to accelerate. This worried him and he realised that he needed to establish a corporate culture that would reflect to MarkPlusers his own values and motivation.

During this period of rapid growth, he saw the need to preserve the firm's intellectual and professional standards. Following the previous demand for MarkPlus's services, it made sense that people would have higher expectations of their expertise, service and quality. While MarkPlus kept targeting high profile clients, it had a difficult time since the firm was still growing.

The difficulty was aggravated by Hermawan's busy schedule, since his involvement in every project was expected by every client. The fact eventually dawned that knowledge and competencies could not only be centered on only one person and needed to be institutionalised.

Even though the various practices in the firm had replicated his abilities and style, that was not enough. Hermawan thus proposed a professional training for the MarkPlus staff. Those with the capabilities and who were able to perform were promoted to senior levels, including being granted Partner or Associate Partner status.

The professional training showed satisfying results, with both Hermawan and MarkPlus's clients becoming more convinced of the staff's abilities. As such, Hermawan need not personally be involved in the projects. In 2004, Hermawan only spent 30 percent of his time on client services while spending the rest of his time developing his writing and public speaking activities.

## THE THREE CORE SERVICES

The three core services that MarkPlus provides are education, research and consultancy, Hermawan had invested considerable time and efforts to build up the knowledge and expertise which is utilised in all the three practices. The knowledge is also presented through the MarkPlus Forum which had more than 480 members in Jakarta and 190 in Surabaya, consisting of Indonesian managers and executives. The Education practice conducts daily workshops and customised training modules. These are highly demanded which make the practice successful and lucrative.

Market research, the firm's second practice, offers fundamental value for various undertakings including strategy formulation. Quantitative and qualitative research are critical to understand complex business factors such as the economy, the market, politics and government, competitors, industry structure, technology, internal conditions, culture, and the customers themselves.

Consultancy aims to help clients address challenges and to succeed. It leverages on the useful information generated from research. Through his writings and speeches on different platforms and to various organisations, Hermawan helped to effectively promote both marketing knowledge and MarkPlus.

## International Expansion

MarkPlus had proven to be able to survive during the hard times. Hermawan advocated three formulae he believed could be useful. The first formula was romancing the brand. This strategy was to keep the brand image from collapsing. In times of crisis, lots of companies went down hill and were not confident enough to invest. Those who dared to spend and invested their money wisely could win. The second formula was rationalising the brand. In order to survive, one should stay rational in keeping the brand image like downgrading the size of a product yet maintaining its fine quality. The last formula could only be done if the two previous formulas did not succeed. It was economising the brand. In this phase, the quality of the product could be low. This can be risky for the brand, but if it is the company's intention to do so during and after the crisis, and perhaps compensate through a lower price, this can be safe to do.

In 2000, MarkPlus decided to go international as it was already the leading marketing consulting firm in Indonesia and there was an impression that the growth of the firm had reached its peak. Building an international image and network could be the next suitable step as MarkPlus already had a number of foreign clients.

Successfully expanding MarkPlus to Jakarta made Hermawan believe that he could also do it in Singapore. In July 2004, MarkPlus established its office in the heart of the city, where the offices of many giant and multinational corporations were located. By doing so, MarkPlus hoped to be able to attract new clients. In its early days, the firm was not able to serve any clients, and most of its activities were only limited to promotions.

It soon became a reality that new opportunities for the firm would not come along easily, as there were already many established consulting firms before MarkPlus even stepped foot in Singapore.

There were also greater risks. MarkPlus would not only have to adapt to different cultures and environment but also a completely different business environment, not to mention competing with other established firms. A deeper reflection throws out a question whether the strategies that had worked very successfully in Jakarta and Surabaya would work as well in Singapore.

Many said that if one wanted to be acknowledged in Southeast Asia, Singapore was the best place to begin. Hermawan was known as someone who passionately wrote and executed marketing strategies through his famous books, but not many people knew about MarkPlus. It had not gained the same amount of fame as its founder had.

As it is not easy to gain access to the media in Singapore which were also strictly regulated one way for MarkPlus to make its mark was through the universities. Hermawan was invited as a guest lecturer in Singapore Management University (SMU) as well as the University of Chicago campus in Singapore and he was also invited as a guest lecturer at the Nanyang Technological University including in its MBA pro-gramme. For two years, Hermawan was able to secure the premises at the University of Chicago, Singapore campus, for its monthly seminars. MarkPlus was also featured as a case study by the Nanyang Business School Asian Business Case Centre.

Overall, given the circumstances, Hermawan decided to focus on other areas. The next stop was Malaysia where Hermawan believed that Malaysians would be more receptive in the sense of having a similar cul-ture to Indonesians. He had a high profile in Malaysia where he became an Adjunct Professor at the Universiti Tunku Abdul Rahman (UTAR), Graduate School of Management and played a role at the Universiti Putra Malaysia (GSM-UPM), and Asia-E-University (AeU).

He was also invited as a speaker by the Asia Strategy and Leadership Institute (ASLI), Malaysia Industry and Government Alliance for High-Tech (MIGHT), and Lengkawi International Dialogue (LID). In recent years, MarkPlus had focused more on huge projects in consulting and research, some of them including projects for Sunway, HeiTech, and 1901.

## From MarkPlus&Co, to MarkPlus Inc

MarkPlus officially changed its original name of MarkPlus&Co after more than a decade to MarkPlus, Inc. In an interview with Jacky Mussry, Deputy Chairman of MarkPlus, Inc, he described the process of changing the company's name as being unique and memorable for him, personally.

The company had used the name MarkPlus&Co for a very long time. In one meeting with a multinational company, attended by Jacky Mussry, he was asked if 'Mr. MarkPlus' was able to attend the meeting.

> *"In that meeting, as soon as I arrived, the client asked if my name was MarkPlus or whether Mr. MarkPlus was there with us, I was so confused at that moment. At this point, I knew the name was somehow bringing some sort of misinterpretation."*

> **Jacky Mussry**

The abbreviation 'Co', may be considered as a catchall phrase for an association of people working together in a commercial or industrial enterprise. The name structure was often used by law firms which may centre on one or more partners. Therefore, the name was finally changed to MarkPlus, Inc to clarify the misinterpretation, and also to signal a new identity. 'Inc' itself is the abbreviation for incorporated. An incorporated company, or corporation, is a separate legal entity from the person or people forming it.

### MarkPlus Inc, Not HK Fan Club

MarkPlusers had always relied on four core passions as their guiding values, called the '4Ps'. These four passions were the breath of every MarkPluser as a fundamental foundation to serve clients respectfully. The first passion was a passion for knowledge, emphasising that every person in the company had to possess the urge to learn and continuously build their knowledge so that MarkPlus would not be a stagnant firm.

MarkPlus had always been a trend setter. Since the beginning when nobody had really believed in marketing, MarkPlus was the only firm that very actively promoted marketing and defined marketing as being the heart of the firm. In order to sustain the passion of knowledge, MarkPlus compiled a library where it collected nearly 3,000 marketing publications, making the MarkPlus Library one of the most integrated resource hubs for marketing in Indonesia, or even in ASEAN.

To further develop its talent pool, MarkPlus, had been giving scholarships to those employees who met the requirements of being capable and most dedicated to the firm. MarkPlus sent its staff to Nanyang, MIT, and Kellogg to earn their masters degrees. MarkPlus staff are the strong backbone of the firm and are strongly encouraged to constantly learn from journals, books, magazines, through conferences, or even by enrolling in business schools. MarkPlus did not just learn from and teach other people's concepts; more than that, it developed and practiced its own models.

The second passion every MarkPluser needed to have was the passion for business, and it could not be separated from the passion of knowledge as these are tied closely together. As what Hermawan emphasised, MarkPlus is a Business Knowledge and a Knowledge Business at the same time.

MarkPlus required its people to have strong faith in being an entrepreneur that would support the firm and sustain its values. The passion for business came after the passion for knowledge for a reason. Hermawan believed that knowledge should always come first and if it was strongly rooted in every MarkPlus staff, it can result in a successful knowledge business.

Having passion for service was just as important; in fact, it was one of the fundamental values of the firm *to serve the clients*. MarkPlus offered service with care, not just service before, during and after the sale. In MarkPlus, everyone, regardless of who they are, should boldly deliver their best service, and on top of that, carry out every service with full care.

MarkPlus is a people-oriented service and a service-based people organisation, where people could not discriminate against clients based on their race, religion, or origin. Passion for knowledge, business, people and service are two inter-mingling values and are used to educate MarkPlusers to be "horizontal" citizens of the world. With the four passions MarkPlus has a very strong foundation in service.

MarkPlusers strongly believe in the concept of growing with excellence. It was not only MarkPlus that had to grow but also every MarkPluser as well. By applying the concept, everyone can achieve excellent growth. Michael Hermawan is a role model in MarkPlus. He spent his high school years in Upland, California, enrolled in UT Austin and graduated with outstanding results. He also worked for Andersen Consulting before embarking on his MBA studies at the Kellogg School of Management in Northwestern University, Chicago. Before he came back to Indonesia and joined MarkPlus, he worked for AT Kearney and is now a Chief Executive Officer for MarkPlus.

Michael Hermawan advocated four values which are considered essential in excellent growth. The first value was commitment and purpose. It's not about winning itself, but about how one chooses to win, and one must consciously choose excellence. Every person in the world has the ability to be excellent in at least one area. The second value was having the right ability, the ability to fit in every competitive place, and that is why excellence is dynamic. Third was being the best that you can be. Being excellent is not a talent given by God. It is something people need to develop to achieve the best outcome. The last element is continuous improvement. MarkPlus sets the bar and continually raised it from time to time. The principle of growth in excellence is that tomorrow should be better than today.

To complete the concept of growing with excellence, Hermawan advocated that combining the four passions (knowledge, business, service, and people) with these four values would result in a real professionalism in service. In addition to that, he also added these with six pillars of character of the Josephson Institute of Ethics, such as trustworthiness, responsibility, respect, fairness, caring, and citizenship. He also emphasised that MarkPlus did not consist only of himself but, bigger than that, every MarkPluser had to contribute and strengthen it internally and externally. Growth with character became a solid guidance for every MarkPluser.

> "We must grow but grow with excellence. Not only with excellence but also with character. Therefore, you have to grow with character."
>
> **Hermawan Kartajaya**

## THE THIRD DECADE — ENCOMPASSING SUSTAINABILITY

During its third decade, MarkPlus has been focusing more on business sustainability. The firm has survived the difficult years, and also has seized many opportunities to grow on a national and international scale which resulted in very significant growth for the firm, during the second decade. After quite a long journey, the firm continuously reviews and formulates the right strategy in order not just to to survive but also to grow, for many more years to come.

In some business life cycles, the third decade is the time when a company enters the shake-out phase, where sales continue to grow but at a slower pace. In this phase, businesses are supposed to come up with new initiatives in order to extend the business life cycle. So did MarkPlus, and one of the most significant initiatives was to restructure the firm.

During the three decades journey, MarkPlus has undergone several rounds of restructuring based on the three core services. At first, the three core services stood as three different business units, which are MarkPlus Consulting, MarkPlus Insight, and MarkPlus Institute. At one point, the three business units were merged with the aim to standardise the whole business process and the skills of its human resources. Each analyst team from the Institute, Insight, and Consulting units became the client engagement consultant (CEC) team. All analysts were expected to be able to handle all training, research, and consulting projects. The team was divided into five main industries, Government and Public Services (GPS), Financial Services Industry (FSI), Automotive, Transportation and Logistic (ATL), High-Tech, Property, and Consumer (HPC) and Resources, Infrastructure, Utilities (RIU). The aim to transform the team into industry verticals instead of project-based was to give a deeper understanding of the industry knowledge and therefore giving a more comprehensive insight and strategy towards all clients.

## MarkPlus Institute Spin-Off

After several years with the Client Engagement Consultant (CEC) structure, MarkPlus initiated another restructuring. The underlying reason was that one of the core businesses, which was even considered as the foundation and original DNA of MarkPlus, which is its education services, was starting to gain less attention. The focus of the team was too much divided into consulting and research projects.

As seminars, training, coaching, and other education services continue to grow in Indonesia, MarkPlus needs to refocus on demand. Therefore, towards the end of its third decade, MarkPlus decided to spin off MarkPlus Institute into a new business unit. This initiative enabled MarkPlus to gain a better understanding of the industry situation and demand.

With a better understanding of the industry, MarkPlus Institute launched multiple new products, provided a more comprehensive curriculum and extended programs to meet the client's needs and expectations. As a result, MarkPlus Institute has grown quite signficantly and is also considered one of the initiators of the e-learning platform in Indonesia.

## MarkPlus, Inc Enhancement

While MarkPlus Institute is now a separate business unit, market research, consultancy, media, and Marketeers remained under one umbrella, MarkPlus, Inc. The reason is that research, and consulting are inseparable.

The structure under MarkPlus, Inc itself was also quite different from the past. The analyst team was no longer divided into several industries. This allows the team to have exposure to multiple projects across industries. The firm has given more attention to the development of the analyst team and supervised directly under the CEO, Iwan Setiawan, who himself also actively handles some consulting projects along with other analysts. The CEO also ensures that the analysts are equipped with comprehensive skills, by holding a research and consulting process workshop for every new analyst.

The measurement of individual performance is also becoming more objective and standardised. Although all the team members are assessed directly by the CEO, there is a 360-degree evaluation system which allows every individual to be evaluated by a colleague that one works closely with, making the assessment more objective and reliable. With the comprehensive skills development and more objective performance evaluation the work quality has gone up even further. Currently, the firm is handling some multinational clients, in addition to Indonesian clients.

## Establishment of MarkPlus Tourism

In the past years, the Indonesian government has been focusing on the tourism industry which has seen significant growth. This is the result of careful policy planning and execution by the Jokowi administration, which rolled out a multi-pronged approach to boost the industry in

2015. In 2014, there were 9.4 million overseas visitors to Indonesia. By 2017, the number had grown to over 14 million and continues to climb.

MarkPlus has recognised the opportunity and decided to seize it. Therefore, the firm has recently established a new business unit that focuses on tourism, called MarkPlus Tourism, and is under the direct supervision of the founder himself. Another reason for establishing MarkPlus Tourism is that the firm had already previously successfully handled many tourism related projects and is therefore well placed to grow this area. MarkPlus has also become the marketing consultant of Indonesia's Ministry of Tourism.

# CHAPTER 5

# MARKPLUS INSTITUTE — ADVANCING TALENT COMPETENCIES

## ESTABLISHMENT OF MARKPLUS INSTITUTE

As mentioned in Chapter 4, MarkPlus started with education as the main core service. Through seminars and forums, its founder, Hermawan Kartajaya, has begun to spread marketing knowledge across many segments and industries. However, the establishment of MarkPlus Institute as an independent business unit was officially formed many years later, along with MarkPlus Insight and MarkPlus Consulting.

During its early years, MarkPlus Institute mainly focused on the development of new frameworks and concepts across topics, from marketing, sales to leadership and with training topics that were in highest demand at that time. As a result, MarkPlus successfully invented its own concepts such as WOW Service, Leadership 3.0, and Sales Breakthrough. At that time, MarkPlus Institute had dedicated analysts that focused on developing these models, called Knowledge Management and Development (KMD). The strategy worked very well at that time. MarkPlus's own original concepts became one of the company's main competitive advantages. One might say that MarkPlus was one of the few training providers in Indonesia that successfully created its own models, whereas many of its competitors relied highly on the training facilitators.

Other than having its own frameworks, the customer-centric business model was also one of MarkPlus Institute's key success factors at that time. MarkPlus Institute was the first division to implement the industry vertical structure. Both the sales and analyst teams were divided across five major industries, Government and Public Services (GPS), Financial Services Industry (FSI), Automotive, Transportation, and Logistic (ATL), High-Tech, Property and Consumer (HPC), and Resources, Infrastructure, Utilities (RIU). The underlying reasons for this are that in the education service, each industry has its own particular issues and needs. The firm would like to gain a deeper understanding of issues, specific to each industry and, therefore, could serve clients even better. Later on, signature programs were developed for each industry that clearly responded effectively to the anxieties and desires of the industry's players.

MarkPlus Institute not only implemented the industry vertical organisation but also complemented it with support from industry professionals, as exclusive facilitators. This created higher values for MarkPlus Institute, as these facilitators deliver practical approaches, based on their years of experience in the related industries.

After operating with this model for a few years, MarkPlus decided to merge the sales and analyst teams of all its business units — MarkPlus Institute, MarkPlus Insight, and MarkPlus Consulting. The aim of this consolidation was to provide end-to-end services for clients. The reason is that most of the time, an important issue can be comprehensively solved only by multiple approaches that include research, consultation, and training. This would also help to standardise the skills and knowledge of all analysts.

## FROM TRAINING VENDOR TO LEARNING PLATFORM

Although MarkPlus Institute was successfully becoming one of the most reputable and reliable training providers in Indonesia, MarkPlus realised that there were always improvements to be made, in order to grow even further. For many years, MarkPlus only acted as a one-time service training provider in providing its education services, only developing training modules based on the client's request and delivering the training.

The initial analysis of the training needs and the results from the training was not a main concern, because there were so many factors along the process that were not in their control. This naturally affected the quality of the training and client's trust level toward MarkPlus's capabilities.

In order to address these issues, it decided to spin off MarkPlus Institute as an independent business unit. The main concern was that it would be very ineffective to focus on education services by the same team that also handled research and consulting responsibilities. After approximately a year, MarkPlus Institute had grown to become a learning platform, where it provided end-to-end services starting from competencies mapping, training needs analysis and pre-assessment, training delivery as well as post-training monitoring or coaching processes. This enabled MarkPlus to have more control over the quality of training delivered, because the team is engaged in every stage of the training process.

With the progress of the range of services offered and which is supported by experienced facilitators, MarkPlus Institute has successfully developed knowledge-based solutions that balance conceptual models with practical insights. The training programs also incorporate creative and interactive methodologies such as role-playing, simulations, case studies, and field assignments to create a participatory learning atmosphere and enhance human capital development. This enhances the value delivered by MarkPlus Institute, as seen in Figure 5.1, where the training is conceptually rigorous and practically relevant.

People development requires a unique approach — a combination of robust theory and strong practical business background. MarkPlus Institute's training programs are a balanced integration of both. It is aimed at building expected competencies for participants that include

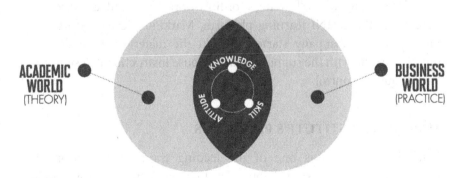

Figure 5.1. Conceptually Rigorous, Practically Relevant

knowledge, skills, and attitude that are powered by the analyst team and supported by experienced facilitators, MarkPlus Institute provides an experiential action-learning approach and contextual case studies that are customised for clients.

## OMNI LEARNING

During its third decade, MarkPlus Institute started to provide OMNI learning. This was initiated as many companies started to consider online training platforms for efficiency and effectiveness purposes. Online learning might have higher setup cost, but it would be very effective for a company with a large number of employees. With this product, the company only needs to purchase one syllabus which can be used by many employees for unlimited times.

Despite its high demand, they still found full online training not completely effective. MarkPlus places great emphasis on the training quality and the results of the training itself. Based on the company's experience, it is tough to determine the extent to which participants fully understand the materials. In order to ensure the quality of the training and that participants can absorb the content properly, MarkPlus introduced OMNI learning — a combination of online and offline training delivery.

Through OMNI learning, MarkPlus designed a full program and decided which stage could be delivered online and which steps required offline interactions. Most of the cases and training delivery could be done in online platforms, followed by offline workshops and exercises. In developing the OMNI learning platform, MarkPlus developed its own programs. The company started to craft the materials, then develop online learning with the support of an in-house instructional designer, as part of quality control.

## MARKPLUS INSTITUTE'S PROGRAMS

MarkPlus Institute, as one of the leading training institutions in Indonesia, provides various people-development solutions, from Public Education Programs (PEP), In-Company Education (ICE) Programs, to Professional Certification Programs.

## Public Training

*Public Education Programs (PEP)*

The PEP is MarkPlus's homemade training program that is specially designed to meet industry competency development needs. MarkPlus has developed a range of topics that will enhance human capital performance at the operational and strategic levels. The materials are prepared by its own team to solve problems typically faced by practitioners across industries.

*Action Learning Program (ALP)*

ALP is a training program that is specially designed for those at the managerial level. The program focuses on direct practice, using tools that have initially been developed by MarkPlus, based on real industrial practices. Participants of this program receive comprehensive materials, as well as hands-on exercises.

*Executive Education Program (EEP)*

The EEP is tailored particularly for executives. This program discusses sales, brand, service, integrating marketing, finance, and marketing comprehensively and are of five days duration. This program is designed specifically for executives who have less than 10 years of experience and are preparing for leadership positions in their company. In this program, participants can learn about topics with the help of seasoned facilitators and lecturers who hold top-level management positions. The program is directly led by Hermawan Kartajaya.

## In-company Education (ICE) Programs

MarkPlus ICE Programs are uniquely customised training solutions for corporate clients. MarkPlus served five industry groups, each of which is supported by a dedicated team of consultants and client relations executives to understand the clients' needs better and prepare relevant solutions. The programs can be delivered in-house at the company's premises, which helps to reduce travel and accommodation expenses, or conducted at the MarkPlus campus where multiple participants can be trained at the same time. Clients can benefit from structured training and education programs that are tailored to specific business objectives.

- **Training Needs Analysis**

  ICE starts with customised training needs analysis, from which specific human capital development needs for clients are discovered. MarkPlus usually conducts direct engagement with the training participants, to clearly understand what is the needed syllabus and how the training is expected to be delivered.

- **Module Development and Training Delivery**

  After completing the training needs analysis, the training modules and delivery methods are customised to fit the client's training needs.

- **Training Evaluation**

  The capabilities of training participants are assessed before and after the training to ensure a successful learning experience.

- **Follow Through/Coaching Program**

  To ensure that the training participants return to their daily jobs with effective practical skills, the training is usually followed by a follow-through assessment and coaching.

## MarkPlus Institute Certification Programs (MICP)

MarkPlus also offers professional certification programs that are focused on sales, service, and brand marketing. The competencies are segmented into operational, management, and strategic levels. At the end of the program, participants are required to clear a test in order to obtain a certification from MarkPlus, which recognises a person's competency on a specific subject. For the operational level, the examination is conducted by the Professional Certification Board (LSP Pemasaran) in order to obtain national recognition. At the international level, MarkPlus Institute also provides tutorials and examinations for the Certified Professional Marketer (Asia) qualification, which enables participants to achieve international recognition.

## MarkPlus Institute License Partner (MILP)

After developing many breakthrough concepts, MarkPlus wanted to spread its marketing knowledge in Indonesia as much as possible. MarkPlus aims to allow as many people as possible to benefit from its framework and models, which contributes to the proliferation of marketing knowledge and to businesses in Indonesia. As such, MarkPlus initiated the MILP, where the program allows anyone who is passionate in marketing or learning to be an official partner of MarkPlus Institute and gives them the license to conduct training using MarkPlus's concepts and framework. The partner is first required to go through a certification program to ensure the quality of the training delivered and standardise the skills of each partner. This program has successfully allowed MarkPlus to reach more extensively to various areas in Indonesia.

## Special Programs in Partnership with the School of Business and Management, Institut Teknologi Bandung (SBM ITB)

The Executive MBA (EMBA) in Strategic Marketing is one of MarkPlus's most prestigious special education programs. This is launched in collaboration with SBM ITB, which is one of Indonesia's premier institute of higher learning. This EMBA is the first and only post-graduate program available in Strategic Marketing in Indonesia. It offers a rigorous program and updated marketing concepts that are relevant with the current and future business landscape.

## GARUDA INDONESIA — SHAPING WORLD-CLASS TALENT

Garuda is one of MarkPlus's clients and the following case shows how both work together for competency development.

### Aviation Industry Dynamics

The aviation business is in one of the most uncertain industries. It is highly affected by exchange rates, natural conditions, airport availability, and regulations, and the uncertainty is aggravated by keen competition, particularly in certain airline routes. The more profitable a route, the more airlines would operate in it and flight frequencies can be intensive.

Regulations, and these can be subject to changes, directly affect the company's financial performance because it is closely related to passenger capacity and flight operational costs. Managing flight operational costs, where 60% of the costs can be impacted by the US dollar — Rupiah exchange rate is one of the most challenging tasks in this industry.

Garuda is a state-owned enterprise that succeeded in transforming the company using the quantum leap approach. The main programs it undertook were on fleet rejuvenation, routes addition, and quality services enchantment. One of Garuda's remarkable achievements was when it won the Best Cabin Crew Award in 2014; another mark of its success was the reopening of the international route to Europe, which was once suspended because of the lack of safety standards. In March 2014, Garuda Indonesia made it to the SkyTeam Alliance that allows it to code share the routes among its member airlines and optimise ticket sales.

## Customer Purchasing Process

In the aviation industry, there are at least three variables considered by the customers before ordering tickets. One is whether the airline flies to the targeted destination. Another is the flight availability and schedule and yet another is the cost of the air ticket.

A deep understanding of the customer's behaviour and factors that will influence their purchase decision can help the company to set up effective marketing communications toward their customers. With a strong knowledge in identifying the customers' anxieties and desires, a brand can strengthen its positioning and differentiation.

Garuda Indonesia had positioned itself as a full service airline and hence they needed to deliver competitive service value. It is involved in not only competition at the national level, but internationally too. As such, they need to develop every employee's competence in order to provide consistently high value to their customers, in particular the frontline employees who are in constant interactions with customers.

## Selling Process

Garuda Indonesia's service performance was outstanding and this was recognised by an award from SkyTrax 5-Star Airline. Garuda Indonesia also collaborates with All Nippon Airways (ANA), Asiana Airlines,

Cathay Pacific Airways, Qatar Airways, and Singapore Airlines. As Garuda won more prestigious rewards, people expected even higher service standards. This also applies to its salespeople when they sell the flight tickets. Many people anticipated advanced technologies when it transitioned to online ticket sales. With economic growth in various regions, the group and business traveler segments also grew; these segments have their own expectations too.

Garuda's branch offices in the various territories have the same responsibility as one another in looking for potential customers. They also needed to creatively think of coming out with traveling programs that would attract their customers. The approach made by the marketing team in every branch office served two customer segments, one being the travel agent segment and the other the corporate customer segment. In the travel agent segment, the marketing method is to give relevant and sufficient incentives to each travel agent, to fulfill its sales target. In the corporate partner segment, sales were conducted through contract arrangements and benefits offered include special fares and extra baggage capacity.

*Sales Professional Development Program*

To support the quantum leap transformation, competent human resources were needed to run the various programs. Without excellent human resources, even the best product could not be delivered and would not be well received. Regardless of Garuda's strong branding, creative initiatives from the sales force were still needed to meet the target.

To sufficiently cover the operational costs, every flight should have an average of 80% load factor. So, if the capacity of one airline could accommodate 200 passengers, they needed at least 160 passengers to reach a breakeven point. The pressure was on to increase the load factor to a maximum degree possible. This is a consistent challenge for Garuda, which has to rely on its travel agents and corporate customers.

To optimise sales, Garuda Indonesia Training center designed a program to prepare its sales force. The team analysed the corporate values of Garuda Indonesia, which would influence the expected behaviour of every Garuda employee. They would then be followed by understanding the work processes of the sales executives, sales managers, and district managers. Such information would be collected in designing the integrated curriculum in the Marketing and Sales Academy. A distinctive aspect of the Corporate University of Garuda Indonesia is that the functional director is the same person leading its functional academic system. This showed that every quality of human resources in one department became a responsibility under one person's supervision.

In the beginning, the program was divided into two stages: the sales manager level and the sales executive level. The designated program consisted of two methods, a comprehensive approach that would include in-class learning and field training. In-class learning was conducted in a way to deliver conceptual and practical learning for the participants and would be constantly highly supervised to assure that the new behaviour would be developed.

MarkPlus also conducted training needs analysis by interviewing each participant with the aim to formulate a program content that is suitable for an effective and sustained development of human resources. In the process of the training needs analysis, MarkPlus conducted in-depth interviews to gain insights into possible obstacles participants would likely face during their work. The results from such studies were used to organise relevant and customised training modules for the sales force of Garuda Indonesia. The final stage would be the presentation of the outcome of these in-class lessons and field training.

To begin the program at the sales executive level, the first phase was mainly focused on basic techniques in marketing, starting from developing a successful sales mindset, gaining knowledge of the market segment, and the decision making process which is also main factor that influences every segment (Figure 5.2). A sales executive had to be skillful in prospecting, probing, presentation, and negotiation to build a post-relation with customers.

There was also a prepared role-play scenario to get the participants to act directly in practicing their technical skills, giving them the opportunity to instantly receive feedback from the facilitators. The participants would present their analysis on certain business segments where they had to start from determining the customer's destination, frequency of the trip, and the position of the customer (staff, manager, or director). Each participant was also needed to prepare to give an immediate response to every client's question regarding the service of Garuda

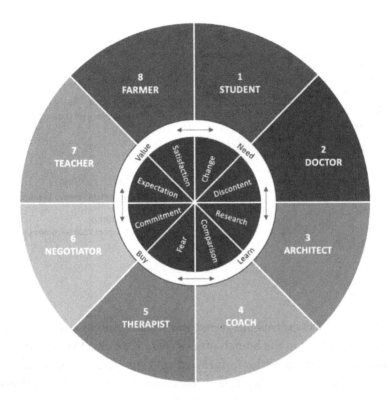

Figure 5.2. Customer-Focused Selling

Indonesia and also technical questions on the purchasing process of an appointed travel agent.

The second phase of the sales executive program was an in-depth understanding in managing an account. The participants were required to have a good understanding of how to approach the decision-making units in a company. Afterward, they had to be able to communicate the company's value proposition and competitive advantage and to try to ensure that the client's loyalty toward Garuda was secured.

The second-level program designed for the sales managers began with the critical role of management — how to lead the marketing team in achieving the target and to make a creative approach in promotion, that is appropriate with the communications strategy, aimed at end-customers. Moreover, the program that was created was synchronised between the sales executives and the sales managers' phase, so that the

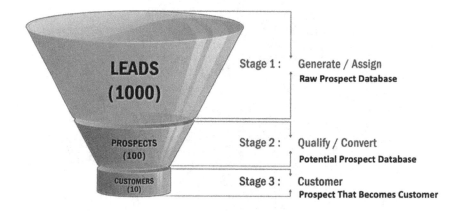

Figure 5.3. Sales Funnel Concept

managerial process is well integrated and would result in a strong operational relationship in the branch office. There is an effective type of synchronisation called the sales funnel concept (Figure 5.3), where the sales managers play a significant role in ensuring that every sales executive activity can create a conversion to turn possible sales into consistent sales.

In the second phase of the sales manager program, the participants were given an understanding of how to analyse macro trends that could possibly affect sales performance in one industry. From a macro perspective, a manager is expected to prepare various tactical responses to deal with the market situation. This a critical role where sales managers would need to guide sales executives on how to respond to every market situation. Effective leadership is essential to help build a well-established work motivation and productivity culture.

The training's execution uses the adult learning approach that focuses on the participants' active participation. The training also included simulation and case studies to boost learning effectiveness. Before the program ended, tools and assignments reports were required and to be completed in two months. Follow-throughs would be conducted as a follow-up to the post-training phase, to develop a long-term learning habit that increases productivity.

*Post-Training*

The post-training activity aims to analyse the progress of the company, particularly in terms of its system, culture, control, and incentive schemes given to the sales force. MarkPlus monitored each branch office to observe the advancement of the employee. The observation results would be reported back to the client, as a basis to introduce more improvements. The output of the program can also be used to plan for the participants' career development. On top of all, competency development is a continuous and sustainable effort to help prepare every employee to compete globally.

# CHAPTER 6

# MARKPLUS INC. — OVERCOMING CLIENT CHALLENGES

## REDEFINING CONSULTING SERVICE

Out of the three core services that MarkPlus offers, education was the first to be established. The founder himself, had always wanted to become a teacher. He started the business with the spirit of spreading marketing knowledge to Indonesians. MarkPlus's first project was a comprehensive training program for Sampoerna, with Hermawan himself as the trainer. Nevertheless, Hermawan always envisioned MarkPlus as a firm that provides a comprehensive solution for all businesses' marketing problems. Therefore, consulting and research services were also subsequently added.

After handling several training projects, participating in several seminars and even establishing his own marketing forum, one day Hermawan was asked if he had his own marketing model and framework. This question hit him hard and prompted him to prove that he could develop his own models and frameworks based on his original ideas and thinking. The result — he introduced the 4C, positioning-differentiation-brand, and nine core elements of marketing models, as his original marketing concept.

These marketing concepts guided the way MarkPlus served its clients. The concepts were developed into a training syllabus, which gave MarkPlus an important differentiation from other competitors. Apart from being incorporated into the training syllabus, the concept was also adopted as the main framework in consulting projects. This concept became MarkPlus's trademark in solving clients' marketing problems and challenges.

The process of handling consulting projects back then was far different from what it is today. Instead of the conventional consultation, it was more like a workshop, where they could discuss any issues that the clients faced. As time went by and they gained more experience, MarkPlus would eventually develop very comprehensive marketing strategies that could deal with any problem that the client faced. Whether a client has issues with sales, or communications, or anything marketing related, MarkPlus would be able to offer various solutions, ranging from industry analysis to marketing communications programs and placements.

Although the style of handling consulting projects in the past, using a combination of training and workshop techniques, worked very well and successfully built a strong client engagement, adjustments and improvements were needed in order to adapt to changing times. The whole process changed when Hermawan Kartajaya's son, Michael Hermawan, joined MarkPlus. Michael Hermawan completed his bachelor's degree at the University of Texas at Austin (UT Austin), in the USA. He achieved this in just six semesters, and with a grade point average (GPA) of 3.97. After he graduated, he worked at Andersen Consulting (currently known as Accenture) before continuing his master's degree at the Kellogg School of Management, Northwestern University. His knowledge and experience working as a consultant at Andersen Consulting helped MarkPlus redefine the consulting process.

When Michael Hermawan joined MarkPlus, he introduced the issue-based problem-solving approach. The idea was to ensure that MarkPlus had a deeper understanding of the client's problems and provide a more focused solution. The original concepts and framework were still useful. The difference is that MarkPlus would not have to provide very comprehensive end-to-end marketing strategies at that time. Instead, MarkPlus would map out the necessary analysis, based on the client's issues. The consulting process significantly changed ever since Michael joined MarkPlus. The process of migrating to a new mentality, system, and processes was not as smooth, because understandably, a miracle cannot happen overnight, and habits do not change all of a sudden. Accepting changes in the work culture is tough for any employee. Not all staff can happily adapt to organisational changes. But the changes were needed for growth and MarkPlusers had no choice but to cope with the new workflow (Figure 6.1).

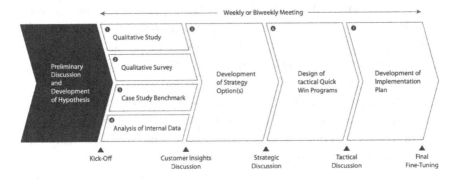

Figure 6.1. Typical Consulting Project Work Flow

Michael Hermawan conducted training and workshop sessions for all MarkPlus's analysts. Many resisted, but some were very passionate about learning the new approach. One analyst who was able to absorb the new information very well *and* showed outstanding performance was Iwan Setiawan, who later became the CEO of MarkPlus, Inc.

## THE URGE TO DISCOVER CUSTOMER INSIGHTS

As a reputable marketing consultancy firm in Indonesia, MarkPlus needs to have strong market research capabilities. However, establishing a market research unit can be quite challenging. Unlike education and consultation services, market research requires a lot of resources in order to meaningfully conduct insightful research of a certain scale. For a company like MarkPlus, this was naturally very difficult. During its first decade, MarkPlus only had less than 50 employees. It was almost impossible to compete with other specialised market research agencies.

However, MarkPlus benefited from the fact that it had handled multiple projects, and most of these consulting projects required preliminary research, prior to forming the right strategic recommendations. This led to the establishment of MarkPlus Insight. The firm believed that insights should come from not only the team's secondary analysis, but also deep insights into the real market conditions which can only be obtained from primary data. The first major research project was a retail audit of

Indofood, one of the biggest fast-moving consumer goods (FMCG) companies in Indonesia. Although MarkPlus faced quite a few challenges due to a lack of capabilities in conducting market research, the team still managed to perform well and deliver the expected results.

During the early days, MarkPlus Insight focused on syndicate research; one of them was "Most Popular Brand," which is based on the customer's top of mind. The syndicated research was considered successful. In its second decade, MarkPlus Insight decided to focus more on customer-based ad hoc research, taking into account that there had been a significant increase in the number of clients handled. These clients required varied research with different methodologies. Such an approach strengthened the firm's portfolio and potentially enables the firm to gain more clients in the future.

Along the way, MarkPlus Insight grew its capability to conduct tailored research for clients in all phases of their business, starting from new product development (idea, product, and pricing test), performance evaluation (service and loyalty, sales and distribution, brand and communication) to market expansion (marketing and strategy) as well as social and opinion research. The range of services that can be offered grew significantly and this is supported by a very comprehensive package of research methodologies, as seen in Figure 6.2.

In its third decade, MarkPlus reinvented its syndicated research. MarkPlus could offer even more added-value since it had developed its own model and metrics. The model was inspired by the increased usage of social media and users and the emergence of new media platforms that provide marketers with new approaches and cheaper alternatives for branding.

The WOW Marketing concept, also known as the 5As (Aware, Appeal, Ask, Act, Advocate), is a breakthrough concept that was popularised through the book, *Marketing 4.0*.

Today in 2020, the research arm of MarkPlus, Inc., MarkPlus Insight, which is a corporate member of ESOMAR, has emerged as a respected Southeast Asia-based research firm, focusing on marketing and social research. As a leading research service provider based in Indonesia, MarkPlus is committed to not only providing reliable information but also relevant customer insights to support clients' decision-making processes.

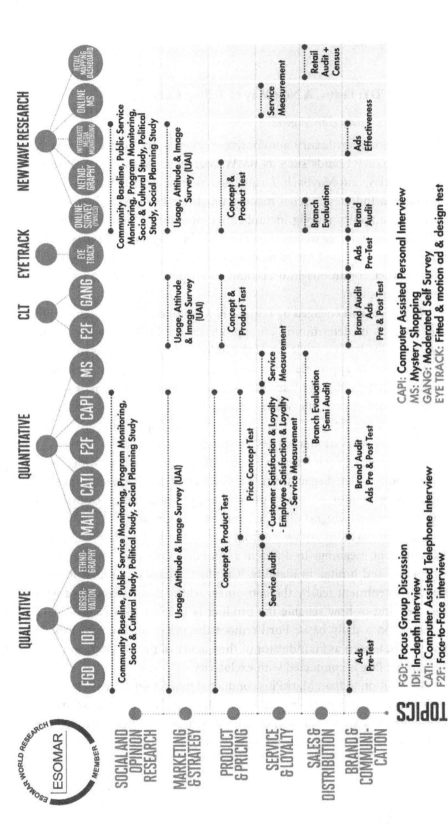

Figure 6.2. MarkPlus Range of Services in Market Research

**CASE STUDY: Lexus, A New Way of Selling Cars**

*Indonesia's Luxury Car Market*

As the Indonesian luxury automotive market is dominated by several Western luxury brands such as BMW, Mercedez-Benz, Jaguar, Ferrari, Audi, Bentley, and Maybach, Lexus encounters a challenging marketing situation in Indonesia. What made it tough for Lexus was the fact that there was a rivalry among incumbent competitors which strengthened their fighting spirit as well as their powerful brand images. Lexus's popularity had not reached the same degree in Indonesia. Lexus had to take such market conditions into account to shape customers' perceptions about its products.

MarkPlus was engaged by Lexus and it conducted wide and in-depth observations in determining an appropriate marketing strategy. Lexus needed an in-depth knowledge of the Indonesian market so as to be able to formulate an appropriate marketing approach. To gain such knowledge, MarkPlus employed several research methods such as in-depth customer and expert interviews, competitors' showroom observations, comparative studies of Lexus showrooms in Taipei, Singapore, and Bangkok, and also conducted desk research.

The result of such extensive and intensive research provided four main findings that began from the *Concept* of the luxurious value of Lexus; *Segmentation* of luxury car market; *Image* branding from Lexus competitors; and *Insights* into each marketing approach.

Perceptions of luxury varied from one respondent to another. Luxury had different meanings to different respondents, such as comfort, ease, expensive, and limited availability. 'Comfort' relates to a sense of emotional contentment felt by the consumers while 'Ease' is connoted with the meaning of how reliable the product is to cater to the consumers' activities on a daily basis. Furthermore the price, or how expensive a product is, is seen as an indicator of the quality of the product, and limited availability is connected with exclusivity.

In addition to that, MarkPlus conducted market segmentation analysis for luxury car consumers and found out that there were six segments relevant to Lexus's global segmentation (Figure 6.3). These included the consumer's lifestyle, values, and objectives.

**Lifestyle/Values**

|  | Conformist<br>Status Quo | Non-Conformist<br>Liberal |
|---|---|---|
| Show off my status to the society | **The Socialite**<br><br>"Look at me, I am rich and successful" | **The Prominent**<br><br>"I am a different kind of socialite; I want people to know that I am always in tune with the trend" |
| Reflect my status | **The Established**<br><br>"People know that I am rich and successful, thus I ought to have the things that rich and successful people should have" | **The Wise**<br><br>"I need to have nice things that reflect my wealth/success, but it has to be well-spent" |
| Appreciate craftmanship and sophistication | **The Elite**<br><br>"I can get all the finest things in life" | **The Avant-Garde**<br><br>"I truly appreciate and want to learn about and experience the latest, best things in life" |

*(Left axis label: I buy luxury car to)*

Figure 6.3. Indonesian Luxury Market Segmentation

## The Socialite

This segment had the objective of showing off their wealth and mostly focused on escalating their social status whenever and wherever they needed to. Therefore, they seek social recognition and products which make them look exquisite, among others.

## The Prominent

Unlike The Socialite, members of The Prominent segment focused on how people perceive them as those who always kept up with the trend, which is also in line with maintaining their social status. In any possible way, they want to be a trendsetter.

## The Established

The Established is acknowledged to be the wealthy and successful group among the community. It is essential for them to have always everything rich people should have, to reflect their social status. They tend to possess or desire anything the members of their community have and symbols of their social status.

### The Wise

This segment refers to those who prefer to keep a low profile, yet at the same time do not ignore their social status. Therefore, they always think about how to wisely spend their money on certain products. They value whether the product they purchase will be beneficial very highly. They will probably learn a lot about a product before spending money on it.

### The Elite

Upholding social status is not the most important focus of this segment. What they seek is the product's exclusivity. The elegance of the product is the top value in their community.

### The Avant-Garde

This type does not pay too much attention to themselves or the perceptions of people toward them. Instead, they seek the best experiences in life and they highly appreciate the beauty and ingenuity of a product.

Insights were obtained about some perceptions of competitors in this luxury automotive industry. At that time, for the respondents in general, Mercedes-Benz represented elegance, BMW and Audi were symbols of sophisticated performance, and Jaguar was the top classic car. Perceptions of Lexus ranged from good to bad. Generally, The Established, The Wise, The Elite, and The Avant-Garde provided favorable views. The Socialite provided average ratings as they thought that Lexus is not able to reflect their social status in Indonesia. Furthermore, MarkPlus examined the automotive industry's service at each touchpoint and views of Lexus's competitors in several countries. Such insights enabled MarkPlus to design a marketing strategy for Lexus in Indonesia.

### Total Lexus Experience

According to MarkPlus's assessment, Lexus should set The Avant-Garde as their main target segment, followed by The Elite, The Wise, and The Established. This took into consideration the competition and

Indonesian consumers' behaviour. When Lexus gained the best position in the Indonesian market, MarkPlus extended their considerations to the last two segments, The Prominent and The Socialite.

Lexus did not just simply compete for the community of people who sought social recognition; it focused more on a properly established group who had long owned various luxury cars. Targeting The Avant-Garde segment would be beneficial, for they certainly would have taken very good care of the exceptional products that they possess.

In order to obtain the ideal Lexus position in Indonesian market, MarkPlus designed holistic marketing approaches where Lexus adjusted the product–customer–brand Management chain by aligning the global approach to fit the Indonesian market. *The Relentless Pursuit of Perfection* was Lexus's prominent tagline which helped it win over its consumers' heart. This was supported by its L-finesse philosophy, which underlines its base operations in the industry.

Lexus delivered strong services in the Indonesian market that enriched its customer and brand management. The summarised approach can be seen in Figure 6.4.

Since Lexus's first release in the Indonesian market, it had been positioned as the one product for Indonesian consumers to aspire for. It was presented not just for its luxury but also for its artistry.

In advertising the product, Lexus had not depended on just Above the Line (ATL) and Below the Line (BTL) campaigns or a massive campaign on media publications. More than that, they relied more on an individual approach.

Focusing on craftsmanship and artistry, Lexus built a gallery, instead of a typical car showroom, where various other arts pieces were curated and displayed together. The design of the Lexus Gallery is such that it offered visitors a different experience. Although its parent company, Toyota had its initial doubts about the concept of a gallery, these were subsequently laid to rest.

The approach adopted by Lexus provided significant points of differentiation from its competitors. Lexus engaged curators instead of typical car salespersons. They were the ones who soothed customer's anxieties and probed their desires. Lexus was really strict in the selection of each potential curator. They had to go through intensive training and

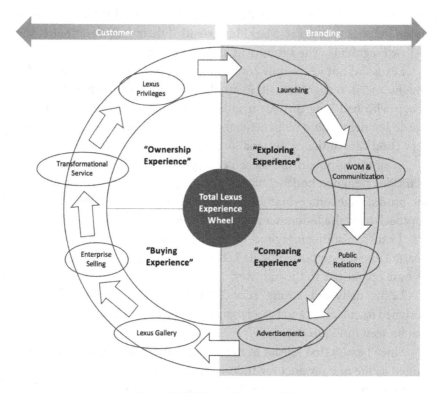

Figure 6.4. Total Lexus Experience Wheel

also gain experiences from visiting several fancy stores and boutiques to learn the best service to provide for their future customers. Every curator should be able to deliver flexible services and made sure that their customers never felt less than satisfied. This method caught the attention of Lexus board members in Japan and they wanted to apply the same strategy to their channels in other countries which did not meet their expectations.

Later on, Lexus presented another touch-points strategy, called Intersect. Unlike the Lexus Gallery, in Intersect, they would not be displaying any Lexus products. Instead, they offered different types of beverages, clothing, and also held various events that had zero correlation to the automotive industry. In 2013, Lexus launched its first Intersect in Japan and planned to expand this to Dubai and New York.

**CASE STUDY: The Body Shop Indonesia, Introducing the New Meaning of "Beauty."**

It was back in 2012, when MarkPlus started to cooperate with The Body Shop in Indonesia. Represented by Hermawan, MarkPlus delivered a brief yet impressive proposal presentation to The Body Shop team. This led to a meaningful collaboration between the two companies. It was generally known that a primary reason why a company would decide to choose MarkPlus over another is when it has serious concerns about its future. This could be due changes in the business landscape including competition.

While The Body Shop Indonesia was clearly in a pretty stable phase of business, it needed assistance to face future challenges. After The Body Shop Indonesia was acquired by L'Oreal in 2006, it needed to be more aggressive in revenue and profit growth. Such new targets were believed to be a source of concern in a company where ethical values was a strong focus, for many years. L'Oreal's expectations posed an issue to The Body Shop Indonesia, as its customer segment was somewhat limited.

The Body Shop had a strong image of being a retailer of imported cosmetics and their main target segment comprises the elite group who valued the products more than others. By comparison, the elites are relatively small in numbers and focusing on them alone might mean the company would lose out on the middle class who may have high aspirations to purchase its products.

There are several companies in this industry — some focusing on treating the products as prestige products and others who positioned themselves as products for the masses. Furthermore, some focus on modern technology in developing their products while others focus more on natural substances. The Body Shop was perceived to be a prestige brand using natural substances (Figure 6.5). This was considered as an inadequate choice, if the company wished to expand its market. Targeting the middle class needed a new approach that would promise quick results, which seems contradictory to its original selling point of natural ingredients, which were projected to take a long time to win over the market.

By 2017, The Body Shop Indonesia had a target revenue of up to IDR 1 billion, twice its revenue in 2012. To achieve such a goal, The

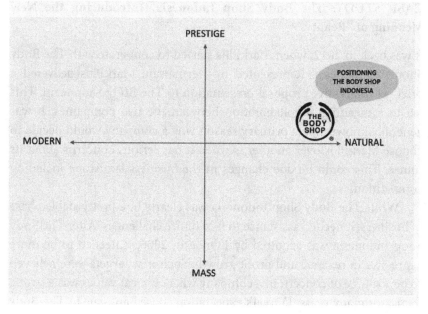

Figure 6.5. Positioning The Body Shop Indonesia

Body Shop had to come up with suitable marketing strategies. Based on organic growth and existing channels, they had to increase the number of stores from 80 to 140 by the end of 2017.

**What did MarkPlus do?**

MarkPlus conducted a comprehensive study over three months, that included quantitative and qualitative research, to understand the needs, expectations, and insecurity feelings of customers toward beauty products.

Quantitative research results would take the form of demographic, psychographic, and consumer behaviour studies, while qualitative research would focus more on sensing trends happening in the industry and also gauging consumers' reactions to the brand-new ideas offered by The Body Shop Indonesia.

In order to analyse the industry landscape, MarkPlus used the 4C Framework (Figure 6.6). Four perspectives were discovered, following the research analysis.

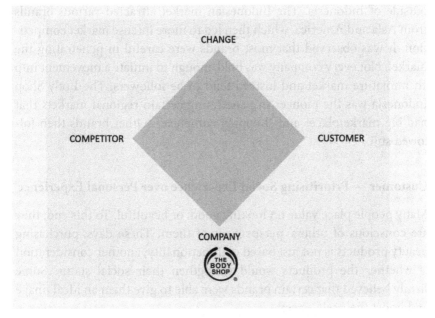

Figure 6.6. 4C The Body Shop

## Change — More Specialised and Personalised

In the past, many consumers did not seem to pay too much attention to the trivial aspects of a product such as different soap fragrances as these did not seem to be the most important. As time passed by, women started to consider more aspects such as the brand of soap, the scent, color, shape, and the background story of a product. Surprisingly, it was not only women but also several men who had such considerations in mind. Men were found to purchase the same products as most women, as there were not many options for beauty products that were specially catered to men. As a result, the overall market turned out to be more specialised and personalised which is quite in line with an urban mindset and lifestyle.

## Competitor — Doubtful to be Bold

Business competition in the beauty products is not as keen in earlier times. Several new brands started to emerge and most of them originated outside of Indonesia. The Indonesian market attracted various brands from Asia and America, which then led to more intense market competition. It was observed that most brands were careful in penetrating the market. Not every company was bold enough to initiate a movement into an immature market and instead tend to be followers. The Body Shop Indonesia was the pioneer in penetrating certain regional markets that had big marketplaces and shopping complexes. Other brands then followed suit.

### Customer — Prioritising Social Experience over Personal Experience

Many people place value on looking good, or beautiful. To this end, they are conscious of others' perspectives of them. These days, purchasing beauty products is not just based on functionality; another consideration is whether the products would strengthen their social status. Some firmly believed that certain brands were able to give them an ideal image and boost their self-esteem.

Based on these three perspectives, several marketing actions were taken to achieve the targeted growth of the company:

### 1. Market Segmentation

In order to accomplish a big enough market, The Body Shop had to target a wider range of consumers, instead of just relying on their fans and customers. Penetrating the market and targeting a new segment could help the company cover the IDR 600 billion gap in its revenue goal. A potential target would be the youths.

Over the years, The Body Shop had been widely dominated by the senior market segment that was able to afford its prestigious products. Apart from their renowned products, The Body Shop was known to have an interior design that was not deemed attractive to youths. This youth segment, which ranged from high school students to those employed in their first job, was the one that the company decided to pay attention to.

In modern times, the middle-class group is expected to grow and should not be abandoned. Though the middle class may not match the high-profile group in terms of income, they are willing to spend. They aspire to have prestige goods, and MarkPlus had assessed that The Body Shop products are desired by this group. However, catering to this middle segment may have an impact on The Body Shop's image of a highly prestigious brand whose loyal customers come from the elite. Hence, a challenge for the company is to maintain its image while also trying to penetrate the middle-class market.

## 2. Positioning

A position based on *values with values* was believed to be the key to targeting the middle-class and youth groups. The sense of value was expected to deliver a clear message that the products were worth buying, regardless of the consumer. Every consumer could have various perspectives and values, including perceived ones, regarding the products they purchase. By positioning on value, The Body Shop could target the middle-class segment without negatively affecting its image. The following points are The Body Shop's philosophical values:

- Promote Self-Esteem
- Protect the Planet
- Defend Human Rights
- Support Community Trade
- Against Animal Testing

These values mean that The Body Shop is not only paying attention to the customer's sense of beauty but also to contributing to the conservation of the earth and environment. As such, being a customer of The Body Shop would give them a sense of having done the right thing.

## 3. Differentiation

Reinforcing the *positioning of values with values* needs a robust differentiation. The Body Shop's overall differentiation strategy covers the management of product, customer, and brand, and comprises three aspects — productivity, connectivity, and creativity (see Figure 6.7).

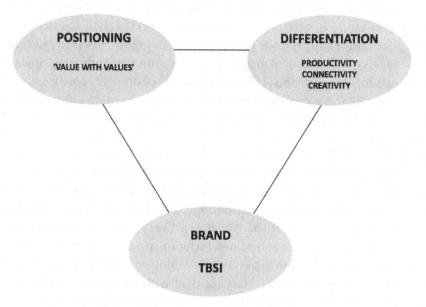

Figure 6.7. Positioning-Differentiation-Brand The Body Shop

### Product Management — *Productivity*

The Body Shop defined productivity as a way to help the consumer to be more productive, for example, by saving time. To accommodate its target segments, the company offered the products through various marketing channels.

### Customer Management — *Connectivity*

The Body Shop facilitated greater connectivity between it and its customers and among its customers. Customers are allowed access to the flow of information and knowledge about its products and other aspects.

### Brand Management — *Creativity*

The Body Shop made it possible for the consumers to actively participate in several social activities, where their contributions would also have a direct positive impact on society. By so doing, it gave opportunities for its consumers to be more creative while also feeling being a part of The Body Shop family. The above three aspects succeeded in enhancing the business growth of The Body Shop as providing exceptional and reputable beauty products in Indonesia.

## 4. Strategic Actions

In implementing its formulated strategy, The Body Shop started to take some strategic actions as part of a practical movement to achieve the current goal of the company. MarkPlus called this strategic action model to *cover broadly but dive deeply,* as seen in Figure 6.8. The company had to keep on developing the market and undertaking constant innovations, toward their channels. Every channel The Body Shop created should always be aligned with their overall strategy, and they should provide several alternatives. With that being said, The Body Shop would not only rely on offline stores but also rely on other means, such as direct selling. This was what *cover broadly* is about.

There are times, when a company is too aggressive and too engrossed in expanding the market, at the expense of ignoring the quality of its products and the needs of its customers. This was certainly unlikely to happen to The Body Shop, as they continuously engaged customers through creative activities to maintain customer connectivity. This was called *deep diving.*

## Results

From 2013 to 2014, transformation in the industry was inevitable. Constant changes were happening in the business landscape be they in the economic or political fields or in the competitive and customer behaviour sectors. Yet, The Body Shop was able to cope and deal with all these, through adjusting its a creative marketing strategy which was advised by MarkPlus and with the personal attention of Hermawan Kartajaya.

Several brick and mortar stores were launched in many market-places and shopping complexes. The Body Shop did not stop right

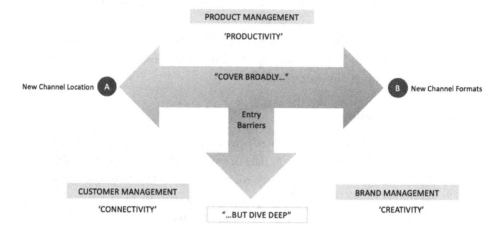

Figure 6.8. Strategic Actions of The Body Shop Indonesia

there, as the company continued to improve other marketing channels, like e-commerce. Moreover, The Body Shop adjusted its branding and image to suit the local culture. Recruiting local talents to be its brand ambassadors was one of the methods adopted. These new marketing practices helped the company to increase its revenue by up to IDR 1 billion, as early as in 2015. This remarkable accomplishment was achieved after two years of cooperation with MarkPlus, through a well-executed and effective marketing strategy.

# CHAPTER 7

# MARKETEERS — MARKETING MEETS CREATIVITY

## ESTABLISHMENT OF MARKETEERS

The establishment of the MarkPlus Forum greatly helped MarkPlus's success during its first decade. It was considered an effective platform to promote MarkPlus Professional Service. Although it was quite difficult at first, as time goes by, the forum was able to attract national class speakers to address the forum. As mentioned in Chapter 4, within a relatively short one-year period, the MarkPlus Forum had gained 60 prominent members.

As the forum became more successful and gained even more members, it became more attractive for managers and executives from various companies. This helped to create a prestigious image for the MarkPlus Forum. Some years later, MarkPlus's Founder, Hermawan Kartajaya, considered it necessary to broaden the scope of the MarkPlus Forum as it became an effective platform for publicity. He wanted to establish a new forum, particularly for younger segments that cannot be reached by the MarkPlus Forum. This is precisely how Marketeers was established. Long before it offered its current core business, media, Marketeers first focused on the community. As time passed by, Marketeers grew even more and broadened its services to include the media and business events and activities such as Meetings, Incentives, Conventions and Exhibitions (MICE) .

111

## MARKETEERS TODAY: INDONESIA'S #1 MARKETING MEDIA AND MICE

Marketeers today is acting as a connecting platform for marketing enthusiasts in Indonesia and beyond. The organisation itself consisted of different departments inside the Marketeers business unit, such as Magazine, Community, TV, Net and Brand Activation (Figure 7.1). The media unit runs the *Marketeers Magazine*, which caters to cool inspiring and progressive business and marketing professionals. The award-winning magazine provides the latest dynamic content on news and views from the business and political world and is available nationwide in modern and digital outlets. It also runs the Marketeers Net online portal, a hugely popular website offering fresh daily content on marketing-related topics.

MarkPlus has stepped up to integrate the online and offline platforms where it enables marketing enthusiasts in Indonesia to connect. Marketeers proves to be the most progressive marketing network platform with an omni-channel presence spanning the mainstream (print), online (website), and social media platforms. It conveys an all-inclusive scope of the most recent marketing information and insights to marketeers in Indonesia and beyond.

The presence of the Marketeers Community which is classified into Campus, Executive, Badan Usaha Milik Negara (BUMN) or state-owned enterprises (SOEs), and Chief Marketing Officer (CMO) Clubs empowers MarkPlus to serve as a connector among thousands of campus students, professionals, and elite C-level executives with the aim to propagate the latest insights on the marketing world and to pick up new ideas and perspectives from inspiring C-suite executives. Marketeers can connect with over 50,000 marketing enthusiasts with its content delivery and event organising divisions and community platforms.

Figure 7.1. Marketeers Structure

## Marketeers Magazine

The Marketeers Magazine has been awarded three gold medals — the Indonesia Print Media Award in the local news/business/politics magazine category, the Gold Winner at Asian Media Awards (Figure 7.3), and the Gold Medal from World Association of Newspapers and News Publishers (WAN-IFRA), (Figure 7.2) for being highly rated in the industry for fresh, inspiring, and progressive information for marketing enthusiasts. It is available nationwide in modern outlets as well as on digital outlets.

Figure 7.2. WAN-IFRA Awards

## Marketeers News Portal

MarkPlus offers a comprehensive coverage of stories and views on business and marketing-related topics in several industries and sectors through Marketeers.com, the most prominent online portal for marketing enthusiasts in Indonesia.

## Marketeers TV

Marketeers TV, the primary dedicated professional YouTube channel for marketing enthusiasts, is an enticing audio-visual platform where ideas and perspectives from various speakers and influencers are shared, including live streaming, sneak peeks of MarkPlus events, and marketing tips are widely provided. Marketeers TV is highly accessible on YouTube and through Marketeers.com. A new show called *15*

**Edition:**
*August 2012*

**Edition:**
*December 2012*

**Edition:**
*November 2013*

**Edition:**
*September 2014*

Figure 7.3. Asian Media Awards

*Minutes with Marketeers* hits a rapid number of viewers for it brings various personalities from different industry backgrounds, to enable them to share insights on their work and latest industry developments.

## MARKETEERS COMMUNITY

The ability to connect, inspire, and engage with people is well performed by the Marketeers Community. This officially provides MarkPlus with an unparalleled reach to the students, professionals, and C-suite executive community.

Campus Marketeers Club (CMC) has the aim to reach out to the Next Great Marketeers, particularly to those who get attracted the most by Marketeers cool content, take part in Experience Field Trips and industry events.

The MX Campus club seeks to bring together young, dynamic marketing enthusiasts from campuses to participate in Experience Field Trip organised by MarkPlus Industry Centers. This club also aims to re-connect marketing enthusiasts among campus alumni from college campuses in Indonesia.

The Executive Marketeers Club is a community where business professionals who yearn to gain brand-new insider views on the latest news from the marketing world gathered. The club is for those who are passionate about marketing, ready to engage with marketing-related topics and trends, and participate in various events organised by Marketeers MICE. The members also get to participate in a company visit and engage with a dynamic industry.

The BUMN Marketeers Club helps people to learn from each other through sharing of ideas and marketing knowledge to achieve accelerate growth in SOEs. It is a platform where marketing enthusiasts from state-owned enterprises gathered to share knowledge, updates, and insights. Gatherings are regularly held every month on different topics from various industries. Hermawan Kertajaya acts as the host in every meeting.

The Jakarta CMO Club was officiated by the Philip Kotler Center for ASEAN Marketing (PKCAM) in February 2008 and was established as a platform to promote strategic marketing to high-level executives, beyond the functional level. It is an exclusive chief-level community, with only highly regarded business and marketing leaders invited to become members. It periodically organises gatherings for C-level executives where members can share and discuss about various topics of interest. Members of the Jakarta CMO alternate in hosting gatherings to share their experiences in applying marketing at the strategic level. In order to maintain the network's quality, the host and the Center invite influential keynote speakers and special invitees to discuss specific topics at particular industry gatherings.

## PHILIP KOTLER CENTER FOR ASEAN MARKETING (PKCAM)

The PKCAM was launched at the ASEAN Secretariat in Jakarta in October 2005 by the then Secretary-General of ASEAN, HE Ong Keng

Yong. The Tri-Founders; Philip Kotler, Hermawan Kartajaya, and Hooi Den Huan have pledged for the Center to achieve two main objectives:

- To enhance the competitiveness of the ASEAN region
- To strengthen and promote the role of marketing in the ASEAN region.

## MARKETEERS MICE

The Marketeers MICE division is accountable for the organisation and management of all events held by MarkPlus, including the WOW Brand Festive Day in March, the Jakarta Marketing Week (JMW) in May, the ASEAN Marketing Summit in September and eventually wrapping the year with MarkPlus's Mega Event: The Annual MarkPlus Conference, KIN ASEAN Forum, and WOW Night Performance Gala Celebration.

In addition, MarkPlus organises over 550 communal events in 18 Indonesian cities annually, making it the largest network to promote marketing to enthusiasts in Indonesia. These include the Indonesia Marketeers Festival (IMF), which is organised in 17 cities across Indonesia, the Gebyar UKM Indonesia (GUKMI), which is organised in 34 cities spanning Indonesia, to share ideas on the expansion and development of small and medium enterprises (SMEs).

With a track record in organising many events, MarkPlus' Marketeers MICE team has newly donned the hat of an incidental Organiser (EO) for external clients, but one with a difference! MarkPlus strongly believes in Style with Substance, and hence, Marketeers MICE division works relentlessly to not only organise the most sophisticated yet hospitable events, but also enrich it with relevant knowledge and exciting content.

The whole MICE team not only gets pleasure from the vast knowledge gained as a result of running a full-fledged media service on market and business trends, but also works closely with a team of extraordinary in-house consultants. These consultants bring the most effective ideas to the table, for developing engaging content and in-depth industry knowledge, to support MarkPlus clients' core objectives for organising an event.

## MarkPlus Conference

The MarkPlus Conference is an annual grand marketing event held by MarkPlus, Inc. since 2006. It provides a comprehensive and concrete picture of marketing development as well as predictions of future marketing trends in Indonesia. The plenary session presents a picture of Indonesia's Marketing scenario in the next year and the breakout sessions feature specific themes and allow participants to choose which suits their preference to attend. The MarkPlus Conference is indeed unique among many other events.

The MarkPlus Conference is attended by approximately 5,000 participants annually and they comprise business executives, marketers, academicians, students, and international participants from the ASEAN, Asian, and other countries. In addition, around 500 companies participate, and typically around 50 speakers who are experts in their field share their knowledge and experiences. The success of the events in 14 consecutive years has made the MarkPlus Conference the most awaited and perhaps the biggest marketing event in Southeast Asia.

## WOW Brand Festive Day

On March 2016, the first WOW Brand Festive Day with the theme 'Brand-X Is Human: Are You In?' was the platform to commemorate WOW Brand 300 — a league of 300 brands across industries in Indonesia with the highest Brand Advocacy Ratio (BAR). The winners on this festive day were judged based on surveys done by MarkPlus Insight. MarkPlus was recognising the 300 top WOW brands and the top 30 Brand Champions who have been working relentlessly to make the brands, the most advocated in their categories.

## Jakarta Marketing Week (JMW)

JMW is an annual event dedicated to marketing enthusiasts in Jakarta where it attracted thousands of spectators to a week-long celebration. Visitors are provided with mindful and interesting presentations, performances, award ceremonies, and many other sessions.

## Indonesia Marketeers Festival (IMF)

The IMF is an annual event organised by Marketeers in 17 cities across Indonesia. IMF is a platform for marketeers and marketing enthusiasts to gather under one roof and discuss some of the winning marketing strategies employed by national and international businesses. The idea is to spur creativity in the local community and encourage companies and people in the region to help advance the business world. Marketeers of the Year from each city are also awarded during the event.

## The ASEAN Marketing Summit

This annual event is dedicated to a gathering of marketing people from ASEAN to discuss the significance, opportunities, and challenges of competing in the ASEAN Economic Community (AEC) environment. There are over 700 participants who come to discuss strategies and tactics to succeed and grow sustainably.

## The Ubud Royal Weekend

The Ubud Royal Weekend is organised in Collaboration with the Jakarta CMO Club, under the PKCAM together with the Museum of Puri Lukisan and Museum of Marketing 3.0. Ubud makes an obvious choice for C-level executives, businesspeople, and influential personalities as the venue, because there is arguably no better place than Ubud for people to engage in history, arts and culture, spirituality, and business management simultaneously. The Ubud Royal Weekend is also aimed at introducing the culture of Ubud to a broader audience.

## Gebyar UKM Indonesia

MarkPlus collaborated with Indonesia's Ministry of Cooperatives, and SME and the International Council for Small Business (ICSB) to organise Gebyar UKM Indonesia (GUKMI). The events serve as a platform for SMEs to prepare themselves for growth and become more competitive. Three program modules are conducted and these consist of Seminar & Award,

Curation of Smes WOW!, and Exhibition. The business ideas and topics by SMEs are curated by a board of curators, based on creativity, productivity, and entrepreneurship. The selected "WOW Smes" are provided with opportunities to display their products at Galeri Indonesia WOW!, SMESCO and are also rewarded with promotion and copyright assistance.

## INDONESIA'S BIGGEST MARKETING NETWORK PLATFORM

MarkPlus is known as the pioneer and the largest homegrown firm dedicated to the marketing discipline and one of its goals is to provide the best platform for Indonesia's Biggest Marketing Network.

MarkPlus has created a marketing network platform for present and future marketeers of Indonesia and to achieve its vision in advancing marketing as an integrated business function. MarkPlus events gather industry insiders, global marketing experts, strategic business thinkers, and renowned government representatives to share ideas and perspectives. MarkPlus also established a unique set-up where brands can connect, interact, and engage with their customers and potential partners optimally. To do these, MarkPlus activates Indonesia's Biggest Marketing Network Platform through its annual events, community events, and MarkPlus industry-based centers.

## INDUSTRY-BASED MARKPLUS CENTERS

The MarkPlus Centers are committed to driving industry growth through better productivity and creativity. The centers actively engage the business community with a series of events, publications, and community activities to provide learning, research, and advice. By establishing MarkPlus Centers, MarkPlus aims to connect policymakers, industry leaders, and influencers in regular discussions and provide relevant, practical, and readily useful business and industry insights.

### MarkPlus Center for Tourism and Hospitality

The MarkPlus Center for Tourism and Hospitality (MPCTH) is committed to supporting the Ministry of Tourism and Hospitality and industry players in formulating relevant business solutions through its consultancy services, comprehensively understanding Indonesia tourism through insightful research, and building the capability of the tourism and hospitality's human resources through participative learning. Inaugurated on November 8, 2014, by Dr. Ir. Arief Yahya, Indonesia's Minister of Tourism, the MPCTH, has been supporting the tourism ecosystem in Indonesia with in-depth insights and strategic advice to compete globally and to become world class, by having regular and relevant gatherings and workshops. The Center is also tasked with preparing an annual whitepaper on the Indonesia Tourism Ministry's achievements and challenges which is presented directly to the Ministry.

**MarkPlus Center for Public Services**

The MarkPlus Center for Public Services is a professional platform that connects government officials and the public, to develop accountable public services, to improve public trust, and to market Indonesia to the world. Seminars, discussion forums, and workshops are routinely organised, featuring pertinent figures from Indonesia's public services and stimulating dialogues among various stakeholders, in the interests of the public.

**MarkPlus Center for Transportation and Logistics**

The MarkPlus Center for Transportation and Logistics works closely with the Ministry of Transportation of the Republic of Indonesia since 2015, to facilitate exchange forums with the aim to bridge the Ministry with all stakeholders, including state-owned enterprises, private companies, or associations engaged in the automotive and transportation industries. The Center organises discussion forums to provide feedback and industry insights from players in the automotive and transportation industries.

**MarkPlus Center for Technology and Creativity**

The MarkPlus Center for Technology and Creativity (MPCTC) is a professional center that facilitates interactions among technology and creative players, to develop smart global citizens of Indonesia. The MPCTC was launched on April 10, 2015, in Bandung by Rudiantara, Minister of Communications and Information Technology of Republic Indonesia, Ridwan Kamil, Former Mayor of Bandung, and Hermawan Kartajaya, Founder and Chairman of MarkPlus, Inc.

## MarkPlus Center for Retail and Consumer

The MarkPlus Center for Retail and Consumer strives to bring together retail and consumer industry players to encourage cooperation and engagement in dialogues so as to strengthen their position in the market. It facilitates and connects companies, both state-owned enterprises and private companies, and the industry associations to discuss specific industry challenges.

## MarkPlus Center for Economy and Business

The MarkPlus Center for Economy and Business is a professional center that connects policymakers, industry leaders, and influencers in shaping industry agendas. It was inaugurated by the Minister of National Development Planning, Andrinof Chaniago on May 25, 2015. The first gathering was attended by 80 participants. Among others who attended were Peter Jacobs, Bank Indonesia's Director of Communication, and Arif Budisusilo, the Editor in Chief of *Bisnis Indonesia*.

## MarkPlus Center for Brand for Good

The MarkPlus Center for Brand for Good (MBfG) was newly conceived as an offshoot, after MarkPlus Insight's WOW Brand Study. This recognition is presented to brands that earn superior advocacy (recommendations) from their customers, not only by way of their products and services, but also from their do-good acts, whether for the society, community, or environment. Brands that have earned their place in the MBfG Club are poised to have regular gatherings.

# CHAPTER 8

# MARKPLUS TOURISM — LEVELING UP LOCAL COMPETITIVENESS

## ESTABLISHMENT OF MARKPLUS TOURISM

Long before the establishment of MarkPlus Tourism (MT), MarkPlus has handled multiple tourism projects from the public to the private sectors. A decision was made to officially establish the MarkPlus Centre for Tourism and Hospitality (MPCTH) in 2014, with the aim to further develop Indonesia's tourism industry. The inauguration of MPCTH was attended by Dr. Ir. Arief Yahya, the former Indonesian Minister of Tourism.

The MPCTH is based in Bali, one of the world's top tourist's destinations. Bali is also considered as a region in Indonesia that generated the highest tourism and hospitality income. In Bali, MarkPlus actively conducts forums and monthly gatherings for all industry experts and players to discuss pre-determined tourism-related topics. These are well attended by 80–100 participants each month.

Besides forums and the monthly gatherings, the MPCTH also held multiple events, one of the biggest of which is the Ubud Royal Weekend. This event is organised in collaboration with the Jakarta CMO Club, under the Philip Kotler Center for ASEAN Marketing (PKCAM), together with the Museum of Puri Lukisan and the Museum of Marketing 3.0. C-level executives, businessmen, and influential personalities gather for this weekend event in the heart of Bali, where they share their experiences, stories, and insights in fun yet serene settings. Ubud makes an obvious travel destination because there is arguably no better place than Ubud for people to simultaneously engage in history, arts and culture, spirituality,

Figure 8.1. MarkPlus Tourism Logo

and business management. The Ubud Royal Weekend is also aimed at introducing the culture of Ubud to a wider audience.

Under President Jokowi's administration, the government paid a great deal of attention to the tourism and hospitality industry and MarkPlus would like to contribute more to the growth of these sectors. Past experiences and recognising the upcoming opportunities were important drivers for MarkPlus to establish this new business unit called MarkPlus Tourism (see Figure 8.1).

MT is committed to formulating relevant business solutions -through its consultancy services, comprehensively understanding Indonesia tourism through insightful research, and building the capability of the tourism and hospitality' industry's human resources through participative learning. Additionally, MT helps destinations or institutions to promote their cultural vibrancy and authenticity, by organising relevant robust events. MT also supports the tourism ecosystem with in-depth insights and strategic advice, to compete on a global scale.

## MARKPLUS'S GUIDELINE TO SUSTAINABLE TOURISM

MT is on a mission to help Indonesia actualise its Sustainable Tourism for the industry. MT engages with various stakeholders covering destinations, hospitality, and tour and travel in order to promote dialogue and discussions on ideas pertaining to the development of Sustainable Tourism in Indonesia. Moreover, as a thought-leader in marketing, MarkPlus through MT has developed its own conceptual model related to sustainable tourism, called OMNI Destination Marketing and

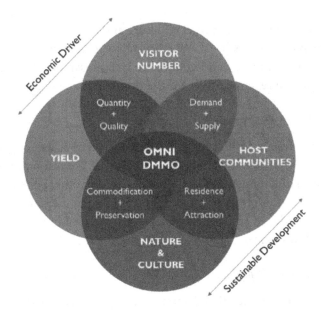

Figure 8.2. MarkPlus OMNI DMMO Model

Management Organization (DMMO), as seen in Figure 8.2. The model combines tourism as a tool for development of social and environmental aspects and as an economic driver.

- *Quantity + Quality*

  Quantity and quality are often considered to be opposites. For the past years, Indonesia's tourism industry was more focused on quantity, where the key performance indicators were mainly on the number of visitors. However, the focus is now shifting, where Indonesia's tourism industry is putting more attention on quality, with monetary value as a primary key performance indicator. Many players within this industry believed that it is challenging to gain both quality and quantity. Therefore, MT aspires to help stakeholders in balancing quantity and quality for the tourism industry.

- *Commodification + Preservation*

  Profits generated from the tourism industry should be allocated not only to improve the natural ecosystem to become an important attraction but also to preserve nature and culture. The players in the industry should realise that it is crucial to prevent unwanted damages. Therefore, if nature and culture are well preserved, it will become a sustainable revenue driver for the destination.

- *Residence + Attraction*

In Indonesia, community culture is considered as a strong attraction for tourists. The host community's way of life is a natural, unique point of differentiation that cannot be found in other places. Therefore, the host community plays an important role in the tourism industry. Both residence and attraction are considered to have mutually beneficial influence.

- *Demand + Supply*

We all have learned that demand and supply across industries should be balanced to achieve market equilibrium, and so too in the tourism industry. There should be a control mechanism to prevent excess demand or supply as this may lead to another problematic condition. For example, an excess in demand may lead to a surge in property prices, making it more difficult for the host community to have access to residence ownership.

Not only does MT have its own models, it has also become the official training partner of the Global Sustainable Tourism Council (GSTC) in Indonesia. MT delivers training on sustainable tourism criteria and indicators based on GSTC's standard. The training programs are also equipped with relevant case studies and field trips. After successfully completing the training program with MarkPlus and passing the examination, participants will obtain a sustainable tourism certification issued by the GSTC.

## CASE STUDY: A GUIDEBOOK FOR NATIONAL PARK DESTINATIONS

MT has assisted Indonesia's Ministry of Environment and Forestry in developing a sustainable tourism guidebook for 54 national parks in

Indonesia. This project serves an essential role in Indonesia's tourism industry, as it aims to achieve three main objectives. First, the guidebook would be used to provide the necessary information and analysis, to support the strategic decision-making process. Secondly, the guidebook would also be used to inspire innovations of national park areas that are oriented to sustainable tourism. Lastly, the guidebook is a useful tool to analyse the conditions of national parks and to help compile the vision and mission of the park which can later be translated into concrete action plans.

MT conducted a direct observation and study on four national parks in Indonesia and developed a sustainable tourism model for national parks in Indonesia (Figure 8.3).

• *Visitor Management*

The first element of the model is visitor management. Visitor management is an approach that focuses on customers, and in this case, visitors or tourists. Visitor management is about various matters related to tourists. The main factor in this strategy is customer segmentation. It is important to first identify the target of each national park in order to be able to set the right positioning.

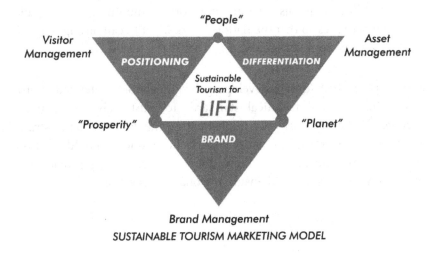

Figure 8.3. Sustainable Tourism Marketing Model for Indonesia National Parks

- *Asset Management*

   Asset Management is everything related to destination development, and in this case, national parks. There are at least three main components of asset management (at the destination): Attractions, Accessibility, and Amenities. These three things are the hygiene factors of a qualified destination. The attraction is the pull factor of a destination, or the main reason why tourists visit an area. Accessibility is related to the infrastructure and access for tourists to reach a destination, whereas amenities are the support for a destination, which include accommodation, restaurants, and others. These three factors are needed to assess the readiness of an area to become an ideal tourist destination.

- *Brand Management*

   Brand Management is defined as the efforts by managers (in this context, it is the national park manager and the relevant stakeholders therein) in communicating a destination to potential tourists. From a marketing perspective, it is related to efforts in establishing a strong brand and attracting targeted tourists. There are many strategies that can be done to strengthen the brand identity of a national park. Some of them are organising promotional activities through both online and offline platforms, encouraging word-of-mouth promotion, and other activities so that the national park identity can be aligned with the targeted tourist segment.

MarkPlus's participation in developing the guidebook is intended to provide guidelines and technical standards for sustainable tourism for Indonesia's national parks. By implementing the comprehensive strategies provided by MarkPlus, national parks in Indonesia should meet the criteria and principles of sustainable tourism management, provide better community welfare, and ensure regional preservation.

# Part III

## FORMULA: Thought and Practice Leader

Hermawan Kartajaya's enthusiasm in marketing, his background as a teacher, and his passion for knowledge shaped MarkPlus's core business as primarily focusing on knowledge and practice. In MarkPlus's early years, Hermawan focused on speaking in forums and gave seminars and lectures about marketing and business. He used popular concepts that were advocated by experts such as Philip Kotler, Al Ries, Jack Trout, Warren Keegan and others. One day, one of the participants in his class praised him for his teaching and asked why he did not develop his own model. This question prompted him to try to do so and he began to do extensive research on this field, by reading books, journals, and articles from renowned experts, as he tried to synthesise his marketing model.

This was not easy, particularly in the early days. Some would challenge him, asking whether his concept was reliable. Many marketers in Indonesia at that time believed that the only reliable source of marketing theories and concepts was renowned global textbooks. The opportunity to validate his model came during the World Marketing Conference in Moscow in 1998. There, Hermawan met none other than the Father of Marketing, Professor Philip Kotler, and presented his model to him. For almost 2 hours of deep discussions with Philip Kotler, Hermawan felt like his model was tested. Finally, Philip Kotler saw merits in his thinking and model and agreed to write a book with him, entitled *Repositioning Asia: From Bubble to Sustainable Economy*. That book marked the beginning of Hermawan Kartajaya's relationship with Philip Kotler, as an Asian and an American expert in marketing, as well as friends. Subsequently, he co-authored many books with Philip Kotler, which contained many practical marketing frameworks that are widely used globally.

This part covers the most popular frameworks from Hermawan Kartajaya and MarkPlus such as *The Anatomy of Change, 4C Diamond Model, P-D-B Triangle, The 9 Core Elements of Marketing, and New Wave Marketing*. The concepts are comprehensively elaborated in international publications such as *Rethinking Marketing (2003), Think ASEAN (2007), Think New ASEAN (2014), Marketing for Competitiveness (2017)* and *Asian Competitors (2019)*. Other concepts such as the Value-based Matrix Model and 5A Customer Path are elaborated on in international publications such as *Marketing 3.0 (2010)* and *Marketing 4.0 (2016)* which are published by Wiley. These books are authored or co-authored by Hermawan Kartajaya himself, along with Philip Kotler and others. All of these concepts are also used as the basis for MarkPlus's consulting, research, and training services to serve local, national, and even international clients. The concepts act as the main frameworks — to diagnose problems, determine the research approach, create training modules, and provide solutions.

## Further Reading

Kotler, P, H Kartajaya and Hooi, D. H. (2003). *Rethinking Marketing: Sustainable Marketing Enterprise in Asia*. Singapore: Prentice-Hall.

Kotler, P, H Kartajaya, and Hooi, D. H. (2007). *Think ASEAN*. Singapore: McGraw-Hill.

Kotler, P, H Kartajaya, and I. Setiawan (2010). *Marketing 3.0: From Products to Customers to The Human Spirit*. Hoboken: John Wiley & Sons, Inc.

Kotler, P, H Kartajaya, and Hooi, D. H. (2014). *Think New ASEAN*. Singapore: McGraw-Hill.

Kotler, P., H. Kartajaya, and I. Setiawan. (2016). *Marketing 4.0: Moving from Traditional to Digital*. New Jersey: John Wiley & Sons.

Kotler, P., H. Kartajaya, and Hooi, D. H. (2017). *Marketing for Competitiveness*. Singapore: World Scientific.

Kotler, P., H. Kartajaya, and Hooi, D. H. (2019). *Asian Competitors*. Singapore: World Scientific.

# CHAPTER 9

# THE ANATOMY OF CHANGE

Marketing is often mistaken as merely a tactical approach to beat the competition. Hence, many companies and marketers only observe micro-factors surrounding the business competition. Some might only observe its competitors' movements in a particular area, to determine the company's overall strategy. Some may just follow the customers' needs and wants. Some may even just focus solely on their companies' capability in delivering values to beat the competition — without taking macro-factors into account. Many might take the view that macro-factors such as economic or political conditions possess little effect on a company's business. Hermawan argues that marketing is the core of business strategy, and when formulating a business strategy, it is not enough just to consider only the micro-factors in the business landscape. The ultimate goal of a company is not only beating the current competition but winning the future. Hence, identification and analysis of macro-factors surrounding the business landscape is crucial.

## THE FOURTH "C"

A Japanese professor and management consultant whom Hermawan strongly admires is Kenichi Ohmae. He is admired for his practical thinking ability, which makes him a highly sought-after consultant, who provides pragmatic and actionable solutions for his clients. Hermawan contends that a consultant does not have to come up with a highly sophisticated, and often complicated solution, which in the end may not end up with practical recommendations. When it is not actionable and just a sophisticated proposal, one may end up with a situation called, "paralysis by analysis." In reality, an effective consultant is one who is able to provide a simple and actionable solution to a problem, however complex it may be.

> *"Kenichi Ohmae really influenced my thinking. Even in the book Mind of a Strategist, he seems to want to simplify complex concepts, not the other way around, complicate the simple things."*
>
> **Hermawan Kartajaya**

Among Kenichi Ohmae's concepts is one renowned model, called the "3C" model, which inspired Hermawan. According to Ohmae, a company's strategy needs to be based on three options: company, customer, and competitor.

First, the company-based strategy. This approach emphasises the company's capability in creating a competitive advantage to win the competition by identifying the company's strengths and weaknesses, then formulating a strategy that can utilise the company's strengths to overcome its shortcomings.

The second approach is customer-based strategy, which is based on the customer's needs and wants. This approach focuses on offering products and services that provide benefits for the customers. Still, the offerings must have their own differentiation compared to others to avoid the commodity trap.

Finally, the third approach is competitor-based strategy. A company's strategy can be formulated based on competitors' movements. The practice could be following what the competitor offers, including the product and the price, or it could be offering the same products or services at a discount or premium price; or even offer something that is never seen before in the market.

To summarise, Ohmae suggests that a company could formulate its strategy by taking advantage of its own strengths to serve its customers' needs and wants and by looking out for its competitors' movements. Once again, an applicable and straightforward approach to solve business problems.

Hermawan continued to observe and study on Kenichi Ohmae's thoughts and ideas through another of Ohmae's books, *Borderless World* (1990). It is understandable why that book became a world best seller at that time. Ohmae envisioned that the world would become a world without borders, even though the use of the internet had not been as advanced as today, and platforms such as social media and video streaming services were not widely-used. In that book, Ohmae described the changing business landscape, where competitions no longer take place just in the local sphere, but the global one. Both threats and opportunities, competitors, and customers could come from anywhere in the world as happens nowadays, which Ohmae defined as being "borderless." This concept inspired Hermawan to complete Ohmae's 3C model by adding the fourth "C" — "Change." Changes in the business landscape need to be identified and put into consideration in formulating a sustainable business strategy.

*"Finally, I came up with an idea to complete Ohmae's 3C model, by adding a fourth C, CHANGE. The reason? It's actually quite simple; if we only make a strategy based on the first 3C that reflects current conditions, the strategy might not be sustainable!"*

**Hermawan Kartajaya**

## ANATOMY OF CHANGE — THE MODEL

A deep understanding of the business landscape situation is crucial in determining a company's overall strategy. A classic saying is that it is no use to paddle harder if we are heading in the wrong direction. The company needs to analyse current and upcoming changes in the business landscape to ensure that the decisions taken will be relevant to the current business condition, and the strategy remains sustainable over time. Therefore, *change* serves as a *value migrator* for a company since various changes outside the organisation's ecosystem could increase value to a company's offerings or the complete opposite (Figure 9.1).

The forces or drivers of *change* itself consist of five main aspects — *technology, political–legal, economy, social–cultural,* and *market.* The drivers are categorised based on two variables: *the immediacy of impact* and *tangibility of impact.* The immediacy of impact is time-based, which describes whether the forces of change are *immediate* or *incremental.* *Political–legal* forces are categorised as immediate. Meanwhile, *social–cultural* forces are incremental. The *tangibility of impact* variable is based

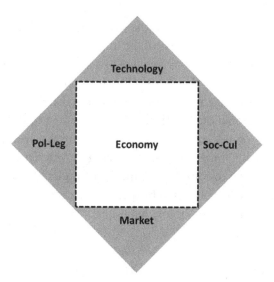

Figure 9.1. The Anatomy of Change

on how directly the drivers impact the industry or business. Therefore, *technology* forces are categorised as *the primary driver* and market forces as *the ultimate driver*. In the center of the model, economy forces are called *the central driver*.

> *"Change, that is not the element of the Customer and Competitor, often 'forces' the Company to change its strategy. Therefore, it is better if Change is considered first in formulating strategy."*
>
> **Hermawan Kartajaya**

## Technology: The Primary Driver

As mentioned in the previous section, *technology* is called *the primary driver* of *change* since it often becomes the main source and driver of the other change aspects. This in the end will impact customers, competitors, and the company.

> *"Technology is often an aspect of triggering major changes in other aspects of change. In the end, it has a big influence on our lives."*
>
> **Hermawan Kartajaya**

Take the industrial revolution, for example. The first industrial revolution, which began in the 18th century, was marked by the introduction and the use of the steam-powered engine for mechanisation of production. Steam power was already known at that time. The breakthrough was the use of it for industrial purposes to increase human productivity. One of the major results of the first industrial revolution was the invention and development of steam-powered locomotive, which enabled humans and goods to move great distances in a shorter time, boosting business effectiveness and efficiency, and acting as a driver for the economy.

The second industrial revolution in the 19th century, which began through the discovery of electricity and assembly-line production for mass production, had brought another empowerment to companies' productivity. One renowned automobile brand founder, Henry Ford, took advantage of this revolution and altered his company's production processes, going from having one station at the factory which built the whole vehicles to producing vehicles by parts on a conveyor belt. This made the manufacturing process significantly faster at a lower cost. Along with mass production, more jobs were created, and workers began to move to urban areas to find jobs in factories. By 1900, 40% of the U.S. population lived in cities, compared to just 6% in the 1800s. Along with an increasing rate of urbanisation, inventions such as the radio, lighting, and telephone transformed the way people lived and communicated at that time.

Between the 1950s and 2000, the third industrial revolution happened through the utilisation of computers and electronics to perform partial or full automation. The revolution allowed industries to perform fully automated production, such as the use of programmed robots in manufacturing. This condition changed the business landscape by redefining companies' competitive advantages. It was no longer the number of skilled workers, but the quality of educated workers.

Finally came the fourth, and most recent, industrial revolution, also known as "Industry 4.0." Inventions in this era include cyber-physical systems (CPS), internet of things (IoT), and industrial internet of things (IIoT), which enable companies to improve their productivity, efficiency, and flexibility, as well as increasing intimacy with the customer through enhanced customer experience.

However, the impact of *technological forces* as the *primary driver* of business landscape changes is indirect and intangible as it influences *social–cultural, economy, political–legal,* or *market* aspects before it really affects companies.

### Political–Legal: The Immediate Driver

During both the classical and modern eras as in current days, *political–legal* forces continue to possess a great influence on the other aspects of *change* as well as toward the business landscape itself. *Political–legal* forces have an immediate effect; once the government takes a stance or a policy is implemented, the impacts almost immediately affect the industry. Any technological advancement, economic condition, and market situation could change if the government imposed certain policies.

> *"A pro-technological political situation that encourages rules that allow the use of technology will accelerate landscape change."*
> **Hermawan Kartajaya**

A company must be able to observe *political–legal* changes in its industry, starting from local, national, regional, and international policies since these possess an immediate impact, especially to the *economy* and *market*.

### Economy: The Central Driver

Economic forces are considered as *central drivers* of change, since they often have the most prominent role in influencing other aspects, and they are the platform on which any sectoral industry is based.

> *"Economy plays a big part in influencing the other drivers of change, and often brings a great shift towards the other drivers!"*
> **Hermawan Kartajaya**

*Economy* plays a big part in determining the bargaining position of a country or region in world politics. In the second half of the 20th century, the economic pendulum began to swing back to the East from the West as Asia's economic situation continued to improve, and the economies of some countries in this region experienced impressive growth and rapid development. Over the past 10 years, the world's economic center of gravity has shifted at a fast pace with the remarkable rise of emerging economies such as China and India. Due to its economic power, China is able to develop strong bilateral and multilateral relations with countries. Economic conditions not only affect international relations, but also influence a country's fiscal and monetary policies as well as its domestic industries.

Thus, it is important that multiple economic indicators such as gross domestic product (GDP), inflation, unemployment rate, etc, in a region are observed as they are among the most definite signs of a possible shift in value.

### Social–Cultural: The Incremental Driver

As the *incremental driver* of change, *social–cultural* forces, including lifestyle, habit, culture, and behavioural trends in society, are gradually evolving over a long period of time. Unlike *political–legal* and *economy* factors that can be clearly identified and measured, *social–cultural* aspects required further and deeper analysis to be understood since it plays a powerful influence in shaping customer behaviour.

Nowadays, it is believed that there are three subcultures that play an essential role in business. These three subcultures include *youth* (the "opposite" of seniors), *women* (the "opposite" of men), and *netizens* (the "opposite" of citizens; Figure 9.2).

*Youth* represents the emerging younger population (Gen-Y, Gen-Z, Gen-Alpha) that plays a vital role in "leading the mind" because they are more attuned to "sense and respond," or have the ability to sniff out the changes in market such as in technological aspects and are quick to adapt to changes, which are getting more difficult to predict and even to control.

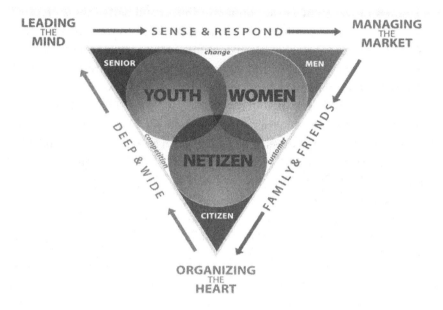

Figure 9.2. Youth–Women–Netizen

*"I believe that at this time, it is the seniors who must learn from the youth. Because the youth are the future!"*

**Hermawan Kartajaya**

The second subculture, *women*, reflects the increasing independence among women in handling finances, both personal and family finances. Most women are the key decision makers for groceries, clothing, and children products and are at least co-decision makers for other products such as electronics and cars in the family. Along with the growing importance of word-of-mouth marketing, the influence of women is rising. Women are able to influence opinions, through word-of-mouth, as some of them like to express their opinions and share information with their friends. Hence, it is not wrong to say that *women* play a role in "managing the market."

*"For marketers, if you want to dominate the market share, then attract women because they buy for family and friends."*

**Hermawan Kartajaya**

*Netizens*, the third subculture, are those who are socially active in online platforms. These people are more able to shape public opinion nowadays compared to mainstream media channels. Internet technology allows netizens to process information "deep and wide." In doing so, *netizens* are able to create and spread opinions that can move millions of people by heart. Therefore, they play a significant role in "organising the heart."

*"If you want to win a heart share, win the hearts of netizens. Because they communicate more with their hearts on the internet."*

**Hermawan Kartajaya**

Therefore, *social–cultural* forces cannot be underestimated since these forces often have a powerful influence on customer preferences and behaviour. Hence, many companies and marketers who are aware of these aspects put a lot of effort into observing, analysing, and even creating *social–cultural* trends.

## Market: The Ultimate Driver

All of the aspects and drivers explained previously will not have a great impact on the business landscape if the *market* does not accept them. Technological advancement will have no impact if it is not adopted by the majority of the market. The imposition of government policies will be in vain if the market keeps rejecting them. An excellent economic condition will have no impact if the situation is not leveraged on, and sociocultural changes will have no use if they does not bring a positive impact on the market. This makes the *market* the *ultimate driver* of change, since market trends are the most tangible forces that can be discerned directly by companies.

The *market* is the platform where supply and demand meet. This is a platform where companies, as *value suppliers*, compete against each other in order to win the *mind share, market share,* and *heart share.* All business and marketing activities are done by companies to create the best engagement with *customers* as *value demanders.* In short, the *market* is a platform that decides the perceived value of offerings, whether an offering is perceived by customers to provide a benefit or not.

> *"Those who succeed in dominating the market have the opportunity to grow and develop."*
> **Hermawan Kartajaya**

Asia is considered as the new market, as the global economic power starts to shift from the West to the East. Emerging countries in Asia account for 67% of the current global growth. The rise of the middle-class market will reach its peak point. According to the Brookings Institute, by 2020, a majority of the world population will be categorised as middle-class or even upper-middle class and above, and Asia will lead the growth of the middle-class populations, while the number will be stagnant in the West. It is forecasted that global domestic consumption will grow at 3.4%, and without emerging Asia's contribution, the growth would only be 1.1%. Even excluding the Asian market giants, China and India, the contribution of emerging Asia countries to world growth already exceeds that of the U.S. and is three times the size of the Euro area.

This circumstance has led businesses to take advantage of the rapid growth of the Asian market. Companies are starting to alter their offerings to compete in the Asian market and to meet Asian customers' needs and wants. On the other hand, companies such as Alibaba and Huawei have already acted on their hometown advantages, resulting in exponential growth for the companies.

## INTERACTIONS AMONG THE DRIVERS OF CHANGE

The forces or drivers of *change* are not individual and independent factors but are related to one another. Changes in one driver or force can influence or trigger changes in other drivers or forces. The rationale behind this is that the drivers are connected to one another (Figure 9.3).

### The Four Major Streams

From the four "major streams" shown the model, the first major stream is the downward stream, which represents *technology–economy–market* interactions. Technological changes often dramatically affect an economic system, which further affects market dynamics, or in the extreme, might even be able to create a new market. An example of this case is the emergence of e-commerce. Advancement in computer and information technology resulted in the creation of platforms which do

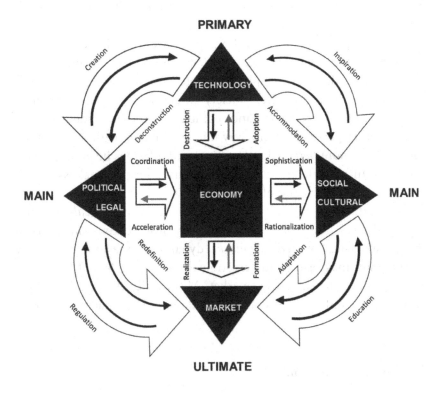

Figure 9.3. Interactions among the Drivers of Change

not require buyers and sellers to meet for transactions to take place. The invention is driving the creation of an entirely new economy, called the digital economy or e-economy, which disrupted the old ways of living and doing business. This influences the dynamics of various markets such as the retail, high-tech, computer, and telecommunication markets.

The second major stream is the rightward stream or the interaction of *political–legal–economy–social–cultural* drivers. For example, the democratisation movement can *coordinate* a completely new and more transparent economic system, which will further influence the *sophistication* process of society.

The third major stream is the reciprocal interaction between *technology* and *social-cultural* drivers. The emergence of new technologies could affect society by providing better *accommodations* as it usually makes life more comfortable and more convenient. On the other hand, it is often that people's lifestyles and the way people behave become sources of *inspiration* for new technology innovations. For example, the invention of the steam engine, electricity, radio, and telecommunication changed the way people commute, communicate, and work. Nowadays, e-commerce offers society an alternative and more convenient way of life since buying and selling activities can be done online. From another perspective, the way humans interact with one another, and demand more personalised services and offerings inspired the creation of artificial intelligence (AI) that is used for personal assistance, and predictive search and offerings.

The last major stream is the interaction between *political–legal* and *market* drivers. As explained in the previous section, *political-legal* changes almost always *redefine market* dynamics. For example, industry deregulation may lead to the creation of new markets and the emergence of new players in the market. Meanwhile, changes in *market* dynamics like industry consolidation will require the enactment of new *regulations*.

### The Four Minor Streams

Interactions between the drivers of *change* are not only limited to the four major streams explained in the previous section. There are several other minor streams as well. The first minor stream is the upward stream or the interaction between *market–economy–technology*, which occurs when the composite growth in all *market* or sectors *form* the cumulative GDP growth of a region. The rate of economic growth will determine the *adoption* level of technology.

The second minor stream is the interaction between *social–cultural–economy–political–legal* drivers or the leftward stream. This interaction takes place when the value that is held by society changes the *rationale* of an economic system, which then *accelerates* the shaping of the new *political–legal* environment.

The third is the interaction between *technology* and *political–legal*. This interaction occurs when *technology* contributes to the *deconstruction* of the *political–legal* system, making the system more transparent and more democratic. At the same time, *political–legal* forces such as patent law can trigger or accelerate the *creation* of new *technology*.

The last minor stream is the interaction between *social-cultural* and *market* drivers. When a new *market* emerges, it contributes to the *education* process of society, forcing society to learn about the new market. For example, the emergence of a technology market drives people to be more "informationalised." On the other hand, changes in social values will force some form of *adaptation* by the market. For example, when society values convenience more, the market for mobile phone and personal computers will start to grow.

In the end, by identifying and analysing the forces of changes and how it influences other aspects in business, companies will be able to determine which *changes* are more critical for their respective industry compared to other elements of *changes*. Hence, the changes could be put under the company's radar and be analysed, in formulating its strategy.

# CHAPTER 10

# 4C DIAMOND ANALYSIS

As mentioned in Chapter 9, both the micro- and macro-factors surrounding the company must be taken into account while formulating a sustainable business and marketing strategy. Four major aspects that have a significant impact on business and that need to be put under the radar are *Company, Competitor, Customer*, according to Kenichi Ohmae's 3C model, and a new element proposed by Hermawan, *Change* — making them 4Cs for business landscape analysis. Although there are some other models or frameworks in analysing the business landscape such as Political, Economic, Social, Technological, Environmental, Legal (PESTEL) Analysis and Porter's Five Forces Analysis, these can be incorporated in this 4Cs model (Figure 10.1) which is comprehensive and yet easy to remember, utilise, and apply.

The 4C model is not only conceptually robust and is applied in many publications, but practically is very useful and is employed in many of MarkPlus's consulting, research, and training projects. It provides an easy to understand framework to help grasp the dynamics of a client's business landscape. Coming up with new models such as this 4C model has helped Hermawan to gain global recognition as evidenced in him being included in the list of "The Fifty Gurus who Shaped the Future of Marketing" by the Chartered Institute of Marketing — United Kingdom (CIM–UK) in 2003.

*"I always adopt the 4Cs model. This caught the attention of one of my friends, Lee Hock Seng, from CIM–UK Singapore who appreciated this model and shared my concepts with the CIM–UK, That's how I ended up being included in the list of 'The Fifty Gurus who Shaped the Future of Marketing'"*

**Hermawan Kartajaya**

## 4C DIAMOND ANALYSIS — THE MODEL

As stated in the name, the 4C Diamond Model consists of four interconnected aspects, which represents the outlook of any particular business landscape. The four Cs, namely *Change, Competitor, Customers,* and *Company,* are placed in a diamond-shaped model, with the first aspect, *Change,* being placed on the top of the *diamond.*

Since the model is designed to analyse the present and future, not the past, the aspect, *Change,* is put on the top, *Change* itself will influence the other three aspects of the model. For example, *Changes* in economic conditions might shift the dynamics of business competition and might alter

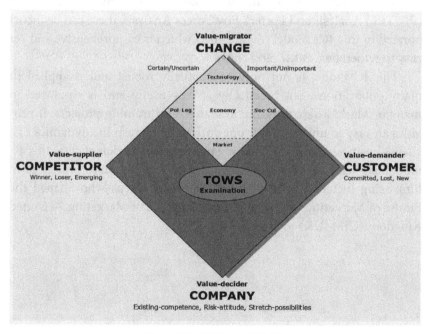

Figure 10.1. 4C Diamond Model

the buying power of customers, which ultimately will impact a company's strategy (Kotler, Kartajaya and Hooi, 2003).

The aspects of *Competitor* and *Customer* are placed at the sides of the diamond, where *Competitor* is on the left side and *Customer* is on the right side. *Competitor* is placed on the same side as *political–legal* since changes in political–legal forces usually affect the dynamics of the competition more. On the other hand, changes in *social–cultural* forces mostly influence the *Customer*. Hence the *Customer* is placed on the same side as *social–cultural* forces.

*The Company* aspect is placed on the bottom of the diamond. The rationale for this is because *Company* needs to observe and understand the other aspects to get a clear picture of the business landscape before formulating its business strategy. A *diamond-shaped* model is used as it represents the view that *Change* is the most significant aspect, which will flow down to influence *Competitor* and *Customer*. The dynamics of *Change, Competitor,* and *Customers* affects how the *Company's* strategy should be formulated and hence, *Company* is placed at the lower tip of the *diamond*.

> *"I put 'Change' at the top because this aspect influences the dynamics in both 'Competitor' and the 'Customer' aspects. This model is designed to create strategies for the future, not for analysing the past. Because the past doesn't guarantee a continuation to the future, right?"*
> **Hermawan Kartajaya**

An analysis of these four aspects of the 4C Diamond Analysis will provide a TOWS (Threats, Opportunities, Weaknesses, and Strengths) assessment of the business landscape.

## CHANGE — VALUE MIGRATOR

*Change* consists of evaluating the five forces that drive the business landscape dynamics — *Technology, Political–legal, Social–cultural, Economy,* and *Market. Change* is termed the *value migrator* because it can affect the *values* of products and services. In other words, the value offered could shift or *migrate* from time to time due to changes in any one or more of the identified dynamics.

*Change* can cause the customer's perceived value of certain products and services to shift, at a particular point in time. For example, during the initial and early phases of the COVID-19 crisis situation in 2020, the value of sanitary products such as masks, gloves, and hand sanitisers shot up, because customers became more conscious of health and sanitary issues and urgently demanded such products. During normal times, the demand, and hence, the value of such products may not be as high.

In the smartphone industry, the rise of social media was also followed by the emergence of a new behaviour in society, the *selfie*, and so-called *digital narcissism*. This social–cultural change shifted up the value of the camera. It triggered the development of built-in front camera technology in smartphones, making such upgraded smartphones more valued by customers who use and enjoy social media on their phones.

*Change* in macro-factor(s) can also alter the dynamics of competition. *Change* in the *Political–legal dynamic*, such as the imposition of free-trade policies in a country or region, could open the gate for competitors to come in, resulting in changes to the competitive landscape — from local to regional, and even international.

BlackBerry was once the leading company in the smartphone industry and happened to control 50% of the smartphone market in the United States and 20% globally at one time (Business Insider, 2019). The success was because of its BlackBerry Messenger (BBM), which provided an instant connection among its exclusive BlackBerry-only users, enabling people to message back and forth almost without limits. It managed to sell 50 million units at its peak, but then demand rapidly declined, and finally it had to stop manufacturing in 2016. It failed to adapt to the *change* in technology, such as the use of touch screens and front camera, which were valued by society as behaviour shifted with the rise of social media and *digital narcissism*.

> *"Of course, there are a lot of changes from time to time. But it doesn't mean that we need to pay attention to all the changes"*
>
> **Hermawan Kartajaya**

It is indeed true that the business landscape is always changing, and there are a lot of aspects of the *Technology, Political–legal, Social–cultural, Economy*, and *Market* dynamics that are constantly changing all the time.

As time and energy are limited, marketers should filter which *change* is relevant to their business by determining whether the *change* is *certain* or *uncertain*, and *important* or *unimportant* for the company. The most significant *change* to any business is one that is *important* and most likely or *certain* to happen.

## COMPETITOR — VALUE SUPPLIER

*Competitors* are termed *value suppliers* because, beside the company, competitors also strive to offer or *supply* good value to the customers. Due to the changing dynamics of the business landscape, a competitors' position in the market changes over time. *Competitors* are categorised into three types: *Winners, Losers,* and *Emerging Competitors.* The *winners* are the competitors who dominate the market. *Losers* are those who cannot compete in the market. Meanwhile, *emerging competitors* are new entrants or new growth competitors (Kotler et al., 2003).

In analysing *Competitors*, there are three key points to be considered:

- **General Information of the Competition landscape**

  The company needs to examine some general information such as the number of competitors within the industry, types of services provided by competitors, range of products offered by competitors, price of their products and services, their distribution channels or place of service, and the promotional activity done by competitors. Besides its direct competitors, a company needs to pay attention to indirect or potential competitors or those who offer substitute products or services.

- **Level of Competitor Aggressiveness**

  Second is the level of competitor aggressiveness. A company needs to look out for every movement made by its competitors, and needs to pay attention to the dynamics of their strategy, changes in its tactical activities, the creativity of competitors, and the risks that competitors are willing to take. This is because competitors who are more agile have the potential to be more *dangerous* compared to those who are stable.

- **Competitor's Capabilities**

This aspect relates to the tangible and intangible assets that competitors possess. Tangible assets include things such as financial resources, equipment, and so on, while intangible assets include items such as technological capabilities, brand name, and so on. A company must also be able to identify strategic alliances and players in the market who may back its competitors with financial or other types of aid.

An example of how competition dynamics affects business is that of Research in Motion (RIM), a Canadian company, that produced the BlackBerry. It underestimated how quickly the smartphone competition landscape was changing. Apple came up with the iPhone, a full touch-screen device, which was a significant leap in innovation in the smartphone industry, while BlackBerry was still using a physical keyboard.

BlackBerry did not fully appreciate the competitive impact of Apple's iPhone or other smartphone manufacturers at that time and still carried on its business as usual. On the other hand, there was a new updated iPhone and other smartphones every year. In 2010, Apple launched its iPhone 4, with sales that surpassed BlackBerry. RIM's global market share began to decline from 20% in 2009 to less than 5% in 2012, and then dropped to a very insignificant percentage in the last quarter of 2016. Of the 432 million of smartphones sold worldwide, only 207,900 of them were BlackBerry devices.

*"For me, the most sustainable way to beat competitors is by satisfying customers!"*

**Hermawan Kartajaya**

## CUSTOMER — VALUE DEMANDER

In the 4C Diamond Model, *Customer* acts as the *value demander*, since customers are the ones who *demand* value that is provided by the *Company* and *Competitors*. There are three categories of *Customers* — *Committed*, *Lost*, and *New Customers*. *Committed Customers* are those who have had a deep relationship with the *Company* for a particular period of time. Lost *Customers* are those who once used a *Company's* products or services but no longer use them. New *Customers* are those who newly use a *Company's* products or services.

Especially in a highly competitive market, customers do not only have needs and wants but also expectations. Understanding the customer's expectations is also important since the *Company* and its *Competitors* compete to offer the best value to *Customers*. With limited buying power, time, and other resources, *Customers* perceive the value of an offering based on their expectations toward the offering itself. In addition, a *Company* needs to understand the behaviour of its customers, in order to predict their purchase considerations.

To understand customer behaviour, there are at least three attributes to be evaluated: *Cognitive* (what is in the mind of the customers), *Affective* (what is the customers' motive), and *Conative* (what is the overt behaviour of the customers).

In the case of BlackBerry, it definitely missed out on some features that appealled to smartphone users in general, as well as to its loyal customers, such as the front and back cameras and the social platform that allows its users to communicate. App developers also did not consider the BlackBerry app store as their primary option to publish their apps, because of the declining number of global users over time. This made the situation worse for BlackBerry, as there were not as many apps as those provided by Apple and Android.

Blackberry's customers felt increasingly more isolated in this connected world, and many felt that they had no other option but to switch to other more inclusive and "connected" smartphone brands. By the time BlackBerry started to innovate it was too late — since its customers were locked into either iPhone or Android, leaving BlackBerry out of the market.

*"It should also be noted that not all customer decisions are straightforward. Their decisions are often influenced by their surroundings or community."*

**Hermawan Kartajaya**

## COMPANY — VALUE DECIDER

The fourth C of the 4C Diamond Model is *Company*. Whereas the first three aspects deal with the external business environment, the *Company* aspect deals with the internal business dimension of an organisation or company. Here, marketers must assess existing and potential resources owned by the *Company* to determine whether they are strengths or weaknesses. Resources come in many forms; typically, it can be classified into three broad categories: *tangible assets, intangible assets,* and *organisational capabilities.*

Tangible assets include all physical resources such as buildings, machines, raw materials, and money — evaluating these resources is not merely counting its quantity but also assessing their usefulness in creating a competitive advantage for the company.

Intangible assets include items such as a company's reputation, brand equity, relationship with its customers and channels, technological knowledge, accumulated experiences, employees' values, behaviour, culture, and intellectual properties. Such assets are most likely to be unique and difficult to imitate by competitors. Hence, they can help a company in creating sustainable competitive advantages.

Meanwhile, organisational capabilities refer to the combination of assets, people, and processes in a company to transform material inputs into output. This includes the ability to maintain process effectiveness and efficiency, to produce goods in good quality, to deliver excellent services, and many more. In many cases, organisational capabilities are the primary source of competitive advantage, which enables a company to use the same input factors as their competitors, but come up with a better product or service or to come up with a similar product or service, but using less inputs.

By assessing these three elements, a company could identify its *existing competencies* and measure its strengths and weaknesses, compared to its competitors. The company can also identify potential risks and hence determine its *risk attitude* — whether the company is willing to take risks or tends to avoid risk. Finally, it also helps the company to understand its *stretch capabilities* to also work with others to pursue specific opportunities in the market.

*"The identification of a company's resources is critical! It determines whether companies can adapt to the changing environment — to seize opportunities and to overcome threats."*

**Hermawan Kartajaya**

## TOWS, NOT SWOT!

Analysing the business landscape through the 4C Diamond Model is a prerequisite to conducting a TOWS evaluation. At a glance, TOWS looks very similar to the popular SWOT (*Strengths–Weaknesses–Opportunities–Threats*) Analysis. In fact, TOWS is not just SWOT in reverse. Many people, including MarkPlus staff, asked Hermawan back then, "What is the significance of reversing the sequence of the SWOT Analysis components?" He replied that by conducting TOWS instead of SWOT, marketers, and companies would be forced to look at the business landscape from an "outside-in" rather than "inside-out" perspective.

*"You must be wondering why I use TOWS, not SWOT? What is the importance of reversing the order? In the end, it is the same, isn't it? For me, this sequence is essential. Conscious or unconsciously, it does matter."*

**Hermawan Kartajaya**

In SWOT Analysis, companies tend to place too much emphasis on internal factors and capabilities and even sometimes become overconfident with what the company had accomplished in the past. They tend to have a very short list of *Weaknesses* because of an inability to identify or accept them. Focusing too much on internal strenghts or weaknesses can impair companies in their identification and assessment of potential *Opportunities* and even *Threats*. As a business should be sustainable and viewed not just from the short-term, but also long-term perspective, its strategy should be formulated based not only on the past and current situations but also the future situation.

This is not to say that companies should not match the external environment with their internal conditions; in fact, companies must do so.

However, by examining potential *Threats* and *Opportunities*, which is derived from analysing *Change, Competitor,* and *Customer* analysis before looking into the *Company's Weaknesses* and *Strengths*, an appropriate and sustainable business strategy is more likely to surface.

The "outside-in" perspective is, in fact, in line with the market-oriented approach as opposed to the product-oriented approach that takes an "inside-out" perspective.

## REFERENCES

Business Insider. (2019). *How BlackBerry Went from Controlling the Smartphone Market to a Phone of the Past.* https://www.businessinsider.com/blackberry-smartphone-rise-fall-mobile-failure-innovate-2019-11?IR=T (last modified November 21, 2019, last accessed March 16, 2020)

Kotler, Kartajaya and Hooi (2003). *Rethinking Marketing: Sustainable Marketing Enterprise in Asia.* Singapore: Prentice-Hall.

# CHAPTER 11

# POSITIONING–
# DIFFERENTIATION–BRAND
## THE MARKETING DNA

In a volatile, uncertain, complex, and ambiguous (VUCA) era, business organisations have to deal with highly complicated and competitive circumstances. Many business organisations may jump straight into tactical executions to score quick wins in their pursuit of short-term profitability, without due regard for a fundamental strategy that will also bring sustainable marketing success. Winning the competition and the future requires a company to win not only the market share but also the mind share and heart share of the customers. A strong alignment and integration between marketing strategy and marketing tactics is critical for a company to be able to deliver good value to its customers. This will also shape the company's marketing DNA.

The marketing DNA is an integration of a company's positioning–differentiation–brand (PDB). Positioning is essentially a promise from a company to its customers, and is the core of marketing strategy. As a promise, the company must fulfill it through delivery of its offers by implementing suitable marketing tactics on how the offers can be received by customers. Differentiation, in terms of content (what to offer), context (how to offer), and infrastructure (enabler) help to ensure a successful marketing tactic. Finally, the company must realise that a brand is more than just a name or logo. The brand gives added value to the company's offerings and prevents the company's products and services from being perceived as mere commodities.

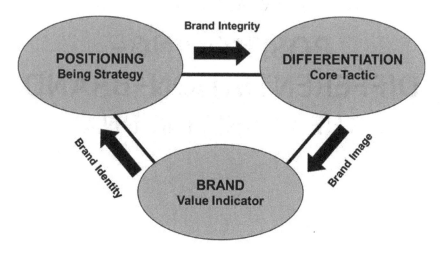

Figure 11.1. The PDB Triangle: Positioning-Differentiation-Brand

Positioning that is supported by solid and concrete differentiation will create brand integrity. This means the company is able to deliver what it promises to its customers. Strong brand integrity results in a strong brand image. A strong brand image will strengthen the predetermined brand positioning resulting in a respectable identity for the brand itself.

If the marketing DNA is built with a solid foundation, it will create a "self-reinforcing mechanism" among its three elements — positioning, differentiation, and brand. The self-reinforcement will further strengthen the brand with a snowball effect, and gives the company an increasingly stronger competitive advantage (Figure 11.1).

## POSITIONING — "BEING STRATEGY"

Positioning is at the very core of marketing strategy and serves as a reason for being, for the products and services offered by a company. According to traditional definition, positioning is often mentioned as a strategy to win and conquer the customer's mind through the company's offerings. Al Ries and Jack Trout (1981), in their book *Positioning: The Battle of Your Mind*, argued that the customer's mind is the battleground for the marketing war. The book defines positioning as what a company does to the mind of its customers, not just what it does to its product. Successful products or brands are those who are able to have a strong and unique position in the minds of customers.

In his book, *Hermawan Kartajaya on Positioning* (2007), Hermawan defines positioning as a "strategy to lead your customer credibly." He emphasises that positioning is as important as building and gaining trust from customers. The more credible and trusted a company is, the stronger the company's positioning. If a company succeeds in gaining its customers' trust, they will feel the existence of the company in their minds. Therefore, positioning is a "being strategy" for a company. It determines the product, brand, and company presence or "being" in the customer's mind.

For example, AirAsia, with its slogan "Now Everyone can Fly," clearly positions itself in the mind of customers as a low-cost air transportation services provider, primarily serving the Asia region. On the other hand, Singapore Airlines, with its tagline "A Great Way to Fly," emphasises its position as a full-service airline, which provides its customers with a satisfying flight experience. These two cases also display the role of positioning using a "frame of reference" — as to where it belongs in the product–service category. The objective of positioning, using a frame of reference, is to avoid comparisons to products, brands, or companies from a different category. In the case of AirAsia and Singapore Airlines, both are airlines competing in the same region of Asia, yet both of them have succeeded in their own category or frame of reference as a "low-cost carrier" and a "full-service airline" respectively.

Positioning is also one of the most effective strategies for companies, to deal with a highly competitive landscape. For example, in the classic case of Coca-Cola versus Pepsi, Coca-Cola positions itself as "The Real Thing" or the real and original cola drink. This may imply that "any other cola drink besides Coca-cola is not the real cola."

Given the circumstances, Pepsi responded with "The Pepsi Generation" advertising program in the early 1970s, which promoted Pepsi as "The Choice of the New Generation," and positioned Pepsi as a cola drink for young generations. This clearly differentiates itself from its most significant competitor. In 2019, Coca-Cola may have a stronger brand valuation than PepsiCo, as it is ranked number 6 on *Forbes* World's Most Valuable brands compared to Pepsi, which is only ranked 29; but

PepsiCo's revenue is twice that of Coca-Cola, with a revenue of US$64.98B compared to Coca-Cola's US$32.25B.

In his book *Positioning Analysis and Strategy*, Yoram Wind, a professor of marketing at the Wharton School of the University of Pennsylvania, also supports the definition of positioning as "reason for being." Positioning is about the definition of a company's identity in the customer's mind. It is no longer only about persuading customers and merely creating perceptions in the customer's mind; it is also about establishing trustworthiness, confidence, and competence for customers.

Earning trust and building credibility becomes the ultimate goal of establishing an effective positioning strategy. Hence companies need to keep in mind that positioning is a promise of delivering certain values to the customers, through its offerings. These promises have to be fulfilled, and the ability to fulfill the promises is an essential part of a sustainably successful marketing strategy. According to Al Ries and Jack Trout, the ultimate goal of positioning is to have a strong association of words to the product, brand, or company; in short, the brand should "own" the words in the customer's mind. Samsung is associated with "innovation," Walmart with "everyday low price," and Ritz-Carlton with "extraordinary customer service." These companies have achieved this ultimate goal because of the consistent use of its positioning statement and ability to fulfill its promises. Positioning must remain relevant over time. As such, a correct and strong positioning is imperative in determining long-term success.

### Recipes of Strong Positioning

Product, brand, and the company positioning are not just a company's promotion tagline though such taglines are strongly related to positioning. A tagline is a summary of a positioning statement that is needed to ensure that members in an organisation have the same vision about the particular product, brand, and company, and how it positions itself in the mind of its target customer. Therefore, it is important to correctly formulate this usually-no-more-than-five-words slogan, which will be stated everywhere on a company's promotion materials and which hopefully will occupy an important space in the customer's mind — to be a top-of-the-mind brand for a particular promise.

According to Tybout and Sternthal (2005) and Kotler, Kartajaya, Hooi and Liu (2003), there are at least five essential elements in developing a positioning statement:

- **Target market:** Profile of segment(s) (geographic, demographic, psychographic, and behaviour) that is targeted as customers by the company to deliver its offerings.

- **Brand name:** Name of a brand, product, or company that delivers value to customers. A brand name should be easy to remember, catchy, and should not create negative perceptions or associated with negative aspects.

- **Frame of reference:** A category or segment in which your product, brand, or company competes or is compared with other players in it.

- **Point of differentiation:** The advantages of your product, brand, or company compared to your competitors.

- **Reason to believe:** Proof that your product, brand, or company can fulfill its promises to customers. This is more crucial if the point of differentiation is relatively abstract.

The positioning statement could be formulated from those five essential elements as follows (Figure 11.2):

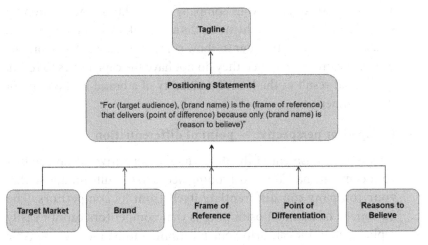

Figure 11.2. Positioning Statement Development

> *For (Target Market), (Brand) is a (Frame of Reference)*
> *that delivers (Point of Differentiation),*
> *because only (Brand) is (Reason to Believe)*

In relation to the positioning statement elements, Hermawan Kartajaya proposed the following considerations based on the four aspects: Customer, Company, Competitor, and Change (4Cs).

- **Customer perspective — reason-to-buy**

  This is an assessment of your customer's reason-to-buy. Your positioning should be perceived positively by customers and become their "reason-to-buy." This will happen if your positioning clearly describes the value proposition that you offer to the customers, and the particular value is perceived as an important value for them. Since positioning is a promise of value, it becomes a determinant for customers in their purchase decision.

  Amazon positions itself as the most convenient book retailer with the biggest selection and lowest price. Its value proposition becomes the reason-to-buy for customers. Giordano positions itself as a "value-for-money" apparel and comfortable shopping experience, meaning these values become its customers' reason-to-buy.

- **Company perspective — internal strengths and weaknesses**

  This is an assessment of your company's capabilities. The positioning should take into account the strengths and weaknesses of the product, brand, or company. In order to show competitive advantages, brands may make promises which they do not have the capabilities to fulfill. This could result in the loss of credibility of a brand in the mind of the customer.

- **Competitor perspective — point of differentiation**

  This is an assessment of the differential competitive advantage that your company has. Your positioning needs to be quite unique so that your company can differentiate itself from its competitors. The advantage of unique positioning is that competitors cannot easily replicate it and it can help your positioning to be more sustainable in the long run.

Starbucks, with its positioning "The World's Finest Coffee Experience," is able to uniquely differentiate itself from its competitors. In contrast to its competitors, Starbucks does not position itself as a coffee shop or a cafe that emphasises just the richness or the taste of its coffee; rather, it positions itself as a brand that provides the coffee drinking experience. Starbucks promises its customers more than just a coffee, but an experience "to see and to be seen."

- **Change perspective — relevance and consistency**

  This is an assessment of how a company stays relevant to the changing environment. A company's positioning and offers have to be relevant to the ever-changing business landscape, be they changes in technology, socio-culture, economy, political–legal, market, competitor, or customer. Once your positioning is no longer relevant to the business landscape, you need to do repositioning.

  Take Burger King as an example, in early 2020, it launched its "Moldy Whopper" preservative-free burger campaign, emphasising the natural ingredients it used in its signature menu, the Whopper. This bold move is a sign that Burger King is starting to move away from using preservatives and artificial flavors, which many fast-food chains have been criticised for. The brand's international chief marketing officer, Fernando Machado, said that Burger King believed that real food tastes better, and they were working hard to remove preservatives, colors, and flavors from artificial sources from the food they serve in all countries around the world. The environment has changed and people are becoming more health-conscious. In addition to tastier food, more people are valuing healthy food and are more likely to avoid unhealthy food.

At the same time, positioning needs to be consistent and cannot change frequently. Positioning creates perceptions and identity in the minds of customers; continuous changes in identity may confuse the customers and create a perception that your company lacks focus.

Samsung owns the word "innovation" in the minds of their customers. Looking at their slogans over the years: "Next is What?" (2007–2010), "The Next is Now" (2011–2013), "The Next Big Thing Is Here" (2013–2017), and "Do What You Can't" (after 2017), there is an implication that

that Samsung wants its customers to imagine things that they could never have thought of before or in short, innovation. Although its slogans keep changing over the years, Samsung consistently maintains its positioning and message as the company that brings innovations to its customers through time and is able to stay relevant to the times.

The positioning that has been developed by management should be internalised within the company, before being communicated to external customers in the form of short, catchy, and easy-to-remember taglines.

The Body Shop succeeds in a crowded and competitive cosmetic industry through the right positioning. Unlike its competitors, instead of campaigning on the beauty effects of its products, The Body Shop positions its products as environmentally friendly cosmetic products. To deliver its promise as an eco-friendly brand, it creates cosmetic products made out of natural ingredients and packed with minimal environmentally unfriendly materials. The Body Shop also positions the company as being against animal testing and shows its care for environmental and social issues. The company spends only a small proportion of its budget on advertising; the bulk of it is spent on providing sponsorships for activities that are aligned with its core values. These are campaigns that raise awareness and care toward global environmental and social issues. To internalise its positioning and its core values, The Body Shop trains its employees about environmental awareness, and the harms of AIDS, alcohol, and narcotics, in addition to product knowledge and customer care. By purchasing its products, customers become part of The Body Shop's actions in protecting the environment and planet. This strong emotional connection becomes the customer's reason-to-buy.

## DIFFERENTIATION — "CORE TACTIC"

As mentioned earlier, positioning is a promise to the customer, which a company would deliver the value that it has committed. In order to do so and to uphold its trustworthiness and credibility, the promise needs to be fulfilled as otherwise, it may end up in an "overpromise-underdeliver" situation. To fulfill the promise, your positioning has to be supported by a strong differentiation and this will help the company to establish a solid brand integrity.

Many experts define differentiation as a set of activities done by a brand or company to make itself different from its competitors. Hermawan Kartajaya, along with Philip Kotler, Hooi Den Huan, and Sandra Liu in the book *Rethinking Marketing: Sustainable Marketing Enterprise in Asia* (2003), went further, in defining differentiation as "integrating the content, context, and infrastructure of what the company offers." A different and unique offering is indeed the core tactic of a company to support its positioning and to deliver competitive value to its customers. Not only must the offerings be *perceived* as unique or different, but they have to *actually* be different in terms of its content, context, and infrastructure. To create a differentiation, companies can either focus on one or more of these three dimensions.

### Dimensions of Differentiation

The three dimensions of differentiation that a company can focus on are content (what to offer), context (how to offer), and infrastructure (the enablers) (Fig. 11.3).

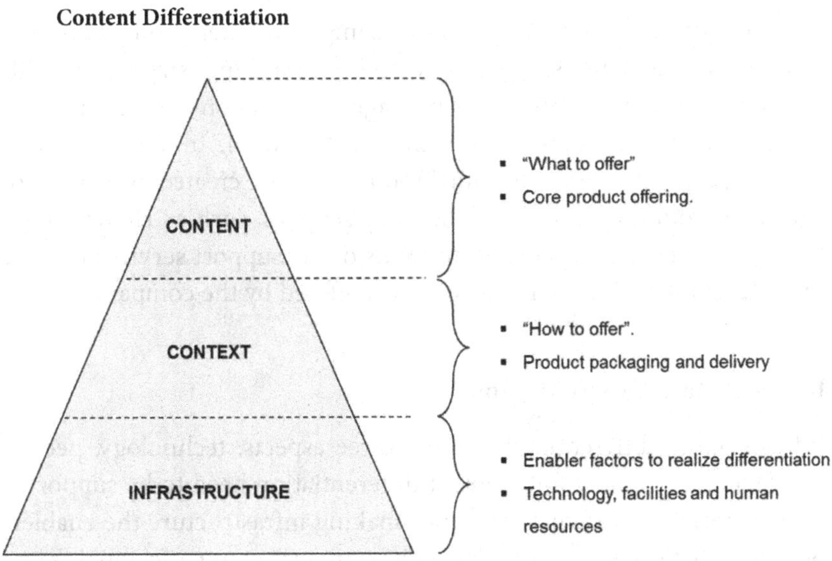

**Content Differentiation**

- "What to offer"
- Core product offering.

- "How to offer".
- Product packaging and delivery

- Enabler factors to realize differentiation
- Technology, facilities and human resources

Figure 11.3. Elements of Differentiation

Content differentiation is, very often, a tangible aspect of differentiation. For example, in food and beverage companies, content would refer to the taste, texture, look, and smell of the product. Both McDonald's and Burger King serve burgers and fries, but the products differ in terms of flavor and appearance. For automotive producers, the content would be about the performance of the engine, fuel efficiency, and top speed of the vehicles that they produce, and so on. The Dodge Challenger, Ford Mustang, and Chevrolet Camaro may be powered by V8 engines, but the difference relies in its overall performance.

As for the services industry, the content differentiation is the core product offered by the company. For hotel businesses, content refers to the rooms they offer; for technology companies, such as Huawei, the content lies in the comprehensive end-to-end network solution provided. Huawei offers a one-stop-shop solution as its B2B clients can get all kinds of hubs, switches, wireless access devices, and other equipment through one channel instead of engaging with many vendors. Hence, it enables a client's business process to be more efficient.

## Context Differentiation

Context differentiation refers to how companies offer products or services to their customers. In the food and beverage industry, context differentiation can be the product's packaging. For automotive companies, the car design becomes its context differentiation. In the hospitality industry, context refers to the hotel room ambience created by its interior and its surroundings. As for technology services, such as Huawei, context differentiation can be seen in terms of the support services that are provided, along with the main solutions offered by the company.

## Infrastructure Differentiation

Infrastructure differentiation covers three aspects: technology, people, and facilities. Content and context differentiation need to be supported by appropriate infrastructure, hence making infrastructure the enablers of differentiation. In order to deliver its signature menu, McDonald's and Burger King have their own skilled labourers to prepare them using their own unique cooking equipment. The layout of its in-store kitchen and system enables the fast service to take place, as promised by these fast-food restaurant chains. Moreover, its well-planned supply chain enables some outlets to perform 24-hour services. The infrastructure of consumer goods businesses relies on its chain of distribution, including its system and people, to make their products available and accessible to customers, through its outlets. For automotive companies, this would mean the production facilities, manned by skilled and educated labourers, to produce products at a certain level of quality. In the hospitality industry, excellent services are enabled by the ability of its people to deliver service quality.

As automotive industry trends starting to move from conventional vehicles to electric vehicles, champions and big players in the automotive industry, such as General Motors Company, Toyota Motor Corporation, Honda Motor Company, Nissan Motor Company, Bavarian Motor Work (BMW), and Volkswagen, are investing in creating electric vehicles (EV) products. In this competitive market, Tesla, one of the pioneers in modern EV lead by Elon Musk, through its Tesla Model 3, was reported to be the world's best-selling EV with 247,011 units sold during 2019. The Tesla Model 3 had almost three times the sales of the world's second best-selling EV, the BAIC EU-Series with 89,162 units sold during 2019, and had more than four times the sale of the world's third best-selling electric vehicle, BYD Yuan/S2 EV with 66,405 units sold during 2019.

Tesla differentiates itself through content, through better performance, in terms, for example, of its acceleration and battery efficiency. The car design, which reflects its context differentiation, is also on the company's focus. Instead of sticking with the standard design of an electric car, which is mainly compact with an impression of an efficient car, Tesla designed its car to look like high-performance and exotic sports cars. Furthermore, Tesla's factory in Fremont, California, is arguably one of the world's most advanced automotive plants, with its highly educated and skilled workforce. These enabled the company to deliver value to its customers.

## BRAND — "VALUE INDICATOR"

According to the book, *Hermawan Kartajaya on Brand*, "Brand is everything." He pointed out that it is a mistake if a company considers a brand as merely a name, logo, or symbol. More than that, a brand is an umbrella for products and services offered by the company to its customers. A brand is a reflection of the value that the company offers; hence, it is called a value indicator of your product or company.

### Value Formula

In the book *Rethinking Marketing*, value is defined as "total get" divided by "total give." There are essentially two benefit components of "total get," namely functional benefit (Fb) and emotional benefit (Eb). On the other hand, "total give" consists of two cost components, namely price (P) and other expenses (Oe). Therefore, value can be formulated as follows:

$$\text{Value} = \frac{Fb + Eb}{P + Oe}$$

### Total Get

Functional benefit refers to the benefits customers can obtain, as a result of a product's features that provide functional utility. Functional benefits usually relate to the functions performed by the product or service. Take a car, for example; its functional benefit can be its performance, safety, comfort, or durability. For smartphone producers, the functional benefits refer to its screen display quality, camera quality, sound quality, battery efficiency, and so on. A company can increase the functional benefits it provides, by improving the performance of its product or adding more features to it.

An emotional benefit, as expected, is one that is based on the emotional utility provided by the product or brand. The feeling of safety while driving a Volvo car, or the sense of prestige while driving a Mercedes-Benz are examples of emotional benefits. Another example and from the food and beverage industry, could be the energetic feeling from soft drinks such as 100 Plus. Emotional benefits can be important customers' reasons to buy a particular product or brand. Apple products sell because people want to be perceived as smart and cool; Harley-Davidson motorcycles sell because people want to feel a sense of belonging to its community. Many makeup products sell because people want to feel as pretty as the brand ambassadors for these products. A company can enhance its emotional benefits offering, through content marketing and using key opinion leaders to promote its product or service.

## Total Give

The first component of total give is price, the direct cost paid by customers to obtain your product and service. This refers to the exact price of the offering. Meanwhile, other expenses are the cost that occurs to the customers when using a product or service. Examples of price and other expenses for automotive products are where the price refers to the vehicle's price, and other expenses refer to the amount of money spent on fuel and maintenance services. For smartphone products, the other expenses are the money that customers spend on text messages, making calls, and internet access.

From the formula presented above, it is clear that how strong a brand is, can be determined by the functional and emotional benefits it could provide to its customers, and the price and other expenses that customers need to bear.

The brand itself is an asset, which adds value offered to customers, increases customer satisfaction, and creates loyalty. If a company is able to build and manage well its brand, the price need no longer depend on the equilibrium of supply and demand. With a strong brand, the company can become a "price maker," and not just a "price taker," since the company can determine the price to levy based on its products' perceived customer value. In this way, the brand enables the company to avoid the commodity trap.

## Building Brand Equity

A brand is an asset for any organisation and its worth could be determined by its brand equity. David Aaker (1996) in his book, *Managing Brand Equity,* suggests that brand equity could be measured by a combination of several attributes: (1) brand awareness, (2) brand loyalty, (3) perceived quality, (4) brand associations, and (5) other proprietary brand assets.

- **Brand awareness**

  Brand awareness refers to the knowledge, awareness, and recall about a brand name among its target customers. It essentially means that the target customers know about the existence of your brand. The highest level of awareness is when customers can recall your brand name without any aid or probe, known as top-of-mind recall. Meanwhile, the lowest level of awareness is a condition where customers need to be aided or even reminded to recall about your brand, or what is known as prompted awareness.

  Building and enhancing brand awareness involve activities that make the brand more visible, heard, and accessible to the customers. This can be done through above the line, below the line, offline, and online media.

- **Brand associations**

  Association is related to the connection that customers have relating your brand to any words that can come to their minds. Associations can arise in relation to the product category, price, promotion, interactions with employees, quality of the product, publicity about the brand, and so on. For example, Mercedes-Benz is associated with the word "prestige," Volvo is associated with "Safety," and Toyota is associated with the word "Efficient." Associations are not only formed by the interactions between a company and its customers, but also by the interactions among customers themselves, which is more difficult to manage. Therefore, it is absolutely crucial for companies to plan interactions with its customers so as to minimise the chance that negative associations emerge among customers. Strong brand associations can help the company communicate its position or differentiation to customers, and reinforces their reason-to-buy.

- **Perceived quality**

  Quality is one of the main reasons for customers to select a brand in all product categories. Perceived quality is customers' perceptions about the overall quality of a brand, which is derived not only from the quality of its product and service offered, but also from the quality of its brand image, as shaped by its marketing communications and publicity. Perceptions about quality play an influential role in determining the pricing strategy. Generally, higher prices can be charged for better quality, actual and perceived.

- **Brand loyalty**

  Traditionally, brand loyalty is defined as repetitive purchase actions, where customers keep choosing the same brand. However, this may not apply for all markets or industries. For example, for many non-fast-moving products such as property or automobiles, it is unlikely that customers will purchase these repeatedly. Loyalty can be indicated when the customer recommends a particular property or its developer or automobiles to their family, friends, and peers.

  Strong brand loyalty brings benefits such as a decrease in marketing expenditure. Repurchase behaviour creates a base of loyal customers who will continuously choose your product or service should they need anything in the same category.

  Customer advocacy increases brand awareness, spreads information about the brand to other potential customers, and creates a reliable and trusted perception among customers since it is endorsed by people known to you. Therefore, loyalty, as one of the essential brand equity elements, needs to be maintained or even triggered by the company, for example, by incentivising repeat orders and advocacy.

- **Other proprietary brand assets**

  Proprietary brand assets include trademarks, patents, relationships with channels, and other assets that are valuable for the brand as they prevent attacks from competitors and decrease in the loyal customer base.

Building a brand is not only about putting advertisements on offline and online media, but also about building good public relations and corporate citizenship activities. Any brand is built through solid segmentation–targeting–positioning, differentiation, marketing mix (product, price, place, promotion), and selling tactics.

All companies must be aware and take care of its actions as these can result in strengthening or weakening its brand equity.

A company's marketing DNA, formulated in the PDB triangle, is extremely important and strategic for a company since it acts as the core essence or guidance for all company marketing activities. Building a solid PDB strategy will help to develop a self-reinforcing system for the company's brand that can be used as a source of competitive advantage.

Positioning without good differentiation is just like empty promises — without the capabilities to deliver value to customers. This can lead to an "overpromise-underdeliver" situation, which will negatively impact the brand's integrity in the eyes of customers.

Differentiation or any marketing tactics without a strong brand is like a set of marketing activities without core value or the "soul." This will result in weakening the brand image. A brand without a solid positioning will be just like a stamp — of the name and logo of the brand — without having a clear position in the minds of the customers.

Hermawan Kartajaya emphasises that PDB is the very fundamental foundation for marketing strategy, tactics, and value. It is the key for companies to win mind share, market share, and the heart share of the customer. Hence, the Nine Core Elements of marketing are labeled as "Marketing DNA."

# References

Aaker, DA (1996). *Building Strong Brand.* New York: The Free Press.

Ries, A, and J Trout (1981). *Positioning: The Battle of Your Minds.* New York: McGraw-Hill.

Business Insider (2020). *Burger King Just Launched a New Ad Campaign Featuring a Moldy Whopper, and it Reflects a Trend Taking Over the Fast-Food Industry.* https://www.forbes.com/sites/panosmourdoukoutas/2019/07/13/pepsi-beats-coke-again/#78788e5b2bad (last modified February 18, 2020, last accessed February 28, 2020)

Clean Technica (2020). *Tesla Model 3 Sales = ~4× Nissan LEAF Sales, World's 2nd Best Selling EV Outside Of China—November EV Sales Report.* https://cleantechnica.com/2020/01/04/tesla-model-3-sales-4x-nissan-leaf-sales-worlds-2nd-best-selling-ev-outside-of-china-november-ev-sales-report/ (last modified January 4, 2020, last accessed February 28, 2020)

Kartajaya, H (2007a). *Hermawan Kartajaya on Positioning.* Jakarta: Mizan.

Kartajaya, H (2007b). *Hermawan Kartajaya on Differentiation.* Jakarta: Mizan.

Kartajaya, H (2007c). *Hermawan Kartajaya on Brand.* Jakarta: Mizan.

Kotler, et al. (2003). *Rethinking Marketing: Sustainable Marketing Enterprise in Asia.* Singapore: Prentice Hall.

Kotler, P, H Kartajaya, and Hooi D. H. (2014). *Think New ASEAN.* Singapore: McGraw-Hills.

Tesla Motors (2020). *Factory.* https://www.tesla.com/factory (last accessed February 29, 2020)

Tybout, AM, and B Sternthal (2005). *Brand Positioning Kellogg on Branding.* New Jersey: John Wiley & Sons.

Wind, (1990). "Positioning Analysis and Strategy", in G. Day, B. Weitz, and R. Wensley (editors), *The Interface of Marketing and Strategy,* London: JAI Press.

# CHAPTER 12

# NINE CORE ELEMENTS OF MARKETING

## MARKETING STRATEGY–TACTIC–VALUE

"We simplify the complex things." Hermawan often repeats this phrase, emphasising the thinking approach that is always used by himself and MarkPlus, Inc. In this fast-paced era, where innovation and technology keeps driving and changing the market, marketing needs to be updated all the time. Many new concepts, approaches, and theories about marketing keep emerging in this new world; it seems that there are hundreds, if not thousands, of new marketing concepts and ideas. Marketing fundamentals, however, remains. Marketing remains centered on customer–product–brand management, as it was for decades. Hermawan believes that it all comes down to nine simple elements; to him, it is much better and more effective to conceptualise scattered elements into one model that is easy to understand. He developed what is known as the Nine Core Elements of Marketing (Figure 12.1). The concept is illustrated in the strategic business triangle or strategy–tactic–value (S–T–V) triangle framework. The framework shows three dimensions of marketing architecture, namely: *Strategy* — "how to win the mind share," *Tactic* — "how to win the market share," and *Value* — "how to win the heart share" (Kotler et al, 2003). To simplify things, these 9 Core Elements of Marketing are divided into three groups reflecting the S–T–V aspects. Each aspect covers three elements of the framework.

*"Marketing must be systematic;*
*from strategy to tactic, from 'strategy to 'how to do,'*
*from winning the war to winning the battle,*
*from the big picture to grass-root, from abstract to concrete."*

**Hermawan Kartajaya**

As a start, the company has to explore the market and view the market creatively by performing segmentation. Then the company needs to decide to target a certain segment of customers; it could be one or more target segments, depends on the needs and capability of a company to serve its customers. After selecting a target market, the company develops a solid positioning, or as mentioned in Chapter 11, a promise of value that will be delivered.

Positioning needs to be supported with differentiation in the form of content (what to offer), context (how to offer), and infrastructure

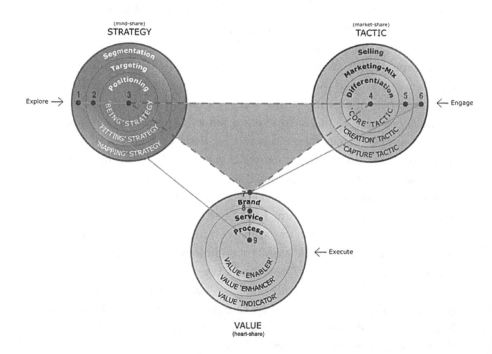

Figure 12.1. The Nine Core Elements of Marketing (S–T–V Triangle)

(enabler) so that the company could deliver what it promised to its customers. Differentiation can then be translated into actionable tactics known as the marketing mix, which consists of product, price, place, and promotion. After that is the selling tactic. Selling is the only element in the marketing tactics that captures value from the market. These three elements focus on how you engage your market.

In support of positioning and differentiation, a brand has to be created and strengthened as the value indicator, and the value of the brand needs to be continuously enhanced through an excellent service strategy, whether it is before-sales, during-sales, or after-sales services. Lastly, comes the value enabler, process. No matter how strong a company is in terms of the other eight elements, it will all fail if the company does not possess good processes. The final three elements deal with how you execute the value.

## MARKETING STRATEGY — "WINNING THE MIND SHARE"

*"Sorting out the market' or segmentation, 'choosing targets' or targeting and 'focusing people's minds' or positioning, are strategies. Without a clear STP, the marketing mix created will have no direction."*

**Hermawan Kartajaya**

The role of the first three elements, segmentation–targeting–positioning (Figure 12.2), is to win the mind share of customers. This is a strategic aspect of marketing as it is strongly related to customer management, and works at the strategic business unit (SBU) level. Segmentation can be defined as a way of viewing the market creatively, where the company strategises to map the market and segments the market into groups of potential customers with similarities in their characteristics and behaviour. After grouping the market, the company selects which segment of the market to enter and serve, based on the size and growth of the segment, as well as the competitive landscape of the targeted market. The last element, positioning, is the presence strategy. After selecting the right segment to serve, the company must define its being in the mind of its customers, as explained in Chapter 11.

Figure 12.2. Marketing Strategy

## SEGMENTATION: VIEW YOUR MARKET CREATIVELY

In order to build a solid marketing approach, a company must formulate its being strategy or positioning, as reflected in its positioning statement. One component of the positioning statement involves asking a question of "who do we serve?" Or, in other words, the target market. In order to decide its target market, the company first needs to divide the market into smaller segments, based on similar characteristics and behaviour.

Segmentation is commonly defined as a process of segmenting or partitioning the market into several segments. For Hermawan, it is really about "viewing the market creatively." The company needs to be creative in finding the right angle to view the market from. It also needs to be able to use appropriate segmentation variables to identify and gain a clear perspective of the market. Segmentation is an art of identifying opportunities in the market and at the same time, a science in viewing the market based on geographic and demographic aspects, as well as psychographic and behaviour aspects. Whatever the basis used in the segmentation process, the grouping must be based on similarities, so that each customer in a particular segment has similar traits.

*"For marketing people, segmentation is the 'key to victory.' I do not agree with the definition of segmentation as 'dividing the market.' In truth, it is about 'how to look at the market creatively.'"*

**Hermawan Kartajaya**

Segmentation plays an important role in the company for various reasons, as outlined below:

- **Enables the company to focus on resource allocation**

  Dividing the market into groups or segments is the initial step, prior to selecting which is the best segment to be served, and whether the company has the greatest competitive advantage. Therefore, segmentation allows a company to focus its resources on the targeted segment to ensure that segment's satisfaction. This will also allow a company to clearly identify who are its competitors that serve the same customer segment and helps it to determine its position in the market.

- **Serves as a basis for determining a company's overall strategy**

  Segmentation is used as the basis of a company's marketing strategy or even its overall strategy, while targeting is the basis to determine the company's positioning in the market. Positioning as a core strategy is then supported by differentiation as the company's core tactic, which is translated into the marketing mix and selling tactic. After these are formulated, they become a reference to help determine the company's service, process, and brand-building strategy.

- **Is a key factor in beating competition**

  Most importantly, segmentation is key factor in beating competition by seeing the market from a unique point of view and different from the competitors. Segmentation does not only use static attributes but also dynamic attributes. Harley-Davidson is able to create and dominate its own market segment and sustainably serve this same segment for decades. In a market where most producers segment their market based on customers' lifestyles (such as whether a vehicle is used for daily commuting or for touring), Harley-Davidson segments the market based on its customers, traits, such as valuing masculinity, being respectable, and being accepted by their community.

## Segmentation Attributes

In performing segmentation, there are several attributes that could be selected as a basis for grouping the market segment. These may reflect the traits of customers in the particular group and may have different levels of effectiveness in predicting the customer's purchase behaviour. The attributes can be categorised as *static attribute* segmentation, *dynamic attribute* segmentation, and *individual* segmentation.

## Static Attribute Segmentation

Static attribute segmentation groups the market based on similar and relatively "static" attributes. This type of segmentation involves *geographic* segmentation and *demographic* segmentation. Though they may not have a very strong correlation with purchase or product usage behaviour, they can still be useful.

Geographic segmentation divides the market based on geographical areas, such as city, province, region, or country. Geographic variables are not as strong as other variables but are still used by some companies. Take McDonald's as an example; in addition to its original menus, the company targets the local market by serving different customised cuisines based on the country it serves. In India, McDonald's serves Chicken Maharaja Mac, and Shahi Paneer McCurry Pan; McNürnburger, a three-bratwurst-mustard-onion burger is served in Germany; while in Indonesia, they serve Burger Rendang, a beef burger with a splash of signature Indonesian flavor.

Demographic segmentation groups the market according to demographic variables, including gender, age group, family size, occupation, education level, religion, and social, economic class. Clothing brands often segment their market according to demographic variables such as age — identifying the products based on kids, and adults' clothing; gender — dividing their products into clothing for men and women. Some players even only serve one particular segment, Tea Collection, a U.S.-based clothing line for kids, sells clothes to children, whose ages range from newborn until 16 years old. The company then further divides the segment into the newborn (6–9 months), baby, toddler, boy and girl, and tween sub-segments. Hence, Tea Collection specialises in serving the kids clothing market, and is able to channel its resources effectively to its target market.

## Dynamic Attribute Segmentation

To view the market creatively, dynamic attribute segmentation plays an important role. One should not only segment the market based on static attributes, which may not have a strong correlation toward purchase decision but should also consider segmenting the market based on similar "dynamic" attributes that may better reflect human characteristics that has a strong influence on a customer's purchase decision. It is called "dynamic" since the attributes may change within individuals over time. Still, these attributes are what define a customer's character as they can reflect the customer's deep-seated anxieties and desires. The attributes in this type of segmentation include *psychographics* and *behaviour*.

Psychographic segmentation groups the market according to the individuals' personalities or lifestyles. A lot of soft drink companies target both genders and customers across almost all age groups. In viewing the market creatively, Coca-Cola divided its customers based on their lifestyles. For example, among their more-than-hundred-types-of-Cola, the original Coca-Cola or Coke is served for customers who want to feel energetic and recharged; meanwhile, Coca-Cola Zero and Diet Coke are for health-conscious people who still want the taste of original Coke but want to minimise their consumption of calories.

Behavioural segmentation groups the market based on the individuals' purchase-related behaviour. For example, Starbucks mainly operates in the form of a coffee shop, but at the same time also produces ready-to-drink (RTD) coffees that are sold in supermarkets and minimarkets. This shows that Starbucks serves both customers who want to enjoy their coffee in the shop, and customers who prefer to *grab-and-go* and who value convenience just as much as enjoying the product.

As successful as its coffee shop chain, its RTD segment dominates North America with 88% market share in the RTD coffee category and 73% market share in the overall RTD category.

Another example is segmenting the market based on benefits sought by the individual. This type of segmentation is widely used in the fast-moving consumer goods (FMCG) industry, especially those which produce personal care products such as toothpaste, shampoo, facial wash, and soap. These companies view the market as being based on the benefit sought, by their customers. For toothpaste customers, the benefit sought could be whitening, teeth protection, sensitive teeth, and fresh breath.

With advances in technology, individual segmentation, the ultimate level of segmentation is possible. This type is where the segmentation is performed on the smallest unit of any market — the individual or what Hermawan called "The segment of one." In the previous decade, this kind of segmentation is challenging to be done. However, the existence of the internet and the advancement of big data analytics allows individual segmentation to be frequently applied nowadays, mainly by internet-based companies such as Google and Amazon. Advanced analytics are used in order to analyse an individual's behaviour in surfing the internet or any web-based platform. This enables the company to understand what keywords are frequently searched by their users, which page of the website the users spend most of their time on, what kind of advertisements do the users click the most, etc. Hence, it is possible for the company to offer personalised offerings to its customers based on very precise analysis.

**Performing Effective Segmentation**

As stated earlier, segmentation is a critical factor in beating the competition and therefore, it is important for companies to formulate an effective segmentation strategy. Effective segmentation should follow these characteristics:

- **Unique Point of View**

  A company must be able to view the market creatively. The ability to see the market uniquely and differently from a competitor may lead a company to find its own niche, where it can establish its own *rules-of-the-game*. If the segment grows, this will no doubt attract competitors. By establishing your own *rules-of-the-game*, competitors are forced to follow the rules that you have established.

- **Reflect Buying or Using Behaviour**

  There are various methods of developing segments, but the best is the one, which can reflect the usage and purchase behaviour of the customers, and that clearly defines customers' *reason-to-buy*. Geographic and demographic segmentation are indeed naturally easier to be performed rather than psychographic, behavioural, or even individual segmentation. However, the nature of such segmentation variables do not provide the company with a clear enough profile of its customers, especially on how the customers choose the product, why they need the product, and what factors do they consider in purchasing that product. As a consequence, it will be challenging to develop marketing tactics that are effective in capturing the segment market share. On the other hand, psychographic and behavioural segmentation variables have more advantages as they give a better understanding of the customers' *reason-to-buy*.

- **Substantial, Actionable, and Measurable**

  Segmentation is the first step in determining marketing strategy and therefore, it has to be able to set a clear direction on where the company wants to go. As mentioned, a company must be able to view the market creatively. At the same time, it must also question itself "Is this segment big enough to be served?" and "Do we have enough resources to exploit this segment?"

  Segments must be substantial enough or have a prospect to grow in the future so that they have the potential to create profits for the company, and at the same time, can be served by the company. More importantly, the identified segment must be measurable and have their characteristics defined, so that positioning, differentiation, marketing mix, selling, and brand-building strategies can be formulated to focus on these characteristics.

## TARGETING: ALLOCATE YOUR RESOURCES EFFECTIVELY

After mapping your potential market segments, the next step is to evaluate the segments and determine which segment or segments your company wishes to target. Traditionally, this process is called *targeting,* which is defined as the process of selecting the right target market for a company's products and services. Hermawan suggests it will be better if we see targeting as "a strategy of allocating the company's resources effectively," given that any company's resources, workforce, time, and money are always limited. Therefore, targeting is selecting a segment whose requirement fits with a company's resources.

It is a common mistake for companies to try to serve the whole world or as broad a market as possible. The idea of targeting is the opposite. In order to serve the market effectively, a company must understand its customer, needs and behaviour. However, if the company targets a segment that is too broad or too many market segments, which have various traits and characteristics, it would be challenging to serve each market segment effectively.

As a generalisation, targeting a relatively narrow market segment rather than a broad one brings more advantages for the company. Your marketing team could create more focused and tailored marketing content for a more specific target segment. For your sales team, it means more relevant prospects being targeted with sales activities, and they could allocate their time and resources on these prospects who look for a solution that fits with your company.

*"Resources are always limited, so you must have priorities. Which segments are the first, second, third priority, even which ones are not the target market! If there are priorities, resources must also be allocated proportionally."*

**Hermawan Kartajaya**

**Determining Target Segment**

In evaluating and determining which segments to target, there are four criteria that companies can use:

- **Segment Size**

  The size of the segment is one of the criteria. The company has to ensure that the market segment it chooses is big enough or profitable enough for the company to allocate its resources. The number of customers in the segment is not the only criterion. Indeed, it may not have to be big. More importantly, is the potential contribution of the segment. It has to be significant enough for the company.

There are companies that survive by serving a small yet profitable market or what is known as a *niche* market. Vegan clothing brands, such as In The Soulshine, Wills Vegan Shoes, and Beyond Skin, sell clothing products that are made from — non-animal materials, such as man-made fibers, synthetic fibers, organic cotton, bamboo, and wood pulp fibers instead of leather, silk, animal feathers, and wool. These brands target customers who are concerned about animal cruelty and offer products which are free from animal cruelty, including keeping and breeding animals in captivity, with inhumane treatment.

- **Segment Growth**

The growth rate of the segment is another criterion. A company may well choose a segment, that my currently be small, but with growth potential in sales and profitability. To do so, a company must examine the potential segment's market outlook — the 4Cs in the marketing framework. A lot of attention needs to be paid on the 4Cs (Customers, Competitors, Company, and Changes) and perhaps more on the *Change* element. By assessing changes in the business landscape of the potential target segment, in terms of changes in technology, socio-cultural, economy, political-legal, and market, a company is able to assess the growth potential of the segment.

Decades ago, mobile phones and smartphones were made for customers in the upper-middle income to affluent segments. Some of the big players like Samsung, Apple, LG, and Sony dominate this market segment. After 2010, the phenomenon called "The Rise of the Cheap Smartphone" emerged, when mostly Chinese smartphone manufacturers, such as Huawei, Xiaomi, and Oppo, launched smartphone products combining low prices with great build quality and features in order to serve the emerging lower to middle income segment in Asia. The rise of the middle class, due to rapid economic growth in many Asian countries, provides a huge market segment for such phones.

- **Company's Competitive Advantage**

  Another criterion in determining the target segment to select is based on the company's competitive advantage. This is to assess whether or not the company has sufficient strength and expertise to capture and dominate the chosen market segment. Segmentation and targeting are complementary actions in determining the company's positioning, which is the promise by a company to its target market. Subsequently, positioning must be supported with differentiation to provide the company with its competitive advantage(s). Differentiation reflects a company's strength and capability to deliver a unique value that is promised to the customers. As such, a company must choose the target segment(s), which it has the capabilities and resources to serve well, in order to avoid any "overpromise-underdeliver" situation. It must also analyse whether serving the chosen market segment is in line with the company's long-term objectives.

- **Segment's Competitive Situation**

  In determining the target market to select, the company must assess the level of competitiveness in the target segment. This will have an impact on how attractive the segment is. Michael Porter's Five Forces model can be employed in assessing the competitive situation, by evaluating the intensity of segment rivalry, potential new entrants, the industry or segment's barriers to entry, the existence of substitute products, the presence of complementary products and buyer and supplier bargaining power.

  Based on the above four criteria, a company can determine whether there is a good fit between the target market and its resources and goals.

## MARKETING TACTIC — "WINNING THE MARKET SHARE"

*"I consider Segmentation, Targeting and Positioning (STP) as the three elements of strategy, and I consider Differentiation Marketing Mix and Selling (DMS) as the three elements of Tactics."*

**Hermawan Kartajaya**

The second component of the Nine Core Elements of Marketing is marketing tactic (Figure 12.3). Differentiation–marketing mix–selling (DMS) plays a critical role in winning the market share.

Differentiation is defined as the *core tactic* since it is the key for differentiating the company's offering in terms of content, context, and infrastructure. The second element, marketing mix, or the *creation tactic* is a crystallisation of the company's differentiation concept in the form of 4Ps — product, price, place, and promotion. These integrate the company's offer, logistics, and communications. The third element is selling, which is defined as the *capture tactic*. It is the element for generating cash flows for the company and integrating customers for a mutually satisfying relationship for both the short and long term.

Conceptually, differentiation is an integration of the offer's "Content, Context, and Infrastructure." Content is the core product offering, that is, "What to offer"; Context refers to the product delivery, packaging, ambience, and so on, that is, "How to offer" and infrastructure refers to the technology, people, facilities, and so on, that is, the enabling factors. Take for example the Xiao Long Baos sold by Din Tai Fung, a famous Taiwanese restaurant chain. The Xiao Long Baos, or the meat buns,

Figure 12.3. Marketing Tactic

represents the "Content," or the core product offering of the franchise. The way the steaming hot buns are packaged in bamboo baskets and delivered by serving staff dressed in white uniform from top to toe, represent the "Context". The skilled staff who prepare these buns represent the "enablers".

## MARKETING MIX: INTEGRATING YOUR OFFER AND ACCESS

After differentiation that is mentioned earlier, the marketing mix is the second element of the marketing tactic. Initially introduced by Jerome McCarthy, the marketing mix elements comprise the 4Ps (Product, Price, Place, and Promotion). Some may, especially in earlier days, consider the 4Ps as what marketing is all about. To MarkPlus, the marketing mix is only one element of tactic. It is only the tip of the iceberg, that is, the parts that are arguably the most visible to the customers and competitors. Marketing mix is really about "integrating a company's *offers* and *access*" (Figure 12.4). The company's offerings, which consists of product and price, must be well integrated with access, which consists of place or distribution channel and with promotion or the communication media that connects the company with its customers and vice versa.

> "*Product is the most important component; that's why Product comes first. After that, the product must be properly valued through, Price, which comes second. The product, with the price that is set, is delivered through the right Place, and finally, all the three components are communicated through Promotion.*"
>
> **Hermawan Kartajaya**

The most tangible aspect of the marketing tactic is product. The product offer is a critical component of value that the company offers to its customers. Product here can mean goods or services or a combination of both. As the company has decided who to target, the product that is offered must fit with the target customers' needs and wants. A company's product should be part of its differentiation that supports its positioning or promise to its customers. Products can be divided into three levels: core products, actual products, and augmented products (Figure 12.5).

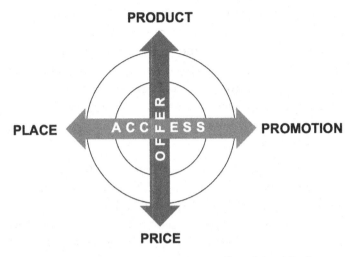

Figure 12.4. Two Dimensions of Marketing Mix: Offer and Access Product

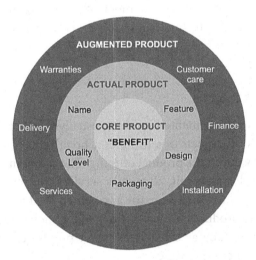

Figure 12.5. Three Levels of Product

- **Core Product**

The core product is actually the principal benefit that is offered to customers. While the product itself can be tangible, the benefit is usually intangible. For example, the core product of any car is the transportation convenience that it offers, since it enables its customer to move from a place to another more easily; another example of a core benefit of a car is time-saving since its customers can use it to cut the travel time from one place to another compared to walking. The core product may be the same for one product category; what actually differs one product from another is the actual and augmented product. The core product or core benefit can be identified by asking a simple question: "why do customers buy this product?"

- **Actual Product**

  The second level, actual product, is the tangible aspect of a product or the physical form of the product itself. This includes the features and design of the product. The actual product could be its size, weight, colour, packaging, features, design, quality, and so on. Returning to the car example, the actual product consists of the design and features of a car, including the car's dimensions, colour, exterior design, interior design, sound system, number of seats, engine capacity, fuel efficiency, built-in technologies such as parking sensor, voice command, and so on. The actual product is often the most visible element of a product.

- **Augmented Product**

  The third level, augmented product, usually refers to the intangible or nonphysical aspects of a product. Though intangible, it can add significant value to the product offering. The augmented product can comprise delivery, credit, after-sales services, warranty, installation, and so on. In the case of a car, the augmented product is the warranty given by the producer or dealer, financing options, additional after-sales services such as car delivery after purchase, or free routine service for a period of time.

## Price

A product needs to be valued in an appropriate way so that it becomes an integrated offering for the customers. Setting prices for a product can make or break a company. In order for it to be formulated in the right way, again, it must fit with the company's segmentation, targeting, and positioning. Setting a price that is too high may cause customers not to buy our products because of insufficient buying power or competitors have a more attractive offer. It could also lead to customers having a high expectation, which can undermine our brand if our product cannot deliver the expected value. Setting the price too low may not only impact our company's profits but could be perceived by the customers as a cheap product with its associate doubts about the product's quality. In determining the right price, there are various considerations a company must account for. With reference to the 4C model, the price can be set, taking into account — company, competitor, customer, and change.

- **Company: Cost-Based Pricing**

  The company can choose to set the price based on how much it costs to make and sell the goods or services, and then add the percentage to achieve the desired margin. In cost-based pricing, there are the "price floor" or the minimum level of the product's selling price would still generate profit for the company, and "price ceiling" or the maximum level of the selling price to avoid customers not being able to afford the company's products. Companies that produce mass products, such as food, textiles, and materials, often adopt the cost-based pricing approach.

- **Competitor: Competition-Based Pricing**

  Competition-based pricing uses competitor's selling price as a benchmark for the company's pricing. After benchmarking, the company may set the product at a price above (premium pricing), or below (discount pricing) that of its competitors. Apart from a head-to-head competition, this type of pricing is often used to differentiate the perception of a product compared to its competitors'. Premium pricing may be used to create a perception that the product possesses higher quality. On the other hand, the use of discount pricing may create a perception that the product is more worthwhile to buy. If a company decides to match the price of their product to the competitor's price, then it eliminates price as a consideration factor for customers. In this case, the product's competitiveness will be determined by other aspects, such as the quality of the product itself, promotional efforts, convenience, and so on.

- **Customer: Value-Based Pricing**

  The third option, value-based pricing, set prices based on the customer's perceived value of a product. Value-based pricing is defined as customer-oriented pricing because the price is set based on how much the customer believes a product is worth. In determining the price based on the customer's perception, a company cannot directly ask, "How much do you want to pay for this product?" since it will be misleading and difficult to answer. Instead, according to Van Westendorp's price sensitivity meter, the company can ask four questions to determine price sensitivity:

  - "At what price would you consider this product to be so inexpensive that you would have doubts about its quality?" (very cheap)
  - "At what price would you still feel this product is inexpensive yet have no doubts as to its quality?" (cheap)
  - "At what price would you begin to feel this product is expensive but still worth buying because of its quality?" (expensive)
  - "At what price would you feel that the product is so expensive that regardless of its quality, it is not worth buying?" (very expensive)

  By asking these questions, the company can determine the points of marginal cheapness and marginal expensiveness, and then calculate the optimum price point.

**Change: Dynamic Pricing**

The final approach that can be used to determine price is by referring to one of the elements of change in the 4Cs model, and that is economy. This relates to the supply and demand of things. In the era of advanced technology, every transaction that happens anywhere in the world can be monitored. Through the internet, it is able to track, in real time, the level of demand for a particular product and the supply. The method is an example of looking at the supply–demand curve, in determining a product's price. When the demand for a product is relatively high, and the supply is decreasing, the price of a product can go up in real time (Figure 12.6). The same thing happens when demand is low; the price can go

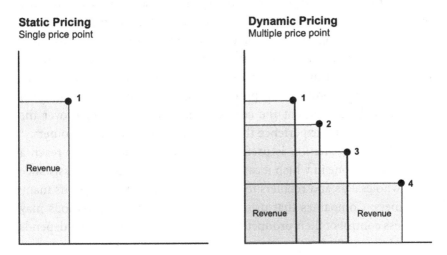

Figure 12.6. Static Pricing versus Dynamic Pricing

down instantly to attract buyers. As an example, ticketing companies, which sell their product online, usually use this method. Dynamic pricing may result in different purchase prices for customers, but from the company's perspective, it is an act of maximising revenue.

## Place

The third component of marketing mix is *place*; this is about where and how the company's product can be purchased. For example, for property developers, a place may refer to the location in which the property is built. It can also refer to the means in which a product can be obtained by the customers, that is, how a product can be, directly or indirectly, transferred from a company to its customers. The transfer process could be done through a single or multiple intermediaries such as distributors, wholesalers, retailers, agents, or the marketplace. For consumer goods companies, place can therefore mean the distribution channel used to move a product from the principal to the end consumer — through distributors, traditional and modern retailers, as well as an e-commerce platform. As for financial services industry, for example, in life insurance, the distribution of its product and service is done by agents.

Hence, this component of the marketing mix relates to *access*, in other words, how the customer can get hold of or gain access to the product.

In determining the type of distribution to undertake, two main options are available for a company — whether it wants to distribute the product directly or indirectly. In direct distribution, the manufacturer or producer directly provides the product to the customers. An advantage of direct distribution is that the company has complete control over the product, price, and experience that it wants to create for its customers.

Indirect distribution is useful for companies who want to reach a broad market, one in which it cannot cover alone, and it needs assistance from wholesalers and retailers to make the product available to its many customers. Companies that use the indirect distribution methods may have less control of their product and price in the market since it depends on the intermediaries.

Different products may require different distribution strategies. In general, there are three types of distribution strategies:

- **Intensive Distribution**

  This strategy involves distributing products as widely as possible, reaching as many customers as the company can, and it usually uses the indirect method. The objective of this distribution strategy is to ensure maximum availability of the product to the market. In general, intensive distribution is effective in distributing relatively low-priced products such as fast-moving consumer goods, or items that are stocked in large numbers such as basic supplies.

- **Selective Distribution**

  With this strategy, products are sold in a number of selected outlets. This strategy fits products with a higher price that still need to be made widely available to the market. Examples products which suit this type of distribution include electronic appliances, mobile phones, and computers.

- **Exclusive Distribution**

  This distribution strategy's objective is to emphasise the exclusivity of a product. Usually, the type of products sold using this type of distribution are products that fetch a relatively high price such as, for example, cars. Car manufacturers distribute their products through their own dealers, although some car dealers may be owned by third parties. Manufacturers will strive to ensure that their product's quality is good, the price set is reasonable, and the customer experience is satisfying, through strict terms and conditions for the third parties.

The place or distribution strategy selected by a company must fit the positioning of the brand. If a brand positions itself as a premium brand, selective or exclusive distribution is suitable since the company has full control of its product in the market. Meanwhile, for a brand that is positioned and targeted to serve the mass market, the company may select intensive distribution to ensure the easy access and availability of the product.

**Promotion**

After making the product available and accessible to the target market, the next challenge is to make sure the target market knows about the product. This is the role of the fourth marketing mix component, *promotion*.

Promotion includes all the activities that the company undertakes to communicate and promote its product and brand to the target market. Promotion plays an essential part in the marketing tactic, as it acts as an information bridge between a company and its customers. In a competitive market, the product may not be easily sold simply due to a favorable price difference. Frequently, customers buy a certain product because of various benefits and it is through the function of promotion that such benefits are well conveyed to potential customers.

There are four main steps in designing a promotion plan:

- **Determine Target Audience**

  The same principles for marketing strategy, which is to start by defining and selecting the target market, can be adopted for promotion. The company will first need to determine its target audience using geographic, demographic, psychographic, and behavioural factors.

This first step is crucial since it helps the company to determine what media the company should select and the relevant message they should adopt.

- **Set Promotion Objective**

The objective of a promotion activity can be categorised based on the 5A customer path, as further discussed in Chapter 15, which are *Aware* (to make the target audience know about your product or brand), *Appeal* (to attract the target audience to your product or brand), *Ask* (to make the target audience want to find out more information about your product or brand), *Act* (to make the target audience perform the purchase transaction), and *Advocate* (to make the target audience willing to recommend your product or brand to their peers).

- **Select Media and Content**

After the promotion objective has been set, the company can choose the suitable media to fulfill the predetermined objectives. In general, the promotion media can be categorised into two main groups, Above the Line (ATL) media and Below the Line (BTL) media (Figure 12.7).

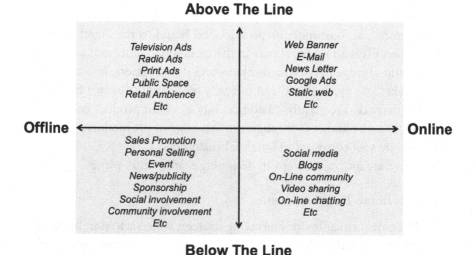

Figure 12.7. Above the Line, Below the Line, Offline, and Online Media

ATL is suitable to reach a wide range of audiences and to raise awareness of a brand or product, while BTL is more suitable for audiences that are more targeted, either geographically, demographically, or by interest. BTL can be used to increase the sales conversion rate.

ATL offline media includes television, radio, print media, out-of-home (OOH), and the use of public spaces and retail malls. ATL online channels include web banner, e-mail, newsletter, Google ads, and static web.

On the other hand, BTL offline media includes sales promotion, personal selling, event, news or publicity, sponsorship, social involvement, and community involvement. BTL online channels included the social media, blogs, online communities, video-sharing platforms, and online chatting platform.

Before selecting the media, the company also needs to ensure that the media fits with the promotion objective (*aware, appeal, ask, act,* and *advocate*). For example, if the company wants to focus on creating awareness, then it could focus on ATL media such as television, radio, and billboards. If the company wants to generate *appeal* to its product or brand, it can continue to use ATL media, with a combination of BTL media such as retail support and creating product demonstration events. To increase *ask,* the company can focus on creating a conversation with customers, which online media such as social media platforms serve the best. In order to improve *act,* the company can focus on promotion activities that trigger impulse buying, such as placing promotion materials in point-of-sales such as retailers' shelves and e-commerce platforms. For *advocacy,* the company can invest in referral programs and community marketing.

The media that is selected by the company will have an impact on the promotion content. The content can be in various forms such as photos, graphic images, short advertisement video clips, running texts, live publications, bumpers etc.

- **Plan the Promotion Roadmap and Budget Allocation**

The last step in establishing the promotion strategy is to plan the roadmap of a series of promotion activities that need to be carried out by a company. A company has to identify the right momentum to perform its promotional activities. The company can choose whether it wants to ride on existing momentums such as deploying promotion activities on national or international occasions, holiday seasons, and New Year, or whether it wants to create its own momentum, such as the company's anniversary. Finally, the company needs to ensure that they have a sufficient budget to implement the promotion activities that have been planned.

## SELLING: INTEGRATING THE RELATIONSHIPS BETWEEN THE COMPANY AND ITS CUSTOMERS

The third component of the marketing tactic, and the sixth element of the 9 Core Elements of Marketing, is selling. Many define *selling* too narrowly as limited to selling activities on a short-term basis. Selling goes beyond this. It is also about creating a long-term relationship with customers, through the company's goods and services. It is a tactic that integrates the relationships between the company and its customers. Hermawan defines *selling* as a *capture tactic* that generates financial returns.

> *"Selling is often mistaken as Marketing. For me it is very clear; selling is a part of marketing. Selling is in the tactic dimension of marketing. Therefore, its existence cannot be separated from the three elements of strategy. It also cannot be separated from differentiation and marketing mix."*
>
> **Hermawan Kartajaya**

Salespeople are often asked to perform sales activities, armed only with product knowledge and a price list. They need to understand the target segment so that their selling efforts can be more effective. In offering products or services, salespeople must understand the product's positioning, along with its differentiation, and marketing mix.

There are three levels of selling — *feature selling, benefit selling*, and *solution selling.*

- **Feature Selling**

  The first and the most basic approach of selling is feature selling, where selling efforts are centered on the product itself. Feature selling is used to present product features, showcasing what the company's product can do compared to its competitors. Hence, they highly rely on product knowledge.

- **Benefit Selling**

  The second approach is in direct contrast to feature selling; it is centered on the customers. Instead of only presenting "what the product can do," this approach emphasises "what can the product do for the customers" or the benefits that are bought to the customers through the product.

- **Solution Selling**

  Benefits do not always provide solutions to customers. Therefore, the company must assure its customers that it understands their problems, and offer the right solution for them. This type of selling focuses not just on the short-term but also on building long-term and valuable relationships between the company and its customers.

The ultimate goal of selling is to build a relationship and convert your customers not only to become loyalists but to also become advocates who willingly give positive recommendations to their peers, friends, and relatives. Back in 1993, many salespeople in Indonesia did not believe that sales could reach the solution-selling level. Back then, the paradigm of selling was still confined to short-term and transaction-oriented selling. At that time, Hermawan said, "Just wait and see, starting from 2000 and beyond, the way of selling will be solution selling." It eventually came true and can be seen in the practice of many companies today.

### MARKETING VALUE — "WINNING THE HEART SHARE"

*"At that time, I was also very inspired by a One Week Workshop I attended at the Wharton School entitled, 'Reengineering Process for Customer Satisfaction.' Through this workshop, I became aware of, and appreciate, the 'correlation' between process and service. If both are done well, it will lead to strong Brand Equity!"*

**Hermawan Kartajaya**

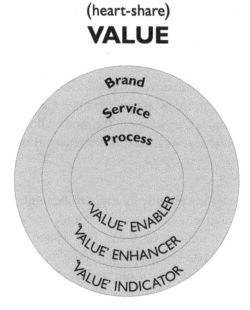

Figure 12.8. Marketing Value

Apart from "strategy" and "tactic," "value" is the third and the last component of the marketing architecture, which consists of three subelements: brand–service–process (BSP), which can enable the company to win the customer's heart share (Figure 12.8). These three elements are strongly related to brand management. Brand is the *value indicator* of a company that enables the company to avoid the commodity trap. Service is the *value enhancer*, and companies should endeavor to meet or even exceed the needs, wants, and expectations of the customers. The last element of marketing value is process or the *value enabler* of a company. Good internal and external processes enable the company to deliver value to its customers and to keep its promise.

## SERVICE: AVOID THE BUSINESS-CATEGORY TRAP

Service itself is not only about after-sales, during-sales, or before-sales services. It is also not merely about a customer service hotline for a company. Often, if a company has already performed that kind of service, they consider their job in providing service to customers done. Service must be seen as a *value enhancer*, a paradigm of a company to create lasting value for customers through products and services.

> *"For me, Service needs to be in the very soul of a company. Service is an attitude to stay at and win the competition in the future. Service is a strategy to avoid the business-category trap."*
>
> **Hermawan Kartajaya**

To be able to set itself free from the business-category trap, your company needs to be a *service business*. Service is with a capital "S" meaning, a company must be fully committed to provide optimum services to their customers. Whether the company's business is restaurants, food, or car manufacturing, it must be a service business. "Why does a company needs to be a service business?"

- **Service is a Solution**

  A company needs to be able to provide real solutions to customer needs. Sometimes, customers may not always show or say what they need. Any company needs to be sensitive and be able to identify the customer's anxieties and desires. Therefore, the right service rendered can become a solution for the customer and creates customer satisfaction and loyalty.

  Consumer goods companies, such as GlaxoSmithKline (GSK), may not be perceived as a company that provides service to its customers. GSK does! It provides service in the form of a solution to its customers who have sensitive teeth. They offer Sensodyne, a toothpaste for customers with sensitive teeth that could build a protective layer over vulnerable areas of their teeth, which is proven to minimise and relieve the pain of sensitivity. Many variants of Sensodyne also provide other benefits for customers such as freshening breath, helping to control plaque, helping to maintain teeth whiteness, and helping to maintain healthy gums. More than just a product, GSK offers a solution for their customers so that they are able to consume foods and beverages that they might not have been able to before.

- **Service as a Memorable Experience**

A memorable experience is a part of emotional benefit offered to the customers. As mentioned in Chapter 11 it has a powerful influence on how a customer perceives the value of a product or service offered by a company. A company can offer not only functional benefits to its customers but by using good service, a company can create a long-lasting and memorable experience for its customers. In short, great service creates a memorable experience.

Speaking of memorable experiences, Hermawan himself had one unforgettable experience on one of his Singapore Airlines (SQ) flights:

*"I was in the middle of a flight in Singapore Airlines, a stewardess accidentally spilled some tea on my suits. It was no problem for me, but it surprised me that the stewardess deeply apologised to me. It was not the end, after the plane landed; a man introduced himself to me as 'chief purser' of the flight, and approached me. He then apologised to me just like the stewardess. After that, he gave me a piece of paper that turned out to be a laundry voucher, and said that I could use that voucher as soon as I arrived."*

That is an example of a WOW service experience that creates a memorable experience for the customers because it connects with customers on an emotional level.

## PROCESS: AVOID THE FUNCTION-ORIENTATION TRAP

Process refers to the process of creating customer value. It is called the *value enabler* since the effectiveness and efficiency of existing processes in the company — starting from raw material procurement, production or manufacturing process, to delivery of the product or service to customers — determines the quality of the product, the cost incurred by the company, as well as the speed of the product or service delivery. How successful a process is can be measured by three keywords, namely, quality, cost, and delivery (QCD). The ability of a company to create value to its customers and differentiate itself from its competitors is determined by how capable a company is in maintaining the quality, cost, and delivery of its offering.

> *"In fact, Philip Kotler once asked me in Moscow in 1998, why is process included in marketing? My answer is that it is good to have the right strategies and tactics to have real value creation. A strong brand, for me, can be created with an excellent service mindset throughout the company. But, this would be useless, if the process 'isn't in line with Service delivery and Brand."*
>
> **Hermawan Kartajaya**

## Quality

In the context of quality, *process* is about how a company is able to establish a system, which in the end can give added quality value to its customers. Therefore, a company needs to pay close attention to its supply chain, starting from the production process from raw material all the way to the finished goods stage. Furthermore, a good *process* requires a company to be *the captain of the supply chain process*. A strong and solid commitment from a company is needed to manage their processes in a way that would strengthen the value-creating activities and reduce or eliminate value-eroding activities within the company.

## Cost

In the context of cost, a company needs to develop a process that can increase efficiency, while providing the best possible quality for the customers. A company may want to differentiate from its competitors by delivering a superior product, but it must also take costs into account because at the end, profitability is also an important pillar that supports the company's sustainability.

## Delivery

In the context of delivery, a company needs to deliver the right products or services at the right time, in the right condition and to the right venue, to ensure their customers' satisfaction. Such a delivery process will create more value for the customers.

In addition, the *process* element requires a company to be *the hub of a network organisation*. A company needs to build good relationships with other organisations, which can result in higher value add for its customers. This strategy is commonly referred to as strategic alliances. The partnering organisations may be the company's suppliers, customers, or even competitors. Most importantly is whether the collaboration can materialise and add value to the company's offerings. Benchmarking, reengineering, outsourcing, and mergers and acquisitions (M&A) are all examples of strategic actions for improving processes.

### References:

Kotler, P, et al. (2003). *Rethinking Marketing: Sustainable Marketing Enterprise in Asia.* Singapore: Prentice-Hall.

# CHAPTER 13

# FROM FUNDAMENTAL MARKETING TO NEW WAVE MARKETING

In the 21st century, technology is increasingly more pervasive, providing more opportunities, to participate, interact, and collaborate. This has lead to more connected networks. What we have seen, experienced, and explored about marketing has changed and shifted over the past 20 years. Marketing has indeed continued to transform. Web 2.0 has changed the structure of the business environment leading to the most remarkable changes in marketing. The impact of the internet and Web 2.0 has indeed made every aspect of the marketing world change entirely as human beings become more humane, more interactive, more participative, and more social.

Hermawan Kartajaya asserts that technology should not turn human beings into robots. In contrast, it should make human beings more wholesome through their emotions, aspirations, feelings, and soul. Marketing should adapt by connecting to the customer's mind, feelings, and soul. The practice of vertical, top-down marketing from companies to customers is no longer relevant in this era. Marketing is entering a new world order that transforms it to become more connected and horizontal — welcome to "New Wave Marketing."

In Chapter 12, Hermawan has stated that marketing has come down to the simple model of the strategy-tactic-value (STV) triangle, which represents the fundamental Nine Core Elements of Marketing.

However, a lot has changed over the past two decades, in particular, digital technology, which has transformed the business landscape. Likewise, marketing should transform and this leads to the birth of what

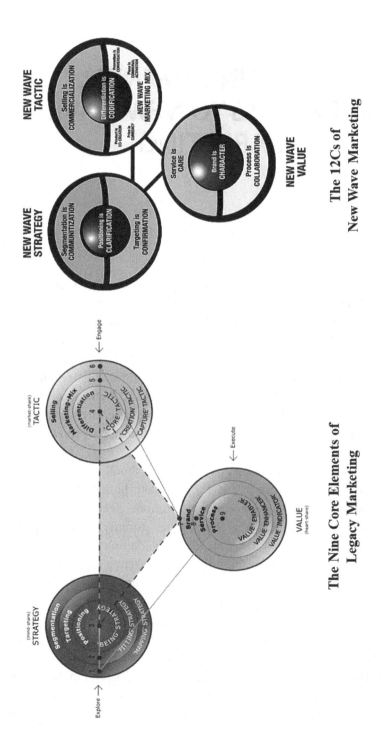

Figure 13.1. Fundamental Marketing and New Wave Marketing

is called the "12Cs of New Wave Marketing," which represents a more horizontal and connected version of the Nine Core Elements of Fundamental Marketing. It is the same, simple STV triangle, but in the context of a more connected world (Figure 13.1).

*"Welcome to the new world marketing order!"*
**Hermawan Kartajaya**

## NEW WAVE MARKETING STRATEGY

In these sections, we will see how the horizontal business landscape in the New Wave era triggers shifts in marketing including the first three elements of marketing to win the customer's mind share through segmentation, targeting, and positioning.

## FROM SEGMENTATION TO COMMUNITISATION

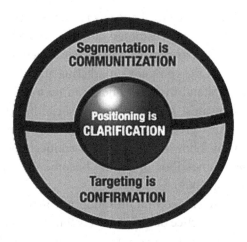

Figure 13.2. New Wave Marketing Strategy

According to traditional marketing, where a company adopts the vertical approach to commissioning, segmentation is seen as a process to explore business opportunities or observing the market creatively by grouping the market into clusters or segments. As explained before, the basis for grouping or segmentation could be one or more static or dynamic attributes or a combination of both attributes. These are done so that segmentation can help companies to manage diversity within a market and aid them in identifying which segments are worth engaging in.

Hermawan said that segmentation is a "vertical" marketing practice because it is done based on a top-down approach, from the company to its customers. The criteria or attributes used in defining the market segment are determined by the company and not based on customers' initiatives. In the New Wave era where everything becomes horizontal, customers need to be considered as subjects or persons rather than merely as objects which the company could exploit to gain market share. Furthermore, technology advancement has shifted the behaviour of customers, where they become more social and less individual. Such circumstances transformed customers' purchase decisions from initially relying only on their own thoughts and considerations into actively taking cues from the people around them in both the physical and virtual environments.

Because of the changing marketing environment, the process of segmentation needs to be revamped. There are two things that need to be considered by marketers and companies. First, the company must be able to recognise the urgent need to change its marketing approach from vertical to horizontal by placing customers at the same level as the company. Instead of being treated as passive objects, customers need to be more actively involved with the company's marketing activities. Second, companies should understand that customers can no longer be regarded as only individuals but must be recognised as social beings who relate to each other and have a greater sense of community. The key to understanding people is by following the bonds or connections between them; therefore, these connections need to become our primary focus (Christakis & Fowler, 2009).

In the New Wave era, communitisation is a new alternative to segmentation. This is a practice of observing customers as a group of people who care for each other, have common purposes, and share the same values and identity. Customer communities can be formed *by design*, that is, by the company's initiative, and *by default*, that is, organically formed by customers' actions. The most crucial thing for communitisation is to ensure the active contribution and involvement of customers as a community to the company's business strategy, and not just become a passive entity in receiving public relations or sponsorship actions. It sums up why communitisation is a part of marketing strategy, not just a tactic.

Speaking of community, one successful example of communitisation is an American motorcycle brand, Harley-Davidson. The company builds its strategy around its customers' community, namely the Harley Owners Group (HOG). This strategy has proven to "save" the company from extinction in 1983. As a result, 25 years later, the company managed to become a top-five global brand valued at US$7.8 Billion. Beyond just changing its marketing programs, Harley-Davidson retooled every aspect of its organisation and reformulated its competitive strategy and business model around a brand community philosophy.

**Segmentation vs. Communitisation**

At a glance, segmentation and communitisation may look similar, because, in practice, both involve dealing with a group of customers with specific characteristics (Table 13.1). Still, there are core differences between the two approaches.

The first and the primary difference is that in segmentation, customers are seen as individuals, whereas in communitisation, customers are seen as social beings and the focus is their relationships with others.

In segmentation, customers are segmented based on static attributes such as geographic and demographic, and dynamic attributes such as psychographic, and behaviour or some combinations. These attributes

**Table 13.1: Segmentation vs. Communitisation**

|  | SEGMENTATION | COMMUNITISATION |
|---|---|---|
| **Paradigm** | Customer as an individual | Customer as a social creature |
| **Factors/ Variable** | Geography, demography, psychography, behaviour | Purpose, values, identity |
| **Company- Customer Relationship** | *Vertical*: customer as passive target segment | *Horizontal*: customers as active community member |
| **Objective** | Customers mapping based on similarity | Community potential identification based on cohesivity and influence |

belong to each individual without the relationships with others. Hence, segments are merely a collection of individuals grouped by specific criteria. On the contrary, communities have purposes, values, and identity (PVI) which bind the members in it — this is the second difference.

Third, as mentioned before, communitisation places customers at the same level with the company, making it the first step of encouraging customers' involvement in business strategies. As for segmentation, it uses a vertical approach and treats customers as passive objects to be categorised and targeted.

Finally, in terms of objective, segmentation's goal is to map customers with similar characteristics so that the segment can be given a particular treatment. The indicator used is merely the similarity of each member of the segment. In communitisation, the objective of a company is to work together with the customers that have the same PVI with the company.

The indicators used are not only the homogeneity among customers but also the extent of the attachment among the community members and the company, as well as the influence of the community on the behaviour of each of its members.

*"Segmentation is communitisation. Marketers should not only divide customers through segmentation. Most importantly, marketers must be able to dive deep into communities, and find the right one to be asked to collaborate horizontally and strategically."*

**Hermawan Kartajaya**

### Community Modelling

Before performing communitisation, marketers and companies must understand the general models of a community that may be formed. A marketing professor, Susan Fournier, mentioned that a community could take the form of *pools*, *hubs*, and *webs*.

- **Pools**

  The most organic and natural form that a community can take is the form of a *pool*. This model of community is formed through shared values and interests, or by the same activities among its members.

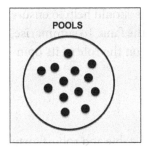 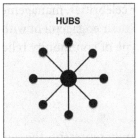 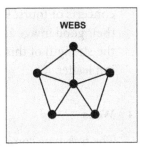

Figure 13.3. Community Affiliation
Source: Fournier & Lee (2009)

This type of community is easily formed either by design or by default. However, the relationship among its members is the weakest, Take for example the community of Apple enthusiasts. The members are only united by the same interest of using Apple products, more than any other brand. Companies that can identify the existence of *pools* in their customers may nurture the community to form a more powerful structure such as *hubs* or *webs*.

- **Hubs**

The second type of community is the *hub*. This type of community is built based on the admiration of its members towards a particular individual or group. This type of community is more potent than *pools* for company involvement, but its weakness is its reliance on a particular figure or icon. Therefore, once the personality of the figure changes from its original nature or no longer exists, the community may fall. An example is a fan club of groups such as sports groups (football, basketball, baseball, etc.) and musical groups (bands, choirs, etc.), or celebrities (actors and actresses, models, comedians, key opinion leaders, brand ambassadors, etc.).

Fans gather together because of their admiration toward the whole group or a certain member of the group. To maintain the strength of this type of community, the company must nurture the appeal of the community icon(s). In the case of sports groups, the management must ensure an admirable performance of the team during championships. For musical groups, management's primary task is to incentivise the group to keep producing its music and performing in concerts or tours. For celebrities, management should help to ensure their good image and their engagement with the fans. To summarise, the strength of this type of community relies on the role of its opinion leader.

- **Webs**

The *web*-type community represents the most stable and robust form of a community because it relies on each member's connections and interactions with one another. *Webs* could be in the form of offline and online communities. An excellent example of offline *web* communities is automotive communities.

Many automobile brands have their "lover" communities. Even when the brand no longer produces a certain type of vehicle, which has become a common "love" interest among its community members, the community would continue to exist. A community of Land Rover 90 lovers gathered not only because of its members' admiration toward the car, but the community could sustain itself because of the relationships among its members. They would still pursue mainly outdoor activities together such as touring and off-road adventures; similar to what HOG of Harley-Davidson motorcycles, do.

As for online communities shaped as *webs*, they tend to be also very much engaged through the social media. Hence, online *web* communities such as Facebook and LinkedIn emerge. Opinion leaders are indeed essential in building strong communities. Still, communities are the strongest when everyone plays a role. The role of a company is to enable the community members to be engaged within the community, by providing support and resources.

## FROM TARGETING TO CONFIRMATION

In fundamental marketing, segmentation is a common practice of mapping market segments based on similar characteristics. After the segments are identified, the next step is to perform an examination and evaluation of the segment to assess whether it is worth serving. This is termed "targeting," which is seen as a way to allocate the company's scarce resources effectively.

In practice, there are four criteria that companies use to evaluate and determine which segment to target. The first criterion is the size of a segment. A company must make sure that the segment is large enough to be served that it would bring income for the company. Second is the growth rate of the segment. A segment might be small, but if the segment has potentially significant growth, it may be worthwhile to target. The third criterion is that targeting must be based on the company's competitive advantage. This is a means to measure whether the company possesses sufficient capabilities to dominate or gain an acceptable market share. Finally, the targeted segment must be assessed based on its competitive situation, which, in the end, affects the attractiveness of a segment.

Hermawan often used the above criteria to show that the practice of targeting is no longer relevant in today's New Wave era. First, because this is done with a top-down or vertical approach by the company without considering whether the customers want to be targetted. Second, the company's initial step in the New Wave era is not merely segmenting or dividing the market into groups (segmenting) but practicing communitisation. It means the company should explore further into which community is suitable to be asked to collaborate with the company. This calls for segmentation to be turned into communitisation. Consequently, targeting should also become confirmation.

## Criteria in Confirming the Community

Along with the practice of changing *targeting the segment* to become *confirming by the community,* the criteria used in confirming by the community also differ from the criteria for targeting. There are three main criteria for confirming by the community: *relevance, activity level,* and *number of community networks (NCNs).*

- **Relevance**

  Relevance would refer to the similarity of PVI between a community and the company's brand. For Harley-Davidson communities, the purpose of its members is to gather and find partners to undertake activities together. The values that unite its members are brotherhood and freedom. Their sense of shared identity is shown on their specially designed costumes that they are proud to wear, whether during community activities or during the members' daily activities.

- **Activity Level**

  As the criterion name suggests, *Activity Level* refers to how actively the community members engage with each other. Community activity could be in the form of offline and online activities. Offline activities would refer to events such as community gatherings, whereas online activities can be actively posting members' activities in the community's social media. The more active the community is, the better potential it carries.

- **Number of Community Networks (NCNs)**

  The last criterion is NCNs. It essentially refers to the reach of the community, meaning the number of networks currently owned by a community or potential network that could exist between a community with other communities or between the members of a community with members of another community.

Among the three criteria, the *relevance* between the community's brand or company's PVI is the most crucial. This is not to say that the *activity level* and *NCNs* are not important. They indeed are, but the level of importance may not be as significant as PVI *relevance*.

If a community has a lot of members and its members actively engage with each other, but turns out that the community does not possess the same PVI as the company, confirmation may not happen. In this circumstance, where a company finds it is too difficult to find a relevant community to collaborate with, the company may eventually form its community (*by design*) that reflects the company's PVI. In the end, it is not only about finding communities that suit the company's objective but to collaborate with communities that are willing to collaborate with the company (Figure 13.4).

### Confirmation is Beyond Permission

It was predicted long ago by marketing author and blogger Seth Godin (1999) that "interruption marketing" would eventually go extinct. In his

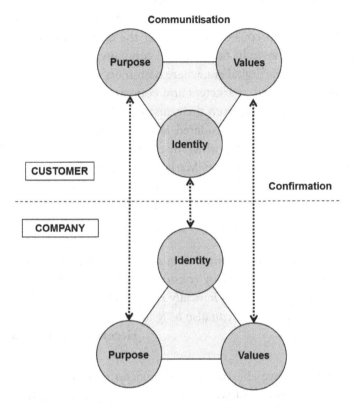

Figure 13.4. Communisation and Confirmation of PVI

book, *Permission Marketing,* the world is seen as rapidly changing and very much different from decades ago when customers still enjoyed being swarmed by tons of information (interruptions) created by marketers and companies. During the early emergence of television, there was a time when people were fascinated with almost all forms of advertising (interruptions) which offered products and services through visual commercials.

According to Godin, on average, a customer was targeted by roughly 3,000 messages a day, which no one would pay attention to all those messages. Considering this, it is no surprise that customers started to ignore the various promotions and marketing activities that they came across. Godin also stated that the biggest problem of mass advertising is the way it treats customers as "strangers" or "objects" rather than "friends."

Marketers would compete with each other to grab the customer's attention by "interrupting" them in any form, at any time, and anywhere. It was all done without considering whether the customers like or dislike and agree or disagree to be targeted by a company.

Nowadays, in the digital era, where customers are more educated and want to be understood, marketers and companies are struggling to get acceptance or permission from their customers, so that their marketing communications are not considered as interference. Therefore, Godin offered an alternative model, which he claimed to be more powerful and friendly one, called Permission Marketing. The concept is in contrast with "interruption marketing" where the company needs to ask for permission from their customers or community prior to conveying advertising messages.

> *"Asking for permission may not guarantee that the marketer is automatically accepted by consumers. Because through permission, marketers can basically request for attention, which can be approved, but can also be ignored."*
>
> **Hermawan Kartajaya**

In the New Wave era, company should do more than just permission-based marketing — it is confirmation-based marketing. In permission-based marketing, the company can only wait for the customers passively until the permission is granted, whereas in confirmation-based marketing, the company may be able to more actively indicate to the customer community, the commonalities that exist between them. This enhances the chances for the company to be well accepted by the community. The company needs to confirm not only its relevance of PVI with the community but also that it would be a "good friend" for the community. That is why Hermawan prefers to use the word "confirmation" and not "permission."

## FROM POSITIONING TO CLARIFICATION

In fundamental marketing, positioning refers to how a company builds credibility in the minds of its customers. By so doing, a company will end up in the customers' minds. In the New Wave era, the practice of positioning is no longer entirely relevant. It is clear that positioning is a company-driven practice, which is a one-way approach to the company's efforts in building up a certain perception about it in the customers' minds. In this new era, where the business landscape has become horizontal, and customers are positioned equal to the company, the company no longer holds a full control toward its brand in the mind of the customers.

In the era of sophistication, customers are more *informationalised* and *enlightened.* Hence, they may no longer perceive a brand, the way the company wants it to be perceived. Customers nowadays no longer entirely believe the vertical communications from the company. On the contrary, with the rise of social media platforms such as Facebook, Instagram, YouTube, and Twitter, customers tend to believe more the expressions made by fellow customers. Hence, the company can no longer just feed its positioning statements to the customers. The company's or brand's positioning statement will be shaped by external opinion that circulates within the customer community. The tagline that is communicated by the company may end up failing to establish the desired customer perception, if opinions surrounding the customers are contrarian.

Therefore, what a company has to do is no longer position its brand towards its target market, but to perform clarification together with and toward the community where it exists. By doing so, a company clarifies its brand persona or character toward the confirmed community.

In performing clarification, companies must be able to answer the questions of who they are and what is their reason for being, to the community. This is essential because, as mentioned, positioning could be formed by external opinions such as by customers, mass media, or even competitors.

## Maintaining Credibility in New Wave Era

Ex-Chief Global Marketing Officer of McDonald's Larry Light (2004) once made a controversial statement while speaking at an advertising industry conference. He said that in McDonald's, the practice of positioning had long been buried, as the practice of identifying and communicating brand positioning was no longer relevant to the current business landscape. He dramatically called upon, "the end of brand positioning as we know it."

Based on research conducted by various consulting firms including McKinsey & Co and Ernst & Young, it is said that 90% of branding failure is caused by the companies' mistakes in positioning its brands. Experts admitted that the mistakes are not due so much to the brand positioning efforts, but with the concept of positioning itself, which is no longer relevant.

McDonald's replaced the concept of positioning with a concept known as Brand Journalism. The concept would refer to the practice of tailoring different products and messages to different target recipients. It was built around the assumption that no single universal message could tell the whole multidimensional story of a mega-brand like McDonald's. The company believes that a brand could possess a different meaning for every individual. Therefore, McDonald's wants to create different perceptions of the firm among different groups of customers; children, teenagers, adults, and the elderly — even having different perceptions during breakfast, lunch, dinner, or during snack time. It sticks to the concept of sending messages via multiple channels to multiple audiences. What McDonald's did is comparable to the content marketing trends that are embraced by start-up companies nowadays — which focus on creating and delivering consistent but relevant content to their clearly defined audiences.

The practice explained above is clarification, which is an evolution of the concept of positioning with a more horizontal approach. There are three main principles of clarification that differentiates itself from positioning, as shown in Table 13.2.

- **Multidimensional Message**

  In positioning practice, the tagline serves as the positioning statement that is communicated through various media and marketing activities

**Table 13.2: Positioning vs. Clarification**

| POSITIONING | CLARIFICATION |
|---|---|
| Focus on penetrating single message | Involving multi-dimensional message |
| Company-oriented content | Customer-oriented content |
| One-way communication | Multiple-way communication |

to all target markets. The objective is to make the customers remember about the message that the company wants to build in the mind of its customers.

In clarification, the tagline only serves as the umbrella or the "cover story" which is later translated contextually to become more relevant to the confirmed community. McDonald's original campaign and tagline "I'm Lovin' It" appeared in over 100 countries in more than 20 languages with different meanings. In Azerbaijan, for example, the tagline literally translates to "See, this is the love." McDonald's does not mind changing the language to adapt to local markets but still emphasises the emotion of love. The company wants its customers to have their own reason to love the brand.

- **Customer-Oriented Content**

In positioning, the focus is to convince customers to use the company's products and services through their competitive edge, which are portrayed as *reasons-to-believe*. Some car manufacturers emphasise their products' engine performance and elegant design in their marketing. Some financial services institutions such as banks focus on excellent customer service in addition to the interest rates that they could offer.

Such approaches may not be entirely relevant anymore because it focuses on the company rather than the customers. In the New Wave era, customers are getting smarter, and they can access all the information they need using information media such as the brand's official website or even getting the information from a current user of the product or service. If they ignore the information that a company thinks is important to them, this may well mean that the company's idea of what its customers value is outdated or irrelevant.

On the contrary, clarification uses customer-oriented content to convince the confirmed community about the company's offerings. Often the content itself may not directly relate to the products or services offered by the company but could provide real benefits to customers. Car manufacturers could, for example, produce and distribute practical tips on taking care the vehicle body and engine maintenance by non-professionals, which many car owners are. Banks may create e-books or webinars on personal financial planning. The principle is to put ourselves in the customers' shoes and ask, "What do I want to know?"

A good example is Unilever's ice cream brand, Paddle Pop. The brand solidly builds the brand mascot's character, Paddle Pop Lion, and then uses the mascot as the main character in their entertainment content. Instead of creating ice cream commercials, Paddle Pop created an adventure video series titled Paddle Pop Adventures, which was released online on YouTube and through television in 30 countries. In addition, the brand also performed offline clarification in the form of Paddle Pop Adventures theme parks, competitions, and sponsorships. In markets where the Paddle Pop brand already existed, customer loyalty reached new heights. In Indonesia, the brand loyalty rose from 65% to 71%. In markets where Paddle Pop was newly launched, brand awareness hit 90%. In India, more than 1.2 million children joined the Paddle Pop Gaming League, and more than 5 million DVDs were redeemed via promotions across Southeast Asia. The program managed to increase Paddle Pop sales globally by 26% in 2011. Meanwhile, in the new markets, Paddle Pop sales grew even more strongly, by 43%.

- **Multiple-Way Communication**

In the past era, communications were done vertically by the company and customers are viewed as receivers of the communications materials. In the New Wave era, technology, particularly social media, enables customers to participate in company–customers communications — making it the real definition of communication, which is essentially a two-way interaction. Customers in their communities could participate in multiple-way communications by sharing their thoughts, stories, and even contents using social media platforms, in the form of comments, reviews, and conversations. This form of communication has played a role in influencing other customers' purchase decisions.

It is best if conversations between the company and its customers arise organically. Interesting content produced by companies will automatically attract customers to contribute to the conversation. On the contrary, companies could also trigger communications by "getting involved" in the social media, and "acting" like a person. Many big companies, such as Netflix, KFC, and Oreo, made use of their Twitter accounts to trigger conversations and advocacy among its followers. A website, Search Engine Journal, even made a list ranking the 12 Funniest Brands on Twitter, showing that interacting with followers on social media has already become the new normal for companies. This strategy makes your brand more entertaining for the communities and helps to position the brand to be on the same level as its customers.

> *"It is important for a brand to clarify its reasons for being in the customer community, as it is getting easier to obtain a blurred perception of a brand. By intensively performing clarification in the connected world, credibility in the New Wave era can be maintained!"*
>
> **Hermawan Kartajaya**

## NEW WAVE MARKETING TACTIC

In the following sub-chapters, we will see how developments in the New Wave era affect the second three elements of marketing, to win the market share through differentiation, marketing mix (product, price, place, promotion), and selling.

## FROM DIFFERENTIATION TO CODIFICATION

In fundamental marketing, as explained in the Nine Core Elements of Marketing chapter, we wrote that brand or company positioning needs to be supported by differentiation. Without a real point of differentiation, the brand might end up stuck in an *over-promise and under-deliver* situation. Hence, the brand would lose its integrity in the minds of its customers. Differentiation itself comprises three major aspects, namely: *content*, *context*, and *infrastructure*. Differentiation *content* would refer to what the company actually offers to its customers. *Context* refers to how the company delivers its offering, whereas *infrastructure* covers what enables the company to bring its offerings to reality, and get them delivered to the customers.

Figure 13.5. New Wave Tactic

In their attempts to avoid losing their brand standing, brands often spend too much time focusing on building not-so-authentic differentiation — merely to be able to stand out among the competition. In the New Wave era, technology has, however, transformed the relationships between a company and its customers to become more inclusive and horizontal and the position of the two to become increasingly aligned.

Nowadays, customers can easily access information regarding the company and determine which of the company's claims are true and which are not. In this age when it is getting easier for one company to copy or replicate another's offerings, authenticity would be more treasured by customers. A company's clarification must be supported by an authentic codification of the brand's DNA to help it maintain its brand integrity in this New Wave era (Figure 13.5). Once the customer community finds out that the company is not as genuine as it claims to be, there is a significant chance that the community would pull itself out from the company's stakeholder ecosystem.

Therefore, to create authentic uniqueness which supports clarification, the brand or company should be able to extend its brand DNA beyond the marketing department. The brand DNA should be the fundamental value of all employees throughout the company, and not only for those who interact with customers. Barlow and Stewart (2004) even stated that it should immerse in all essential processes within the company, including hiring, day-to-day working activities, leadership style, and performance appraisal. All these are needed in order that the codification of the brand DNA becomes the very core of, and throughout, the company. This codification is what a company needs as its customer communities will observe how authentic the product, brand, and the firm that they are collaborating with is.

The Body Shop and its sustainable business practices is an example of authentic brand DNA. They call their program "Enrich" and this resides not only in its marketing department but throughout the company. The Body Shop translates its brand DNA into three main pillars of their sustainability business practice focus: Enrich the Product, People, and Planet. "Enrich Our Products" refers to making environment-friendly products, which uses natural ingredients and are totally against animal testing, as well as reducing carbon footprints in its products and production process. "Enrich Our People" refers to the company's activities in giving back to communities such as helping local communities, and economically vulnerable people. The third practice, "Enrich Our Planet," refers to energy-saving practices, such as commitments in powering their outlets with renewable or carbon-balanced energy that minimises greenhouse gas emissions and reducing in-store energy use by 10%. Hence, when customer communities look at The Body Shop's business, they will find that the company is authentic both on the inside and on the outside.

**Codification of Brand DNA**

Differentiation in terms of *content*, *context*, and *infrastructure* can easily be copied by competitors, in particular, with technological advancement. Beyond differentiation, a company should possess a uniqueness that has been coded, so that it would be difficult for competitors to imitate. Codification itself takes a long time to show results. Therefore, it requires a serious commitment from all stakeholders in a company (Table 13.3).

**Table 13.3: Differentiation vs. Codification**

| DIFFERENTIATION | CODIFICATION |
|---|---|
| Brand differentiation is only the marketing department's concern | Brand DNA has penetrated the whole organisational culture |
| Brand differentiation is considered to be the domain of marketers | The brand DNA is understood and valued and provides meaning to all employees. |
| Brand differentiation is developed in isolation from the service and organisational culture | The brand DNA provides guidelines and context for all service deliveries and employee behaviour |
| Not all leadership practices are aligned with the brand differentiation | Leaders at all levels understand the brand DNA and reflect it in their behaviour |
| Recruitment is driven primarily by knowledge, skills, and experience without considering the candidate-brand fit. | Recruitment also takes into account the candidate's capacity to behave in line with the brand DNA |
| Performance management doesn't incorporate measurement of brand-aligned behaviour | Performance management measures congruence of employee behaviour with the brand DNA |

Codification as a practice immerses the brand DNA throughout the company. The brand DNA has to be well understood and practiced by every employee, and not just marketing department employees. As mentioned before, the purpose of brand DNA is not only to provide guidance in formulating marketing activities but also to act as the essence of the company's organisational culture. Therefore, it acts as a guide not only for marketing activities but also for service delivery and any other organisational practices such as human resources, supply chain, and finance department. Essentially, brand DNA guides the company's employee behaviour. If the codification of brand DNA is done successfully, then every employee will stand as a representative of the company's brand in each of his interaction with a customer. This level of commitment is the root of real authenticity, which attracts customers and is hard to be imitated by competitors. Therefore, it gives the company an upper hand in the competitive market.

In the New Wave era, the key for companies and brands to make customers fall in love with them is through meaningful and authentic customer experiences with every touchpoint of the organisation. Such touchpoints may not be limited only to employees who work in the sales, service, or marketing departments. This is why codification across the whole organisation is essential.

## The Codification Model

The codification of the brand DNA in a company is done by implementation through three layers of the codification model (Figure 13.6). The first and outermost layer is the most tangible aspect and the easiest to be executed. The next two layers represent somewhat intangible aspects but can be seen through the behaviour of the employees in a firm. These two layers require a longer time and more effort to be fully implemented.

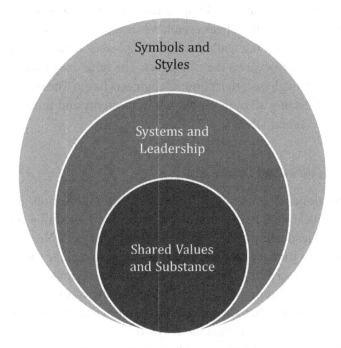

Figure 13.6. The Onion Model of Codification

**Level 1: Symbols and Styles**

The first level of codification is pretty much similar to the *context* aspect of differentiation. It deals with how the company would package its offerings to its customers. Symbols and styles refer to the physical and tangible representation of the brand DNA. They can take the form of artifacts installed within the company which are in tune with the brand DNA. They consist of visual aspects (office ambience including layout and color, decorations, uniform), audio aspects (jingle and background music), and even smell aspects (scent). Symbols and styles may seem to have a minor impact on brand DNA codification. Still, it turns out to be proven to help the employee understand and immerse the brand DNA better in their daily activities and make them practice the expected behaviours.

Take a look at Google's offices, for example. One of the factors making up Google's brand DNA is "innovativeness." Google has taken this philosophy into account when designing its workplace. The digital giant designed its offices with colorful ambiences, with beanbags in addition to regular desks and chairs, providing comfort for its employees while doing their jobs. A few of the offices even have treadmills installed so that the employees can work out while working. Employees are also free to scribble on the walls to express their thoughts. The result may look a little bit chaotic, but Google says that's how its engineers like it. These are Google's ways of immersing all of its employees in creativity and innovation and codifying its brand DNA.

**Level 2: Systems and Leadership**

Artifacts alone are not enough for brand DNA codification. It requires more efforts and more commitments, which are rooted in a company's system and leadership style. This is to allow the brand DNA to immerse in the organisational processes. Systems here also include the processes of employee recruiting, training, performance appraisal, and career advancement. The brand DNA provides guidance of the essence of skills and attitudes that are going to be developed within the company's employees. Leadership means the character of company leaders starting from the top until the bottom of the company's organisation chart who becomes role models for their subordinates and these must be based on the brand DNA.

Starbucks demonstrated a concrete example of brand DNA codification through its systems and leadership. This covers employee recruitment, immersion, communication, and incentives.

- **On-brand Recruiting**

  During its hiring process, Starbucks recruiters will follow a specific guideline, which helps them to filter the candidates who possess attitudes and behaviour that fits with the character of Starbucks as a brand. Hence, the "culture-fit" of a candidate with the company's organisational ecosystem is ensured.

- **Employee Immersion**

  New employees are obliged to attend a full-day paid course on "first impressions," whereas it is mandatory for new retail managers to join a 10-week training program on brand-focused management.

- **Employee Communications**

  Starbucks maintains its transparency from the chairman to managers through dialogue, using offline and online platforms, such as daily meetings or blogs and newsletters.

- **Employee Incentives**

  Starbucks' employees who work more than 20 hours are entitled to a "Starbucks Total Pay Package" consisting of financial and non-financial benefits.

By executing all four practices, Starbucks can shape the character of its employees, starting from filtering the candidates with the desired traits, and developing them through internal training and organisational processes so that they reflect the brand DNA.

**Level 3: Shared Values and Substance**

The third layer and the most difficult to implement within an organisation represents the intangible aspect and yet has a deep impact on codification. The second layer — systems and leadership — plays a role as a "hard control mechanism," which provides rewards for behaviour that is in line with brand DNA. The third layer — shared values and substance — plays its part as a "soft control mechanism" to employees' attitudes and behaviour.

An example of third layer implementation is from one of the best hospitals in the United States, namely the Mayo Clinic. The hospital is known for its "patient first" philosophy, which is the shared value among its medical and non-medical personnel. As a result of this, for example, if a nurse was faced with two choices — to return to their desk on time or deal with a 10-minute delay to fetch a wheelchair for a patient — they would pick the second choice without a thought, even without consulting a head nurse first.

> *"Competitors can emerge at any time with similar advantages as ours. Highlighting differentiation and excellence is no longer enough!*
> *What really needs to be highlighted is the authentic DNA code, which cannot be imitated by competitors."*
> **Hermawan Kartajaya**

There are three methods that a company can implement, to develop codification of its brand DNA. Each method has its own difficulty level of implementation, but also has its own level of impact on the brand DNA codification success. The best way to achieve full brand DNA codification is by implementing all three layers, which a company could start to apply on a layer-by-layer basis. By recognising brand DNA codification, companies and brands will be able to create an authentic uniqueness that can be experienced by customers through more than just the marketing, sales, and service touchpoints.

## FROM PRODUCT TO CO-CREATION

Along with the other elements of fundamental marketing, the horizontalisation phenomenon has brought changes to the marketing mix elements (product, price, place, and promotion). The first component of the marketing mix is the product. The process of new product development always makes an interesting study. New product development possesses high risk. Therefore, it often involves people across various divisions and departments, in addition to the marketing department since, this is a big concern for the company.

In general, the process of new product development mainly consists of *discovery, development,* and *commercialisation. Discovery* is the initial step of new product development where the company begins to study the market, observing competitors, and identifying the needs and wants of customers to generate ideas. The second step, *development,* is a stage where the ideas generated in the previous stage are being researched and developed further to produce a prototype of the minimum viable product to be tested to the market. The first and the second step is more an iteration cycle than a straight phase, meaning the company can go back and forth during idea discovery and product development phase before finally reach the final product. The final stage is where the company launches its product to the market and *commercialises* the product.

In fundamental marketing, the process of new product development is done with a company-centric or product-centric paradigm. This vertical approach of product development makes the company undertake all parts of product design and development, whereas customers are merely asked for opinions and acceptance toward the product.

On the contrary, in the New Wave era, the new product development process is no longer done vertically, but is instead implemented horizontally. This is an approach in which companies give opportunities for customers to participate actively and collaborate in their product development process. Hence, the resulting products are the outcomes of co-creation between a company and its customers.

For the process of co-creation to be effective and efficient, four building blocks need to be considered by companies.

- **Dialogue**

   One of the critical determinants of co-creation success is the active participation between the company and its customers, as collaborators. Therefore, dialogue between both parties is crucial. It symbolises a horizontal process in which both parties are more or less on an equal standing. Dialogue means much more than just listening to the customer's anxiety and desire. It implies shared learning and communications between two equal problem-solving parties. The role of a company is to facilitate the dialogue to take place; to focus on the mutual interests between customers and the company; to provide a forum where dialogue could occur; and to set up rules which allow the productive interactions to take place.

- **Access**

The company needs to consider giving access to customers. Access refers to the information and tools required to make the co-creation happen. Customers can contribute more to the product development process if they are given some company information and even resources. The development of technology in the New Wave era allows such practices of a sharing economy to happen between both parties.

- **Risk Assessment**

In co-creation, customers will also expect companies to share not only information regarding the product itself but also the risk or harms that can occur to the customers. Therefore, companies need to provide not just data, but also appropriate methodologies for assessing risks related to the products and services.

- **Transparency**

The philosophy of co-creation itself is to put both customers and companies as partners in the same horizontal level, which needs reciprocal trust as the base of this collaboration. In order for co-creation to succeed, a company needs to show the openness of its internal information such as product, price, and business model information to enable customers to evaluate the product's business and societal impact.

Businesses may learn from companies such as Starbucks and IKEA, which use co-creation to help them understand what customers want, by involving customers in the process of their product development. With Mystarbucksidea.com, Starbucks managed to gather more than 150,000 ideas in five years; approximately 300 of the ideas were brought into reality and commercialised. In 2018, IKEA launched a co-creation digital platform called "Co-Create IKEA." Customers can suggest furniture or product designs, and if the product is considered to have potential, IKEA may agree to invest in the future product. IKEA also provides incentives for the customers, such as cash rewards and personal exposure as a designer through the world's largest furniture retailers. IKEA even went a step further by offering facilities like test labs and prototype shops to enable customers to develop and fine-tune their ideas. By using this tactic, IKEA managed to put crowd wisdom to work on product innovation — providing the company with useful design insights, while at the same time contributes to a community of loyal and dedicated customers.

*"In the New Wave era, the company provides maximum opportunities for customers to participate in new product development actively. It means the product is a co-creation between the company and its customers."*

**Hermawan Kartajaya**

## FROM PRICE TO CURRENCY

The second element of the marketing mix is price. Hermawan said that price has "superpowers," because it is a significant determinant of a customer's purchase decision. It also plays a crucial role within the company's various departments. For the finance department, pricing is a key concern, because it relates to costs and profits. For the marketing department, pricing has a key relationship with other marketing promotion activities in devising the marketing strategy. For salespeople, their sales performance is strongly impacted by pricing. Price is not only seen as a means to achieve higher sales volume and generate revenue but is also a key variable of profits.

Profit itself is a function of price multiplied by quantity, from which variable and fixed costs are subtracted. In the book *Pricing Advantage*, Michael Marn stated that if price is increased by 1%, *ceteris paribus*, and at the same time both fixed and variable costs remain unchanged, the operating profit of the product could rise by 11%. In comparison, if variable cost is lowered by 1%, operating profit would only increase by 7.3%. On the contrary, if the cost that is being altered is a fixed cost and is reduced by 1%, the impact on operating profit is just 3.2% increase. Another scenario — if sales volume is increased by 1%, its impact will be a 3.7% increase in operating profit. These scenarios demonstrate the importance of pricing.

From a fundamental marketing perspective, there are four mechanisms in determining the price. Pricing could be based on the 4C Diamond model using market-based or dynamic pricing (*Change*), competitor-based pricing (*Competitor*), value-based pricing (*Customer*), and cost-based pricing (*Company*).

In the New Wave era, the 4C model has transformed into the 5C model with the emergence of the fifth C — *Connector*. The existence of the Connector, which enables a more horizontal and interconnected business landscape, illustrates increasing transparency of information to the customers. Nowadays, customers are able to obtain information about costs and price because such information are becoming more accessible. On the contrary, customers also want greater freedom to determine the price that they would pay. This is a new era when a product can result from co-creation, and price has become currency.

Technological advancement has enabled a flexible approach for companies to allow their customers to conduct price customisation. Customers determine the amount of price to be paid according to the features that they need. Most importantly, this kind of customisation would make the value received by customers increasingly relevant to their wants and needs.

There are two approaches to Currency that companies can use:

- **Currency Adaptation**

  The first approach refers to the practice in which a company creates a product that can be customised and personalised based on customers' needs, wants, and desires — resulting in customisable and adjustable prices. Companies only need to indicate their choices with a mechanism to perform customisation and payments.

  A practical example of currency adaptation can be seen from the freemium concept. Tech companies such as LinkedIn and Youtube give their users the freedom to choose between a free or premium (paid) option. Based on users' needs and wants, they can determine whether they only want the basic and limited version of the product and service, or they prefer more advanced features and functions of the product and service. For some companies, the premium option even has more packages or plans to choose, with various levels of features that are priced accordingly.

- **Currency Collaboration**

The second approach for currency is utilising dialogues between companies and customers. Both sides attempt to identify the optimum offerings and prices that would optimally meet each other's needs. The collaboration approach is suitable for customers who cannot easily articulate what they want, and even get frustrated to choose between options provided by the company.

An example of this approach is from the American premier jewelry retailer and design house, Tiffany & Co. A dialogue between customers and the jewelry designer will be conducted to help customers to create the perfect piece of jewelry for their needs. During the dialogue, the customers can consult with the designer not only about the product, but the price as well. Customers can personalise their co-created product, and together determine the price.

*"In the New Wave era, pricing can be set together by companies and customers, since the product itself may be a co-creation in the first place."*
**Hermawan Kartajaya**

### FROM PLACE TO COMMUNAL ACTIVATION

The third element of the marketing mix is Place — not necessarily referring to just the physical point of selling, but also to the distribution channels. Typically, Place refers to the physical platform that connects the company and customers. Traditionally, Place would refer to the company's distribution channels as wholesalers and retailers, whereas for a service company, it could be branch offices. In the New Wave era, the internet has led the creation of alternative distribution channels to the regular physical ones, which are online and mobile channels. The emergence of online and mobile distribution channels enables companies to sell their products directly to customers and eliminate intermediaries.

In the New Wave era, the direct selling model through mobile or online channels has become quite common. What needs to be recognised is that distribution success cannot rely only on online channels. The new era calls for companies to be smarter in devising the right combination of online–offline approaches, in particular, for target customers, who increasingly become communal. As discussed before, technology has driven changes to the marketing–STV triangle. At the strategic level, segmentation has shifted into communitisation. Therefore, at the tactical level, companies need to implement the right initiatives, one of which is aligning the company's distribution channel with the community in terms of PVI. This practice is called communal activation.

In performing communal activation, the role of a company is to become a facilitator that provides a platform for community members to interact with each other and share ideas. Customers nowadays tend to be dominated by people from younger generations, such as Gen-Y, Gen-Z, and even Gen-Alpha. They are digital immigrants and digital natives who are accustomed to digital interactions. Although social media and other online platforms offer community members convenience in interacting with others, still, it could not replace physical interactions. Therefore, companies could provide a platform where its digital customers could interact offline.

Vice versa, if the customers are already part of some routine offline community activities, a company could show its support by creating an online platform to facilitate greater interactions among the members. It can be done through the establishment of a social network platform by utilising social media and online forums.

> *"Communal activation can be done as long as you have a mobile, experiential, and social connecting-platform that exists in the online and offline world."*
>
> **Hermawan Kartajaya**

## FROM PROMOTION TO CONVERSATION

From the fundamental marketing point of view, the goal of promotion is to inform, remind, and convince customers to buy our products or services. Promotion is usually used to inform customers or potential customers of changes in price, launches of new products, or to remind customers where to buy the products, or even to convince customers to switch to the company's brand. Promotion was usually dominated by advertising through conventional media such as television that can reach a vast range of customers within a relatively short time. This may be quite costly.

In the New Wave era, the top-down and one-to-many approach that traditional advertising adopts does not seem to be entirely relevant anymore. This new era of marketing communications puts consumers at the heart of both content and media. Nowadays, customers can produce their own content in various forms, such as pictures, videos, audio files, and writings. In some cases, some content produced by the customers is so entertaining and interesting, it could even compete with the works of a formal creative agency.

As a result of the rise of digital media, customers can also share their content through various media such as social media, blogs, instant messenger platforms, even online marketplace, and app stores, therefore making these more accessible to other users. This phenomenon has been termed user-generated content (UGC). Companies are starting to put in efforts to develop creative and engaging content to trigger conversations among customers, contrary to traditional one-way advertising. Conversation is essential in today's era as it can trigger customers to share the content with other customers. This creates a chain reaction and makes the content to be the buzzword among customers and going viral. Hence, the real challenge for the company is to develop content that can encourage customers to share them voluntarily.

There are at least nine themes, according to Lois Kelly (2007), Co-Founder and Partner of Beeline Labs, that could trigger conversations among customers. The contents can then be packaged in various forms, such as texts, images, and videos. Companies can choose one or more among these themes that are suitable for their products, services, and brand value (Table 13.4).

**Table 13.4: Nine Conversation Themes**

| Conversation Themes | Description | Example |
|---|---|---|
| Aspirations and beliefs | Something inspiring and touching, and big ideas that potentially create meaningful change. | The story of Indian families which came out of poverty as a result of becoming Hindustan Unilever's Shaktipreneurs |
| David vs. Goliath | The story of a small player's struggle against the domination of big powers | How Hyundai attempts to beat Mercedes/BMW |
| Avalanche about to roll/ Trends | Big, emerging trends that could damage a business or industry practice | The emerging trend of how the latest tech products from the likes of Xiaomi are taking off; the rising wave of online transportation companies (Uber, Grab, Gojek, Didi Chuxing, etc.) in Asian countries |
| Anxieties | Information about something that evokes fear, but should be kept in mind because it involves risks that must be avoided | Health messages from soap manufacturers about the dangers of certain endemic diseases |
| Contrarian/ challenging assumptions | An opposing view of conventional wisdom that already exists in the community | A campaign from Dove which features unconventional definitions of feminine beauty |
| Personalities and personal stories | Stories about the private life of successful personalities or inspirational success stories of people (business, political, and social) | How Steve Jobs resurrected Apple after his return |

| How to | Information relating on tips or techniques to do something useful but not yet widely known or practiced | Tips for performing simple financial planning for a family |
|---|---|---|
| Glitz and Glam | Stories about the lives of glamorous celebrities for example, featuring their luxurious lifestyles | Story of celebrities or famous personalities who prefer a particular brand |
| Seasonal/ event-related | Information about special events or important moments that are generally of interest to many people | The launch of new products on special dates such as December 12, 2012. |

*"The New Wave promotions are based not so much on an orientation to convince and promote, but on building Conversations with the customers and make the brand the topic of the conversation among themselves."*

**Hermawan Kartajaya**

## FROM SELLING TO COMMERCIALISATION

Along with changes in the marketing mix elements, selling has also undergone a shift in the New Wave era. In the more horizontal business landscape, salespeople need to dive deeper and better utilise their most valuable asset — social networks, according to Christakis & Fowler (2011). It is defined as a network of social interactions among people who are in some forms of relationships with each other. These can be families, relatives, friends, colleagues, or clients. Given that advertising may be less effective in this era, a more horizontal approach such as customer recommendations plays a larger part in affecting purchase decisions. Hence, social networking is becoming more important.

Nowadays, people tend to have more faith in what other customers say about the product or service as compared to one-way and top-down advertising from the companies. As such, the practice of selling must be transformed into commercialisation which is the optimal utilisation of social network, to acquire new customers and retain existing customers.

The optimisation of social networks does not mean only making more and more connections with a large number of people from various backgrounds. Such actions alone would not provide salespeople with added value; instead, they could become a waste of time, energy, and money in managing numerous relations.

Commercialisation refers to an effective and efficient way of utilising social networks. To that end, the salespeople need to understand the different types of social networks that exist, because each plays a unique role in supporting the process of the commercialisation itself. According to Tuba and David Godes (2006), the process of commercialisation can be mapped into four types:

- **Commercialisation of market place network**

    In the beginning, the salesperson's main goal is to find a potential prospect. A network that is suitable for this stage is one that can introduce the salesperson to numerous customers. This is called the market place network.

    For example, a consumer banking salesperson could build a network with another salesperson, which targets similar customers such as insurance salespeople. Both can establish a mutually beneficial relationship through the exchange of new prospect information.

- **Commercialisation of prospect company network**

    When one has already been introduced to the prospect, the next stage is to gain the potential customer's interest. To do so, a salesperson needs to connect with the right person in the organisation. The salesperson needs to approach the *user* (the party that will use the product), *the technical buyer* (the party that in charge of product specification), and of course the *decision-maker*, who will authorise the purchase. The stronger such a network is built, the higher is its contribution to the success of the commercialisation.

    In B2B selling, there is more than one decision-making unit, and each plays a different role, as explained above. Building a network through various silos in the client's organisation could benefit the B2B salesperson by providing them with many perspectives regarding the client's needs and their perception toward the salesperson's product or even a competitor's product.

- **Commercialisation of internal network**

  This refers to a network among colleagues within the company where a salesperson works. Commercialisation is not an activity that a salesperson can possibly do alone. He needs active collaboration from several parties within his organisation, such as technical support teams that enable customisation of the product or service offering, as well as a customer service team that would provide insights on the customer's expectations.

- **Commercialisation of the customer network**

  The customer network consists of the company's most loyal customers. Such networks of loyal customers do not only positively impact the loyalty of existing customers but can also be leveraged to help the process of closing sales on new customers,

  The company could organise customer gatherings, inviting both existing loyal customers and hot prospects. The customers will voluntarily interact with each other, and loyal customers could provide positive feedback toward the company's products and services. Therefore, it could influence the hot prospect to purchase.

> *"There are at least two main competencies that a salesperson must possess, in this New Wave era. First, is mapping and building effective networks. Second is commercialising the network."*
>
> **Hermawan Kartajaya**

## NEW WAVE MARKETING VALUE

In these last sections, we will see how the New Wave era affects the third and final three elements of marketing to win the heart share, through brand, service, and process.

## FROM BRAND TO CHARACTER

It seems that nowadays, being a famous or viral brand is the goal of most brands in the world. As the world becomes more connected, it becomes

Figure 13.7. New Wave Marketing Strategy

faster and easier for brands to be known by their target customers through digital channels. On the contrary, as the flow of information is getting faster, brands could easily be shifted from the customer's top of mind and forgotten by their audiences.

In this horizontal era, customers' confidence in many organisations, including companies, is starting to decline. Therefore, organisations would need to put more emphasis on its brand identity as a person or human. Organisations could position their brands as a human being, on the same level as their customers and not as an organisation that is above the customers.

As companies can no longer force customers to buy their products and services, a more horizontal and human-oriented approach must be taken. It is through building brand leadership that a company is able to influence the behaviour of other people, in this case, customers. To build brand leadership, what needs to be done is to implement a branding concept with character (Figure 13.7).

A company that wants to build a brand with character needs to consider six aspects. These aspects are adapted from the WOW Leadership Model that Hermawan Kartajaya, along with Ardhi Ridwansyah (2004), developed. The six aspects are physicality, intellectuality, emotionality, sociability, personability, and moral ability.

- **Physicality**

  The first aspect covers all elements that are tangible to the five senses. It shapes the first impression of a brand and hence must be well designed. The physical appearance should reflect the brand's character, whether it would reflect youthfulness, fun, and joyful ambience or on a more serious dimension, professional, and trusted. The brand's physical elements such as its logo, name, typography, image, packaging, as well as its entire physical existence should reflect its character.

- **Intellectuality**

  A brand must have the ability to capture new opportunities and adapt them to the company's product or service. A company must be able to perform rapid experimentation and innovation to develop this aspect. The ability to keep innovating and to come up with more up-to-date offerings causes a brand to be perceived as being more intellectual or smart.

- **Emotionality**

  Aside from physicality, a brand needs to show its personal and emotional human touch to its customers. It can be done by emphasising the emotional benefits that the brand offers to the customers. A brand could tell stories regarding the brand's values and how it relates to the customers. McKee (2003) stated that it is even more potent than providing data and rational facts.

- **Sociability**

  The fourth aspect is related to how a brand could facilitate the interactions among customers, and its ability to socialise with the customers as a human. The advancement of technology, in particular, social media, has made this practice easier as brands could interact easier through social media platforms with its targeted community.

- **Personability**

  Personability refers to the characteristic of a brand which emphasises that its purpose is not only for the pursuit of profit but to care for people and the planet. More than just corporate social responsibility

(CSR), caring for others needs to be the value of the brand itself and be reflected in its everyday business practices.

- **Moral Ability**

  The last aspect is the moral ability. It is related to a brand's responsibility to protect the customer's rights and maintain its integrity. Customer trust is a high-value commodity in the New Wave era because once customers feel disappointed with a brand, they could spread negative rumours which will affect other customers and even potential buyers. If at any time, there arises an issue which could potentially pose a risk to customers, the company must intervene immediately.

  The Branding with Character model represents a new branding philosophy for brand building. The character resembles a leader, who can influence its followers. With such an approach, customers would voluntarily follow the brand. Customers would even choose the brand over the competitors because of the brand's charisma.

*"A brand without character is nothing."*

**Hermawan Kartajaya**

## FROM SERVICE TO CARE

In fundamental marketing, value creation is determined by "brand" as a value indicator, "service" as a value enhancer, and "process" as a value enabler. Service itself is not only about the ability of a company to provide after-sales supports or merely a customer help center. It is a series of initiatives affecting all customer touchpoints and that continuously enhance the value given to the customers. The framework commonly used to analyse the quality of service is called ServQual, which consists of five dimensions: *reliability, assurance, tangibles, empathy*, and *responsiveness*, or in short, RATER. However, this concept was developed in the 1980s. Today, technology is far more advanced than it was four decades ago, and the nature of the business landscape has drastically changed. It is not that ServQual is not relevant anymore; rather, companies need to

**Table 13.5** Service vs. Care

| Dimensions | Service | Care |
|---|---|---|
| Perspective towards customers | Customer is a king | Customer is a friend |
| Focus | Customer's needs and wants | Customer's anxieties and desires |
| Expected outcome | Repurchase | Recommendation |
| Management tools | Standard Operating Procedure (SOP) and service scripts | Values-Based Principles (VBP) |

review its service paradigm. Service excellence is important but it is no longer enough to excel in the competition and win customer, hearts (Table 13.5).

Mayo Clinic, for example, as one of the most renowned medical institutions in the world, always focuses on serving their patients based on what they really need. Their organisational system requires doctors to understand their patients' needs through diagnosis and intense communication and consultation. "The needs of the patient come first" is the motto of Mayo Clinic. It uses the word "need" and not "want" because what matters are the things that patients need and not merely what patients want.

Under the Care concept of New Wave Marketing, customers are not always treated as "king" — the treatment which many companies that claim to be customer-focused try to provide. There are four fundamental differences between Service and Care.

- **Customer is a King vs. Customer is a Friend**

  From the fundamental marketing perspective, the customer is treated like a king, whose wishes are commands for the companies. It reflects a vertical relationship between both parties and places the company under its customers. The customer's dominant position in the traditional service model is illustrated in a famous anecdote about the "two rules" that were popularised by Stew Leonard, a supermarket chain in the United States. Rule number one: the customer is always right. Rule number two: If the customer is ever wrong, refer to rule number one.

As for the Care concept, the customer is considered a friend, meaning for example, sometimes the company ought to alert its customers, when they ask for something that they may not really need.

- **Needs and Wants vs. Anxieties and Desires**

Traditionally, companies have focused on the explicit needs and wants that are stated by the customers. However, it is often the case that customers are unable to express them. Therefore, in the Care concept, the focus of the company is to figure out the deepest anxieties and desires or the unspoken needs and wants of the customers, then offer solutions based on it. Hotels in India are welcoming regular customers by their names at the time of arrival and check-in, whereas for celebrities, the hotel personnel would address them with a pseudonym, respecting their privacy.

- **Repurchase vs. Recommendation**

The traditional service paradigm may focus on creating customer repurchase intention as a measurement of loyalty. On the contrary, the New Wave Care paradigm measures customer loyalty through advocacy, meaning customers' willingness to recommend the company's products and services. As the importance of the horizontal customer voice is increasing along with increasing social media activities, recommendations from customers are becoming the ultimate focus of Care.

- **SOP vs. VBP**

The final difference is located in the management tools used by the company. Traditionally, service provisions are guided by SOPs and service scripts, which elaborately detail the regulations concerning the behaviour of service staff. For Care, the emphasis is on the importance of empowerment and the use of VBP as general guidelines on employee behaviour.

*"In Care, the focus is on providing services that are most relevant to the anxiety and desires of consumers. This will create the "Wow" effect, which makes consumers really appreciate the help given by the company."*

**Hermawan Kartajaya**

## FROM PROCESS TO COLLABORATION

In the fundamental marketing perspective, Process would refer to the quality, cost, and delivery (QCD) of the products or services that the company provides. All of the back-end activities throughout the company's supply chain are designed to meet the standard quality that it has established. The operational process is optimised to be more cost-saving, and the delivery mechanism is established to ensure that customers could obtain quick and easy access to the products or services.

Today, a company's activities in buying raw material, manufacturing, and delivering products or services will eventually become more horizontal because it is supported by connectivity and information technology. In the New Wave era, Process has become Collaboration. Process, which is related to value creation, is no longer just coordinating everything relating to QCD. As the New Wave era is a horizontal era, all internal or interdepartmental processes and the external process should be done collaboratively. This is possible. For example, the emerging horizontal platform connects and synchronises suppliers, manufacturers, different distributors, and end-customers. A company that enters into such a platform will be required to be more open, share information, and in the end, implement the principle of collaboration.

In terms of the supply chain, the Global Commerce Initiative (2008) describes that collaborations could take form in various aspects:

- Multi-partner information sharing among key stakeholders — consumers, suppliers, manufacturers, logistic service providers, and retailers.
- A collaborative warehouse which stores multiple manufacturers products.

- Collaborative logistic and transportation service that will deliver multiple ranges of products to regional consolidation centers or hubs.
- A collaborative non-urban distribution which will cross-dock products for final distributions.

*"Technological devices and platforms have changed the word, but our success in utilising it is determined by our ability to harmonise our business process with it, based on horizontal and collaborative practice."*

**Hermawan Kartajaya**

Collaboration could benefit a company in terms of its bottom line. A study by AMA Research reveals that supply-chain collaboration can add as much as three percentage points to the profit margins for all types of supply chain players. For example, through a joint collaboration between P&G and Wal-Mart using Collaborative Forecasting and Replenishment (CFAR), managers from these respective companies could jointly forecast the demand on P&G products at Wal-Mart stores and plan the replenishment strategies (Chopra & Meindl, 2001). This optimises their profits.

Essentially, the practice of New Wave Marketing is to horizontalise the market by connecting companies and customers through the community. The purpose is more than just giving a chance for communities to participate in marketing tactics and value creation. The primary objective is to treat any customer as a subject and no longer as an object of marketing. The success of New Wave Strategy relies on the marketer's willingness and seriousness in becoming a part of the community — meaning sharing the brand with the community. Together, the company and its customers could create even greater value.

# References

Barlow, J., and P Stewart (2004). *Branded Customer Service: The New Competitive Advantage,* San Fransisco: Berrett-Koehler Publisher, Inc.

Christakis, N.A., and J.H. Fowler (2011). *Connected: The Surprising Power of Our Social Networks and How They Shape Our Lives.* New York: Back Bay Books.

Chopra, S., and P Meindl (2001). *Supply Chain Management: Strategy, Planning, and Operation.* New Jersey: Prentice-Hall Inc.

Fournier, S., and L. Lee (2009). "Getting Brand Community Right", *Harvard Business Review,* April 2009. https://store.hbr.org/product/getting-brand-communities-right/ R0904K

Global Commerce Initiative (GCI) and Capgemini (2008). *2016: The Future Value Chain.* Paris: Global Commerce Initiative.

Godin, S. (1999). *Permission Marketing: Turning Strangers into Friends and Friends into Customers.* New York: Simon & Schuster.

Kartajaya, H., and A Ridwansyah (2014). *WOW Leadership.* Jakarta: Gramedia Pustaka Utama.

Kartajaya, H., and W Darwin (2010). *Connect: Surfing New Wave Marketing.* Jakarta: Gramedia Pustaka Utama.

Kelly, L. (2007). *Beyond Buzz: The Next Generation of Word-of-Mouth Marketing.* New York: AMACOM.

Kotler, et. al. (2003). *Rethinking Marketing: Sustainable Marketing Enterprise in Asia.* Singapore: Prentice Hall.

Light, L. (2004). "The End of Brand Positioning as We Know It" Conference Speech presented at the ANA Annual Conference, cited in *The Ramsey Report: The State of the Online Advertising Industry,* 8 November 2004.

Light, L. (2014). "Brand Journalism Is a Modern Marketing Imperative," *Advertising Age,* July 2014. http://adage.com/article/guest-columnists/brand-journalism-a-modern-marketing-imperative/294206/ (last accessed March 26, 2016).

McKee, R. (2003). "Story Telling that Moves People," *Harvard Business Review* 81 (6), 51-55.

Stewart, J. (2013). "Looking for a Lesson in Google's Perks," *The New York Times,* March 15, 2015. http://www.nytimes.com/2013/03/16/business/at-google-a-place-to-work-and-play.html (last accessed March 31, 2016).

Ustuner, T., and D Godes (2006). "Better Sales Networks," *Harvard Business Review,* July-August 2006. https://store.hbr.org/product/better-sales-networks/R0607H

# Part IV

## FUTURE: Winning the Future

As someone who is passionate about marketing even now, Hermawan Kartajaya still continues to contribute to the development of marketing concepts and practices.

As the founder of MarkPlus, he believes that its 30 years of experience have given it a strong brand and strong organisation, that is led not only by himself alone but also by the council. The council members are Michael Hermawan, Jacky Mussry, Taufik, Iwan Setiawan, Vivie Jericho, and Ence, with help from Stephanie Hermawan and Hendra Warsita as the council at large, and Estania Rimadini, Yosanova Savitry, and Edwin Hardi as the council plus. The council members come from the

Knowledge, Business, and Service teams of MarkPlus and help Hermawan in determining the company's direction.

At the age of 73, Hermawan still contributes to the development of MarkPlus by igniting the entrepreneurial spirit and keep immersing the MarkPlus's values to all the MarkPlusers because he has a vision for the company to be a world-class corporation from Indonesia.

Therefore, he felt the need to keep on preparing the company and its employees to help achieve that goal. In early 2020, the world was shocked by the COVID-19 pandemic that impacted almost all business sectors, MarkPlus included. Once again, Hermawan felt the need to play a role together with others, to lead the company out of this crisis particularly with his experience of the 1998 Asian Crisis. That crisis impacted all businesses in Indonesia including, MarkPlus, which was then in the first decade of its journey.

Hermawan also sees that the world is much different from what it was decades ago since he started to learn about marketing. In today's era of technological advancement and globalisation, he felt the need for a new approach for marketing in order to stay relevant in this digital age. He has developed the concept of Marketing 5.0 with Philip Kotler and Iwan Setiawan. This is in a book, *Marketing 5.0: Technology for Humanity*, that is published by John Wiley. At the same time, Hermawan is also developing another concept of Entrepreneurial Marketing to complement marketers with an entrepreneurial spirit, as marketers cannot rely only on marketing knowledge and practice nowadays.

This chapter elaborates on Hermawan Kartajaya's vision for MarkPlus's future particularly in the next 10 years of its journey, as well as about the future of marketing in this dynamic business landscape.

### Further Reading

Kotler, P., H. Kartajaya, and I. Setiawan. (2021). *Marketing 5.0: Technology for Humanity*. New Jersey: John Wiley & Sons.

# CHAPTER 14

# ENVISIONING MARKPLUS

MarkPlus faced many obstacles and challenges in its last 30 years and like any other company, it had its fair share of ups and downs, along the way. The downs made MarkPlus reflect from its mistakes and improve and the ups made it stronger. Now, already in its 30th year of existence, MarkPlus is heading toward encompassing sustainability.

It is of paramount importance for any company to make sure that its business is sustainable in the long term. There are many factors and ways to build a sustainable business. One of the first things to do in ensuring the sustainability of a business is to define a vision and a set of goals. Having a specific set of goals will help the company move toward the designated direction more efficiently. With a road map on hand, the company can avoid making unnecessary deviations. MarkPlus, a company that always aims to achieve a higher goal, has envisioned its future.

What would MarkPlus do next then? This chapter will give you an glimpse into its future, hence the name **Envisioning MarkPlus.**

## ENCOUNTERING THE COVID-19 CRISIS

The year 2020 marks MarkPlus Inc's 30th anniversary. Thirty years is not a short period of time Not every business is capable of getting to this point; hence this is a significant milestone for MarkPlus. To illustrate, a human who is 30 years old would have been through several ups and downs and experienced many major milestones. The pleasant moments from childhood memories, the struggle during the teenage years, the excitement of being employed for the first time, the first goodbye, the first promotion, the quarter-life crisis, other crises, and the list can go on and on. The 'life' of a business is like a human life; it also has its ups and downs. Inevitably, MarkPlus has experienced many things in the last 30 years. But now in its 30th year, another unexpected crisis came — the coronavirus pandemic, otherwise known as COVID-19.

The COVID-19 outbreak has placed the world in the middle of a global crisis, perhaps the worst in the past few decades. It has been reported to affect more than 200 countries and territories around the world. Millions of people have been affected, and businesses worldwide have taken a hit because of this outbreak. Its spread has caused a disruptive effect on the world economy and left companies around the world with tremendous challenges.

New regulations are being imposed to stop the spread of the virus with social-distancing policies, as an example. Some governments prefer to impose lockdowns to prevent further spreading, whereas others prefer to impose large-scale social limitations and restrictions. The new regulations limit the people's movement. A consequence is that people consume less, particularly for some products and services for various reasons — lower income, being forced to stay at home, etc. This has a spiral effect. Many companies are forced to close, leading to retrenchments and/or their employees bringing home a lower income. Some businesses are not able to attract customers, leaving workers with no pay at all. The COVID-19 outbreak has brought a sudden dynamicshift to the national and global business landscape, and with negative impacts that may last thereafter. The pandemic's significant effect finally hit Indonesia toward the latter part of the first quarter of 2020, affecting even MarkPlus itself.

> *"For humankind, the pandemic is a war against humanity. While for businesses, the crisis is a shifting factor in the market, with impactful changes in the technological, socio-cultural, political-legal, and economic aspects."*
>
> **Hermawan Kartajaya**

One of Indonesia's countermeasures in preventing the spread of the novel coronavirus was to impose large-scale social limitations and restrictions, starting from Jakarta, where MarkPlus's main office is located. Following the government's policies, people were required to work remotely. MarkPlus deployed the work-from-home protocol for all of its employees in Jakarta in the middle of March; similarly, MarkPlus's offices in other cities were asked to adhere to the regional government's policies and act accordingly.

## Time to Shift: OMNI Company

Many businesses experienced a volatile, uncertain, complex and ambiguous (VUCA) environment due to the COVID-19 outbreak spreading relentlessly throughout the world. This raises the urgency in re-analysing decisions during this time of crisis, before taking actions. Business leaders should ensure business continuity and sustainability. It can be done by first analysing all related aspects, from the external market and industry landscape to the internal company's condition and resources.

Amid this pandemic, companies may find themselves facing a dilemma in determining the right actions to take, as the business landscape is changing. Companies may start to consider whether they have to come up with new products or services, or new ways to serve the customers and to beat the competition. Some companies may focus on planning and executing short-term plans for quick wins. Some may think that there is a need to take time to think about the long-term impact of the strategy that should be implemented.

No one predicted that this pandemic would disrupt businesses in so many sectors. Only a handful of industries are not affected by this outbreak. However, consulting and research companies are undoubtedly affected in quite a hard way. Like many other businesses, MarkPlus too faced various dilemmas in overcoming these challenges during the crisis. In normal day-to-day activities, offline interactions dominate. Be it meetings with clients or even discussions amongst the staff, everything is mostly done by face-to-face interactions. Of course, with newly imposed regulations and restrictions, a lot of these interactions these are no longer feasible. Hence, to overcome the crisis and to ensure business continuity and sustainability, MarkPlus, as a company, needs to shift its daily operations into the online-based mode.

With employees working from home, many adjustments need to be made. Constant discussions on how to adapt in this situation are necessary. Quick decision-making and creative thinking are of paramount importance at this time. Trial-and-error is unavoidable in determining the best practices for the company in this situation. All of the business units in MarkPlus started to steadily shift their operations from offline to online during this outbreak.

In MarkPlus Inc., the daily discussions and meetings with clients had moved into online platforms. Data collection is done remotely in accordance with the government's large-scale social limitations and restrictions policy, and daily discussions and brainstorming sessions are conducted online as well.

Within one month into the working-from-home protocol, MarkPlus, Inc. had found the most suitable dynamic for their business units. Everyone had adapted well and knew their roles in this situation. Both the consulting and research divisions have initiated several online approaches in their daily activities. As a result, MarkPlus, Inc. was still being able to operate relatively well despite the unfavourable conditions during the pandemic.

MarkPlus Institute had adapted even faster during this time. Having training as their core product, a quick adaptation is, of course, needed to survive in this outbreak. They were able to migrate their training sessions to an online platform within a short period. Naturally, some concerns and worries may arise from customers regarding the online training delivery method. Still, MarkPlus Institute made sure that the quality of the training stayed stable.

MarkPlus Institute is not only innovating their training delivery methods, but has also developed several new products that are suitable for a pandemic situation. It launched several short courses, focusing on particular topics. One of the examples is "How to sell during the outbreak." These courses are tailored to meet the specific needs of the potential participants in such difficult and tough times.

The other business unit, Marketeers, is also adapting to the transition from offline to an online approach. One of the most significant developments of Marketeers during the pandemic is establishing its capabilities in executing online events. Before COVID-19, they were used to handling offline events, where the organisers and the visitors could meet directly. But now, due to the social-distancing regulations, face-to-face interactions are no longer possible. Hence, amid the outbreak, Marketeers came up with innovations to stay relevant, by organising online events.

They have proven themselves by successfully hosting several online events. All these examples show that MarkPlus took quick and serious actions to respond promptly, in handling and facing the crisis. Arguably, MarkPlus is one of the fastest consulting professional service companies to shift its operations from offline to online. This would not have been possible to achieve without the cooperation and support of all MarkPlusers across the different cities and the MarkPlus leadership team. The staff worked together to find suitable innovations for the pandemic and in identifying creative ways to deliver their newly invented products. A smooth execution of planned strategies to overcome the obstacles that arise from the crisis is critical and so is the need to keep working together in facing these tough times.

When the number of new cases decreased significantly and the curve of the coronavirus cases flattened, the government started to lift the large-scale social limitations and restrictions policy. A new normal will emerge when the situation improves. People will go back to offline inter-actions just like they had before the outbreak, but they will still be leaning on online interactions. The reason is that people have gotten used to the technologies and online platforms and have experienced the ease of inte-grating these into their daily life. Changes in the economic and social order are inevitable.

This new normal will bring new dynamics that are unprecedented and have never been experienced before. The situation post-COVID-19 will not be the same as it was before, and it will not be the same as the time during the outbreak. Thus, another series of adjustments and adap-tations are required not only by people, but also by companies, to get used to the new normal. From a business perspective, one of the ways to cope with the new normal is by shifting toward the OMNI approach.

*"After the outbreak has passed, offline interactions will con-tinue to happen as usual, but also accompanied by the increasing usage of online platforms.*
*Therefore indeed, the **OMNI** approach is suitable."*

**Hermawan Kartajaya**

Hermawan believes that the key to survive the crisis and prepare for the post-COVID-19 situation is to integrate the offline and online means as well as other paradoxes (global and local, human and machine, vertical and horizontal, etc.) in undertaking marketing. Similarly, MarkPlus needs to be a flexible company that can shift and adapt according to the situation and condition at the time. That is what he calls the **OMNI** way. In the OMNI way, we believe that humans and machines could exist side by side, complementing each other. Online would not replace offline totally. In the *post-crisis* period, offline interactions would return to normal, and there will also be increased intensity of online interactions as customers become more accustomed to it. MarkPlus had been and is heading toward becoming an OMNI Company.

**Breakthrough in the Time of Crisis**

Despite the challenges that surfaced during the crisis, MarkPlus succeeded in finding ways to survive and even thrive. MarkPlus's name and reputation is becoming more well-known because of the initiatives that were taken in this crisis time. The various initiatives are well suited to the period of crisis.

The first initiative was a webinar hosted by Hermawan Kartajaya, the first webinar event ever held by MarkPlus. Called *Surviving The Corona, Preparing the Post: It will never be the same again,* its main objective was to give an outlook on how businesses face the coronavirus crisis and included a prediction about the post-coronavirus situation. This was also the first platform where he could introduce his newly developed crisis framework "The SPA 2020" to the public.

The webinar was held at the beginning of April, and it was astoundingly successful. Even though it was a paid event, people were still willing and curious to join the very first webinar held by MarkPlus. The event attracted more than 700 participants, from different cities, industries, and backgrounds. As this was an online-based event, MarkPlus could accommodate many people at the same time. The webinar's success ignited the vigour of all MarkPlusers in facing the crisis and this was a breakthrough event.

Following the webinar's success, MarkPlus then published a whitepaper with the same title (Figure 14.1). It provided more detailed information regarding the webinar and also gave the audience a chance to read through the topic. Not stopping there, MarkPlus later published another whitepaper as a sequel to the previous one. The whitepaper, written by Iwan Setiawan, was called *"Digitalization Strategies Amid COVID-19: One Size Doesn't Fit All"* (Figure 14.1).

This second whitepaper discusses the importance of digitalisation in a time of crisis and the appropriate strategies that could be taken, based on the type of industries. As one strategy does not fit all, business leaders should assess their current state of readiness in dealing with this physically immobilising condition, determine the most suitable plans, and allocate resources wisely according to the new strategic directions. Both whitepapers discussed threats brought about by the pandemic, that businesses should address, and opportunities that they should seize. The right strategic actions will lead businesses to not only survive the crisis but also prepare well for the future.

Having observed that the impact of the crisis is different for each business sector, MarkPlus took the initiative to conduct several industry round tables that cover different industries. The round table aims to take a deep dive into the conditions of the sector and identifies the impact of

Figure 14.1. Published Whitepapers by MarkPlus

the pandemic in each sector — from the experts' and players' points of view. As different business industries might experience different things during the crisis, some may be barely surviving while others may thrive in such conditions. Hence, different approaches are necessary for each respective business sector.

Two different industries were covered in each week, and this will go on for 10 weeks in the industry round table series. The sectors for the round table series are displayed in Table 14.1.

At the end of this, 20 different kinds of industries would be discussed in the round table series. Each of the round table sessions feature invited experts and players from each sector as the speakers in order to get a holistic and complete view of the industry. These round tables are open for the public and anyone can freely join in and acquire the insights from the round table.

The industry round table initiative also gained valuable feedback from the public. Each of the round tables succeeded in attracting more than 500 participants. For every round table session, a survey asking about one specific industry would be distributed beforehand. Then after the session ended, MarkPlus would develop a whitepaper based on the findings of the session and the pre-survey. In the end, the whitepaper would be published and made available to the public. The industry round table was another breakthrough activity achieved by MarkPlus during the crisis.

**Table 14.1 List of Industries for Round Table**

| Resources and Mining | Insurance | Property | Multifinance |
|---|---|---|---|
| Logistics | Government | Commercial Banking | Transportation |
| Telecommunication Services | Infrastructure and Utilities | Broadcast, Pay TV and Media | Pharmaceutical |
| Tourism and Hospitality | Automotive | Retail | Spare Parts and Services |
| Ecommerce | Fast-moving Consumer Goods | Construction | Healthcare Services |

Despite the crisis, MarkPlus was able to develop various initiatives to help companies in getting through the tough times. These kinds of actions will not stop here and the firm will continue to develop and improve in the future.

### MarkPlus's Balance Sheet

After 30 years of being in the business, MarkPlus now has a stable balance sheet. The balance sheet consists of assets, liabilities, and equity as seen in Figure 14.2. Each of these variables has its derivatives.

One item in MarkPlus's balance sheet is "asset". The company's strongest asset is surely its brand. The brand is made up of MarkPlus, Marketeers, and the branding of the founder and leader, Hermawan Kartajaya himself. These three things combined together resulted in a substantial brand equity for MarkPlus, which is widely known in Indonesia today. A strong brand as an asset, of course, will have its obligations to shoulder. Whether the market conditions favour a company or not, the image of the company must remain strong and not waver. Once the image fluctuates, the strong brand that has been built in the past 30 years can crumble. Hence, protecting the brand and showing the right image is of utmost importance for MarkPlus.

Under "liability," lies the customer. It might seem weird to have customers as a liability, but Hermawan Kartajaya has his own beliefs. How

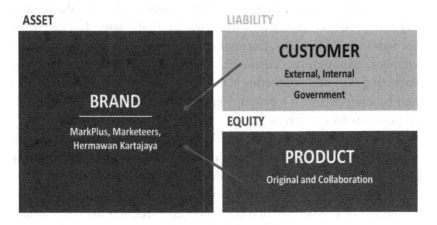

Figure 14.2. Balance Sheet of MarkPlus

can a company consider its customers as its liability? From Hermawan's perspective, the customer is categorised as a liability and not as a debt because of MarkPlus's obligations and responsibility in providing them with quality service. This is aligned with one of the passions that MarkPlus holds firmly, which is the passion for service.

Customers here refer to internal and external customers. The internal customers are those who are usually called "employees" in MarkPlus. It is MarkPlus's responsibility to give guidance, provide directions, and provide suitable development programs for them. Particularly during difficult times, MarkPlus needs to commit to encouraging them to get through this and fight the crisis together as one in unity.

Serving customers is not necessarily always about money. Hermawan believes that the government is one of the entities that a business needs to serve, regardless of whether money is involved or not. The reason is that it is the responsibility of the company to help the government.

As for external customers, Hermawan always remembers one of his mentor's, Pak Ciputra, sayings, which explains that promises to customers are obligations that any business needs to fulfill.

> *"Our promises to customers are our obligations,*
> *and those obligations must be paid."*
> **Pak Ciputra**

The next item is "equity". MarkPlus's equity is its products. There are both the original products and the collaboration products. The original products are those frameworks that were developed by Hermawan and MarkPlus. Examples include the 4C analysis framework (changes, competitor, customer, company), nine core elements, Marketing 3.0, and Marketing 4.0. These original products will also then be equipped with a patent. Hence, the equity of MarkPlus's original products will be strengthened.

For product collaborations, MarkPlus currently has several partnerships with external parties. These collaborations with other reputable parties will also elevate the equity of MarkPlus itself as a company.

After reviewing the current balance sheet of MarkPlus in its 30th year anniversary, it can be seen that customers and products drive MarkPlus's assets.

## M30 : ENABLING MARKETING EXCELLENCE

Today, MarkPlus is in the 30th year of its journey. It is not easy for a local firm that literally started as a one-man-show to survive for 30 years. The first decade of the journey represents the "surviving" phase of the business (Figure 14.3), especially with the Asian Crisis in 1998. The second and third decades of MarkPlus's journey represent the "preparing" phase for the company. It was in these two decades that MarkPlusit started to institutionalise its organisation and began to develop a solid foundation and structure for the company's continuity and sustainability. The forthcoming decade will be an "actualising phase," an era when MarkPlus actualises its true vision and mission as an Indonesian and Asian company. MarkPlus's success is not a story about luck. It is a story of its founder's, along with all MarkPlusers', 30 years of hard work. It is truly a story about the harmony of marketing and entrepreneurship.

### "Surviving" The First Decade

In MarkPlus's first decade, the company could not be separated from the image of its owner, Hermawan Kartajaya. It can be said that MarkPlus's continuity and sustainability relied on Hermawan's thoughts, energy, and spirit. The first decade of its journey was one of the most critical parts of the journey for the company, since the company was still in the very early stage of its development, and it did not even have a solid corporate foundation nor structure at that time. Moreover, towards the end of its first decade, MarkPlus, like many Indonesian and Asian companies, was hit hard by the impact of the 1998 Asian Financial Crisis, making its first decade even more challenging. However, Hermawan's entrepreneurial spirit and marketing thoughts which he put into practice for his company, successfully brought MarkPlus out of this dangerous phase. Subsequently, the firm moved into the next chapter of "preparing" for its future.

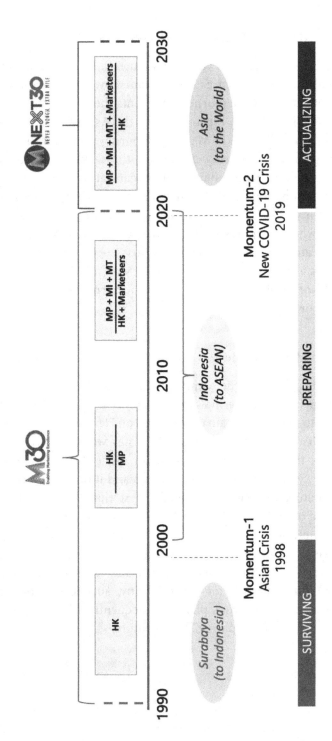

Figure 14.3. MarkPlus's Milestones

### "Preparing" during The Second and Third Decades

This second phase of MarkPlus's development took two decades, where the firm institutionalised itself, shaped its solid foundation and structure, and established its sustainable business model. This began in the second decade of MarkPlus, when Hermawan Kartajaya's son, Michael Hermawan, came back to the company and started to establish three main business units, consulting, research, and training, under the name of MarkPlus Inc. These represented the three main services that MarkPlus provided at that time. It was followed by the establishment of the firm's organisational structure for each business unit, which enabled the firm to become better organised and possessed a clearer vision and mission. The organisational structure itself had undergone several transformations, as part of the process of finding the most suitable combination amongst its various components, knowledge, business, service, and people, to support its goals. During this time, Hermawan still played a big part in shaping the company's image. He possesses a strong image as the Father of Indonesia's marketing, which gave a great leverage to MarkPlus as an eminent marketing consulting, research, and training firm.

Into the third decade, Hermawan was aware that the brand name of MarkPlus is gaining more and more trust among its clients and marketing enthusiasts in Indonesia, Asia, and probably the world. As the founder, he thought that he might need to begin to "separate" his image and MarkPlus's so that the company can stand on its own. This was possible given that the company already has a strong brand image, unlike in the first decade. Hermawan began to strengthen MarkPlus's brand by spinning off MarkPlus Institute (the learning and development division of MarkPlus) from MarkPlus Inc. into a completely different business unit and establishing a new business unit called MarkPlus Tourism (specialising in government and tourism projects), with the support of the media, MICE community, and Marketeers. Hermawan also began to avoid getting too involved in projects, leaving them in the good hands of his council members, including Jacky Mussry, Taufik, Iwan Setiawan, and Michael Hermawan. He believed that he had already prepared them to handle those projects well and that they were indeed way keener than him in solving business and marketing problems. It is not that he was no longer involved in projects, but rather that he acted more as the leader than as a manager involved in the company's day-to-day operations.

Towards the very end of the third decade, a new crisis emerged — the COVID-19 pandemic. As mentioned earlier, this crisis impacted many companies, including MarkPlus's, operational activities. However, Hermawan and the firm's leaders still managed to deal with the situation by starting to transform its business from offline to OMNI (integration between offline and online). The entrepreneurial and leadership spirit of all MarkPlusers became strong values influencing how they faced the situation. These must continue to be held and immersed, to deal with the new, next, and post-normal conditions arising from the impact of the pandemic.

During these two decades, MarkPlus also extended its range of clients not only within Indonesia but also to Asia, including countries such as Malaysia, Vietnam, and Japan. MarkPlus also managed to open its overseas branch offices in some ASEAN countries such as Singapore, Malaysia, Thailand, and Vietnam. MarkPlus then decided to focus more on the Indonesian market which was growing from time to time. Hermawan also became more active in a number of Asian organisations such as the Asia Marketing Federation (AMF), of which he was the president from 1998 to 2000. In 2007, Hermawan, with the support of Professor Philip Kotler, rebranded AMF from its previous name, Asia Pacific Marketing Federation (APMF). He also actively participated in the development of small businesses through the Asia Council for Small Business (ACSB), which he became the president of from 2016 to 2019. All of these actions are the realisation of MarkPlus's journey from Indonesia to ASEAN and Asia. All these milestones represent the phase of "preparing" MarkPlus's future vision and mission in the forthcoming decade.

## M-NEXT 30: NEVER ENOUGH AND EXTRA MILES

Although M30 means the 30 years of MarkPlus' journey (Figure 14.4), M-NEXT 30 means the leap into the next decade for MarkPlus. Today, MarkPlus is planning the next decade of its journey, its "actualising" phase MarkPlus's 30th anniversary on the first of May 1, 2020, marks the "second cycle" of the company. Just like the innovation process in the

Figure 14.4. M30 and M-NEXT 30

product life cycle model, M-NEXT 30 is MarkPlus's new spirit in creating the company's next upward slope, after reaching the current maturity stage (Figure 14.4). It means that MarkPlus is ready to further grow its business in facing the next decade until 2030.

In the last two decades, MarkPlus has prepared itself by competing in Indonesia and even ASEAN and Asia. Now it is ready to actualise itself from Asia to the world. Hermawan believes that in the next decade, MarkPlus Inc., MarkPlus Institute, MarkPlus Tourism, and Marketeers are prominent enough to actualise his and his company's vision, without being associated with his name as it was in the first and second decade. Hermawan will take the position as a leader who keeps inspiring the company and provide enlightenment to all MarkPlusers.

To actualise its great vision for the next 10 years, MarkPlus will immerse itself in the spirit of M-NEXT 30. NEXT itself consists of two aspects; NE means Never Enough, and XT means eXTtra miles. Both aspects are related to MarkPlus's four core passions: Passion for Knowledge, Passion for Business, Passion for Service, and Passion for People.

Hermawan believes that to achieve MarkPlus's goals in the next decade, Passion for Knowledge and Passion for Business are Never Enough. It means that it is imperative for all MarkPlusers to possess the Passion for Knowledge and Business and keep enhancing their passions. Passion for Knowledge is the foundation of MarkPlus's business, and Hermawan often repeats that MarkPlus is a knowledge business. It should be enhanced by continuously searching for the most updated knowledge to cope with the changing business landscape so that all MarkPlusers can keep on providing value to stakeholders related to them. Passion for Business is a must-have, because knowledge needs to be applied to business to become more than just conceptual frameworks or theoretical concepts. In the end, knowledge will be useful for business only if it is practically relevant to the business situation. Passion for Business is also related to the innovative spirit that all MarkPlusers need to have, which is important to develop state-of-the-art products and services to match the ever-changing market needs, which is are the businesses of MarkPlus. All MarkPlusers are given opportunities to be creative and to invent something new. If it is feasible and viable to be done and can bring more value to the company and its customers, the firm's leaders would provide the support and facilitation to make it happen. Hence, that the Passion for Knowledge and for Business is Never Enough, is really well suited to MarkPlus's characteristics as a marketing and entrepreneurship lab, not only for its clients but also for its employees.

On the other side, the Passion for Service and Passion for People needs to be implemented with eXTra miles principles. It means that all MarkPlusers need to possess intimacy with the customers, which allows them to better identify not just their needs and wants, but their anxieties and desires too. This will enable the firm to provide services that are most relevant and valued by customers. MarkPlusers need to be caring not just to customers but also to each other, so that the family atmosphere that surrounds the firm since it was established back in 1990 will still be felt by all MarkPlusers. MarkPlus always wants to have an employee-friendly and human-centric work environment, which will naturally encourage higher productivity and creativity among all employees. This is one essential key to achieve MarkPlus's goals. As MarkPlus's business is a people business, all of its business units' operational activities are related to people. As such, MarkPlusers need to have a Passion for People. To balance out Passion for Knowledge and Business, a more human touch to the organisation is needed. In envisioning the future, the Passion for Service and for People needs to be practiced with eXTra miles principles. It means that caring for both internal and external stakeholders must be done with the heart.

It might seem that the principles have stayed the same since the day MarkPlus was established. People might ask whether it is still relevant in the forthcoming years and in the context of a more digitalised world. Hermawan believes that when MarkPlus aims to reach out to the world, it cannot leave its original values behind. It still needs to carry its values as well as its spirit as an Indonesian firm when it brings itself to the world. In the end, knowledge and business alone are not enough. In a more connected world, where knowledge becomes more accessible and more people and organisations are business-oriented, MarkPlus needs to balance itself with a touch of humanity through its caring and intimate service and human-centered approach to its people.

## VISION AND MISSION

*MarkPlus's Vision*

After three decades of its journey, MarkPlus, Inc. has set a new vision and mission to be achieved in the next 10 years. The vision is not only limited to how the firm can grow significantly in terms of business, but also how the company wants to inspire and allow as many people as possible to gain benefits from its existence. MarkPlus redefined its vision, which now includes two main points:

- **Energy of Indonesia:**

  MarkPlus started as a local consulting firm that began its business in Surabaya. Today, after 30 years of existence, it is arguably one of the best national consulting firms that is able to compete with other global consulting firms in Indonesia, an identity that the company would like to retain. In the forthcoming decade, this is the identity that the company would like to keep. By keeping its identity as a national consulting firm, MarkPlus has contributed to the proliferation of the country's business and marketing for so many years. It has actively participated in and is one of the main drivers for the International Council for Small Business (ICSB) Indonesia, an international organisation that was founded nearly 64 years ago. This indicates the firm's strong determination to do something "beyond business," particularly for SMEs in Indonesia, which contributes highly to the national economic growth. In the upcoming years, MarkPlus will continue to be a business that inspires and empowers, especially for Indonesia, the place where it all started.

- **Asia's Champion for the World's Inspiration:**

  Over the past 30 years, MarkPlus has experienced significant growth. Its growth is very fast-paced, wherein the company has started to enter the international market after only one decade of its establishment. In 2000, MarkPlus officially went international with its founder, Hermawan being elected as the President of the Asia Pacific Marketing Federation (APMF). In July 2004, MarkPlus went international and established its office in Singapore, a city-state where many giant and multinational corporations gathered. Along the journey, the founder, Hermawan, realised that it was too soon to serve the international market. The company had not fully seized the many opportunities in Indonesia's market. Therefore, the company decided to refocus on the national market. As time passes by, although MarkPlus's operational business activities are centered in Jakarta, the business has grown so much that it currently serves multiple global companies around Asia, particularly in Southeast Asia. MarkPlus has also held various international events such as the ASEAN Marketing Summit and the MarkPlus Conference, which many of the firm's partners from various Asian countries such as Singapore, Korea, and Japan have attended. It has finally come to a point where the firm should be able to seize a bigger opportunity by serving a bigger market. Hence, the company aims to be Asia's champion that inspires the world.

*MarkPlus's Mission*

The common definition of mission is a statement that expresses a company's business or defines its scope. However, as the business world becomes more dynamic, the definition of business scope can change very fluidly. Therefore, it is more relevant to define a mission with a much more fundamental intent, which is a company's reason for its being and reflects the company's primary purpose. It is safe to say that the more fundamental the company's mission is, the more sustainable the company will be. MarkPlus's mission for the next decade can be expressed in two main points: integrating marketing and entrepreneurship, a statement that has been firmly rooted for so many years; and promoting OMNI Multilateralism, that always defined MarkPlus's openness towards any principles, ideologies, or stances.

- **Marketing and Entrepreneurship**

Hermawan has always believed that to establish a successful business, at least two things are required. The first is the right marketing strategy, and the second is an entrepreneurial spirit. These have become the guideline for all MarkPlusers in executing the day-to-day business. These have also become the foundation of the firm's models and framework. MarkPlus has developed so many models that have helped people to understand marketing and entrepreneurship in a simpler way. Today in 2020, MarkPlus has begun to register the intellectual property rights for all its marketing and entrepreneurship models.

- **OMNI Multilateralism**

OMNI''s general concept is to integrate things or concepts that may be considered paradoxical, such as online and offline, global and local, liberal and conservative, democracy and monarchy, and so on. MarkPlus always promotes the OMNI idea and avoids take sides on certain aspects or parties. The fundamental reason is that the company believes that there is no one correct side to everything. Therefore, under OMNI Multilateralism, it is important to respect any ideology. This value espouses policies and practices of cooperation which provide mutual benefits to stakeholders involved. Hermawan believes that to expand the business worldwide, MarkPlus should be open to any stances, ideas, and principles.

*MarkPlus's Values*

In running its day-to-day operational business activities and to achieve its vision and mission that has been explained previously, MarkPlus will adhere to the firm's values as represented by the 13 Ethics, Professionalism, and Excellence (EPE) Principles (Figure 14.5). The enforcement of the 13 EPE Principles will help to sharpen human intelligence, including Physical Intelligence (PQ), Intellectual Intelligence (IQ), Emotional Intelligence (EQ), and Spiritual Intelligence (SQ). Each of these intelligences are intercorrelated, and MarkPlus believes that a balanced mixture can help to define one as a true leader.

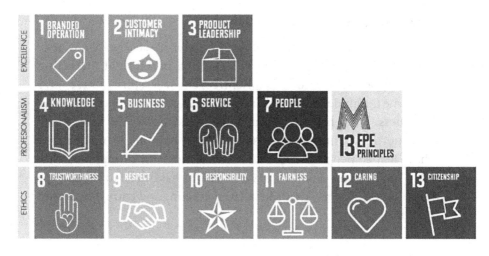

Figure 14.5. The 13 EPE Principles

## EXCELLENCE

### 1. Branded Operational Excellence (Brand Management)

An excellent brand is not found; it is built. It is all achieved in one package: superb and punctual service, lower cost, and expected quality. MarkPlus has always tried to ensure that the results of its work meet or even exceeds the customers' expectations. In terms of cost, the principle is quite simple; operations should always try to keep costs low, wherever possible and without compromising the quality. MarkPlusers also need to deliver every piece of work on time to maintain clients' trust. And lastly, service should be ingrained in every MarkPluser so that excellent service equals satisfied customers. Therefore, MarkPlusers should always perform excellent service to ensure the customers' satisfaction.

### 2. Customer Intimacy Excellence (Customer Management )

Creating value while building intimacy with internal and external customers is not only a must but is also a way of professional life. Each role is equally significant in the business process. The concept of customer management in MarkPlus includes four aspects: Get, Keep, Grow, and

Win Back. First, it is crucial to get the right customers with the right efforts at the right time. Then, Keep. It is essential to remember that having a loyal customer is also very crucial since every market has its limits. It is impossible to gain new customers forever. The next thing to keep in mind is that loyal customers will tend to advocate for the brand. It is important to prolong customers' devotion before encouraging them to make recommendations. And last, to Win Back, MarkPlus believes that there will always be a chance to attract lost customers and encourage them come back to its business.

### 3. Product Leadership Excellence (Product Management)

Customers continually seek quality products. It is in MarkPlusers' nature to practise product leadership strategy. This can be achieved by proposing novel ideas to initiate new products, creating additional value to maximise the product's potential, utilising existing resources to maintain an essential product, and observing the customers' needs and trends, to examine the sustainability of an existing product.

### PROFESSIONALISM

### 4. Passion for Knowledge

As a knowledge business, all MarkPlusers are expected to be dedicated to learning, developing, and sharing knowledge with others. MarkPlus expects its employees not only update and upgrade themselves with the latest information and concepts but to also to practically implement them with proficiency.

### 5. Passion for Business

A passion for business means one should be dedicated to discovering business opportunities, trade, and be concerned about target achievements. MarkPlusers should demonstrate their potencies by participating in selling activities and owning a target-and-cost-conscious attitude. By empowering all MarkPlusers to have a passion for business, the company indirectly stimulates every employee's entrepreneurial spirit.

## 6. Passion for Service

A passion for service means a dedication to flawlessly serve by treating a customer as both a client and a friend. MarkPlusers should sincerely care for and sensitively understand the customer and, where needed, be courageously apologetic and immediately help to provide service recovery to solve or minimise customers' dissatisfaction. For all these years, this is the foundation for every MarkPlusers to deliver excellent service for their customers.

## 7. Passion for People

A passion for people means a dedication to socialise and build relationships. MarkPlusers must be confident in interactions, quick to initiate conversation, establish good connections, and eager to be part of social activities and to meet new people. Having a passion for people is considered very important and with this, MarkPlus has become a firm that has extensive networks not only with national companies but also is able to connect with global companies and organisations across the world.

## ETHICS

## 8. Trustworthiness

An ethical point that all MarkPlusers must have is trustworthiness. It is imperative for all MarkPlusers to be honest and to never conduct any actions that deceive, cheat, or steal. Moreover, every MarkPlusers should be reliable and always have the courage to do the right thing. This is very important to build an excellent reputation for the firm.

## 9. Respect

All MarkPlusers are also required to follow the golden rule, to treat others with respect. They need to be tolerant and accepting of differences. Good manners and not using bad language is are expected. They should be considerate of the feelings of others and should not threaten, hit, or hurt anyone; rather, they should try and to peacefully deal with anger, insults, and disagreements.

## 10. Responsibility

Another ethical point that should be embraced by all MarkPlusers is responsibility. All MarkPlusers should be reliable and be responsible for their actions. To be reliable, it is essential to have action plans and be disciplined. Perseverance is also they should never stop trying and always consider the consequences of their actions. All are expected to have a strong sense of self-control and be accountable for their own choices.

## 11. Fairness

Treating all people fairly is one crucial trait in MarkPlus. MarkPlusers should be open-minded and have the ability to listen to others. By having this ability, people would see things more clearly and objectively and avoid blaming others carelessly. It is also important to take turns and be willing to share.

## 12. Caring

MarkPlus also encourages its people to always be kind. Be compassionate and show others that you care. MarkPlusers should express gratitude and forgive others. The willingness to always help others in need is also required.

## 13. Citizenship

The last pillar of ethics is citizenship. It means that MarkPlusers are expected to cooperate and be involved in community affairs. Always stay connected and be well-informed. To be a good citizen, MarkPlusers should obey laws and rules and respect authority.

Printed in the United States
by Baker & Taylor Publisher Services